Two Nations, Indivisible

Two Nations, Indivisible

A History of Inequality in America

JAMIE L. BRONSTEIN

 PRAEGER™

An Imprint of ABC-CLIO, LLC

Santa Barbara, California • Denver, Colorado

Library of Congress Cataloging-in-Publication Data

Names: Bronstein, Jamie L., 1968– author.
Title: Two nations, indivisible : a history of inequality in America /
    Jamie L. Bronstein.
Description: Santa Barbara, California : Praeger, an imprint of ABC-CLIO,
    LLC, [2016] | Includes bibliographical references and index.
Identifiers: LCCN 2016025051 (print) | LCCN 2016040150 (ebook) | ISBN
    9781440838286 (hardback : acid-free paper) | ISBN 9781440838293 (ebook)
Subjects: LCSH: Income distribution—United States—History. | United States—
    Economic conditions. | United States—Economic policy. | United States—
    Social policy. | Social classes—United States—History. | Wealth—United States—
    History. | Poverty—United States—History. | Labor—United States—History. |
    Liberalism—United States—History.
Classification: LCC HC110.I5 B66 2016 (print) | LCC HC110.I5 (ebook) |
    DDC 339.2/20973—dc23
LC record available at https://lccn.loc.gov/2016025051

ISBN: 978-1-4408-3828-6
EISBN: 978-1-4408-3829-3

20 19 18 17 16   1 2 3 4 5

This book is also available as an eBook.

Praeger
An Imprint of ABC-CLIO, LLC

ABC-CLIO, LLC
130 Cremona Drive, P.O. Box 1911
Santa Barbara, California 93116-1911
www.abc-clio.com

This book is printed on acid-free paper ∞

Manufactured in the United States of America

Contents

Acknowledgments

Academic projects are never completed in a vacuum. My New Mexico State University (NMSU) colleague Mark Walker, who was writing a book on the Basic Income Guarantee as I wrote this one, first encouraged me to consider inequality from a historical perspective. The NMSU conference that Mark organized on the Basic Income Guarantee in 2014 introduced me to scholars who have long worked on the philosophy of contemporary inequality. Simultaneously, participation in an ad hoc reading group facilitated by NMSU student Alan Dicker on Thomas Piketty's *Capital in the Twenty-First Century* helped to get my thoughts flowing My NMSU colleagues Lori Keleher, Peter Kopp, and Julie Rice, and my former graduate student Ryan MacLennan, all provided helpful suggestions at crucial moments. In the later stages of the project's completion, Tim Ketelaar of the psychology department at NMSU gave me the opportunity to present the ideas contained in this book to a wider general audience, allowing me to better focus my message.

This project could never have been completed without the assistance of NMSU's tireless interlibrary loan department. Mike Zigmond and Evan Zigmond respectively read parts of the manuscript and participated in some wide-ranging conversations about inequality that convince me that the future is, at least in part, in good hands. My biggest debts are to my friend Dawn Rafferty, who read and edited the entire manuscript, and to editor James Ciment, who reviewed this book and provided extremely helpful guidance on its revision. Finally, I'd like to thank the NMSU students to whom I've taught American history for the past 20 years. This book is for you.

Introduction

In 1845 Benjamin Disraeli, novelist and member of Parliament, published *Sybil: Or the Two Nations*, a "social novel" that considered the gulf between the wealthy and the poor in Victorian Britain. The majority of Britons had not yet been granted the right to vote, many of the cities suffered from overcrowded slum housing and pollution, and the children of the poor worked rather than going to school. This life contrasted with the dazzling wealth of the aristocracy and the solid prosperity of a growing middle class. So it made sense that Disraeli would have one of his characters refer to Britain as

> Two nations: between whom there is no intercourse and no sympathy; who are as ignorant of each other's habits, thoughts and feelings, as if they were dwellers in different zones, or inhabitants of different planets; who are formed by a different breeding, and are fed by a different food, are ordered by different manners, and are not governed by the same laws ... THE RICH AND THE POOR.[1]

Britain's status as a class society was well known throughout the nineteenth century; American thinkers conjured the specter of British aristocracy when they warned against looming American inequality or when they celebrated American exceptionalism.

Now the tables have largely turned. In the words of historian James L. Huston, the United States has become what it once despised:

> Europeans come to the United States to witness the social distance between rich and poor, to observe homelessness and unendurable poverty, to see a political system of republicanism that elicits either apathy or outright hostility from the

majority of its citizens, to research rampant crime and the world's largest population of prison inmates, to record the antics and frivolities of the inordinately
wealthy.[2]

Despite the growth of labor-force participation by new groups, including
women; better access to higher education than at other times in American history; and transfers from the federal government, income and wealth inequality have worsened since 1983, particularly for the bottom 40 percent of the
population.[3] Members of one family, the heirs to the Walton fortune, had
amassed $90 billion in wealth by 2012, the same as the bottom 30 percent
of the U.S. population.[4] As the Figure I.1 indicates, America's poorest suffer
under a much less progressive tax system than their European counterparts or
than Americans in 1960 when payroll taxes, state and local sales taxes, the cap
on taxation of incomes for Social Security, and the lower rate assessed on
capital gains are all taken into consideration. Those in the lowest quintile of
income earned have an effective tax rate of 27 percent; those in the highest
quintile have an effective tax rate of 9 percent.[5]

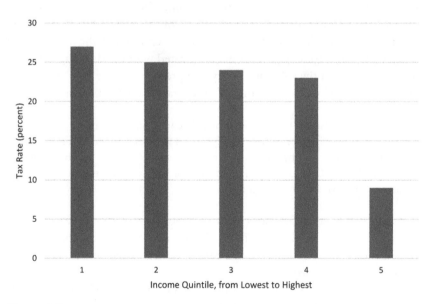

Figure I.1
**Effective Tax Rate from all Sources (Percent), 2012. (Computed from Bret N.
Bogenschneider, "Income Inequality and Regressive Taxation in the United
States,"** *Interdisciplinary Journal of Economics and Business Law* **vol. 4 no. 3
(2015): 8–28, at 12.)**

Poor Americans' chances for economic mobility are lower than those of the poor in many other countries, America's reputation as a "land of opportunity" to the contrary.[6]

Why should we care? Social science research reveals that income inequality correlates with a host of social problems: "Higher crime rates, lower life expectancy, less charitable giving, worse school performance, greater incidence of obesity, and slower economic growth."[7] Moreover, a republic depends on the participation of citizens who are independent enough to achieve a certain level of political knowledge and to assert their own opinions. That independence is so important that some commentators have absurdly suggested that people who collect income support should lose the right to vote.[8] The other, more palatable, logical conclusion is that if we are committed to a participatory republic, we should work to ensure that extremes of wealth and poverty do not undermine broad political participation.

As this book will show, economic inequality has been a persistent, detrimental feature in the United States since its founding, although the extent of the exploitation has changed over time. At the same time, a critique of inequality has also been ubiquitous, growing louder during some periods (the Depression years, for example) and more muted in others. Cyclically, the topic of inequality in the United States has emerged again in the twenty-first century. The *New York Times* in 2005 ran a series of articles on class, pointing out for its readership that, contrary to popular belief, the United States is not the most upwardly mobile country in the world.[9]

A number of recent books question the notion that deregulation, budget cuts to safety nets, free trade promotion, and privatization have promoted growth to benefit all.[10] Despite its length and serious subject matter, economist Thomas Piketty's *Capital in the Twenty-First Century* (2014) was widely read and reviewed. Historian Steven Fraser's *Age of Acquiescence* (2015) compared the modern American public unfavorably with Americans in the late nineteenth and early twentieth centuries, who were not afraid to call out class warfare against the working poor when they saw it.[11] Former Secretary of Labor Robert Reich's documentary *Inequality for All* (2013) reached a wide audience, with an accessible message: the prosperity of the United States hinges on the middle class having an income to spend. After all, a multimillionaire can only drive one car at a time, wear one change of clothing at a time, sleep on one or two pillows at a time. Democratic presidential hopeful Bernie Sanders made economic inequality one of the cornerstones of his unexpectedly popular campaign: "Unchecked growth—especially when 99 percent of all new income goes to the top 1 percent—is absurd...Where we've got to move is not growth for the sake of growth, but we've got to move to a society that provides a high quality of life for our people." Sanders mentioned free college tuition and single-payer health care as important initiatives in this regard.[12]

At the same time that Americans seem to be grasping for answers to the problem of inequality, the history of American beliefs about, and policies toward, inequality remains understudied.[13] In one of the few exceptions to this rule, *Securing the Fruits of Labor* (1998), James L. Huston argued that from 1765 to 1900, Americans believed that equality and democracy were inseparable but saw the solution to that problem in political measures rather than economic ones. Nineteenth-century Americans observed European aristocracies protected by laws like entail and primogeniture, wealth gained through crown-granted monopolies, and aristocratic chokeholds on landholdings. In the United States, in contrast, small government promoted economic equality, since North America abounded in the natural resource most associated with independence: land. In an agrarian republic, although people's talents might vary, if they were allowed to keep "the fruits of their labor" without the coercion of taxation, relative equality would follow. Huston's interpretation is attractive; if early Americans were basically united in their belief that economic problems had political solutions, then certain actions, like granting freed African Americans the vote in 1870 but failing to economically redistribute in their favor, make sense. Huston blames the Founding Fathers for constructing what he calls a "haunted house"—they based their republic on an expectation of equality, and yet never, in the first 125 years of its existence, made a move to create any redistributive economic institutions.[14]

I think Huston presents too optimistic a picture. In the pages that follow I argue that inequality has always been a feature of the American experience. The myth that the United States provided unique opportunities for upward mobility was forged in the nineteenth century, when intergenerational occupational mobility for white males was higher in the United States than in Europe. Indeed, the United States had some attractive features for white male economic mobility, including the ability and willingness to unseat large numbers of Native Americans from their ancestral homelands and turn that land into farms. But such nominal equality as existed depended on the complete marginalization of others (indigenous people, African Americans, and women). In the twentieth century, any advantage the United States had disappeared, but crucially, Americans continued to buy into the opportunity myth, and it restricted the scope of palatable social welfare initiatives.[15]

Even statistical arguments about American inequality have tended to miss the important point that most historical calculations of economic welfare leave out some groups. Economists and economic historians use a measure of inequality called the Gini coefficient, derived by plotting the percentage of American households on the X axis of a graph and the proportion of their national income or their wealth on the Y axis, as shown in Figure I.2. Then one measures the way the actual curve compares with both a "perfect equality" scenario (one in which all households have the same income or wealth) and a "perfect inequality" scenario (one in which one household has 100 percent of the income or wealth and the other households have 0). A Gini coefficient of zero represents perfect equality; a coefficient of 1 represents perfect inequality.[16]

Peter Lindert and Jeffrey Williamson, the most-cited economic historians to write about American inequality, claim that inequality followed this trajectory: a period of relative equality during the American Revolution was followed by growing inequality before the Civil War, high levels of inequality at the turn of the century, and then finally a leveling off of inequality in the middle decades of the twentieth century. While this is the dominant view, economic historian Carole Shammas showed that Williamson and Lindert omitted from their calculations married women (subject to laws that excluded them from ownership of most property, so without a claim to income in most cases) and African Americans (the vast majority of them slaves, and thus without income at all). Whatever "equality" means, it cannot mean a nation in which over half the population has no claim to income or to wealth.[17]

Shammas argued that historians of inequality should focus on wealth rather than income, since in her estimation wealth is even more likely to be lopsided

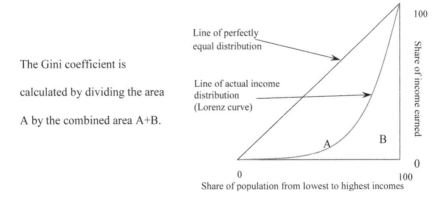

Figure I.2
The Ginny Coefficient Is Calculated by Dividing the Area A by the Combined Area A+B.

than income, and more likely to confer political power. She recalculated Gini coefficients for the period from 1774 to 1986 and showed that throughout that entire period, the Gini coefficient was at least 0.72, rising to 0.83 during the 1850s and 1860s. For the purposes of comparison, the Gini coefficient of wealth for the United States in 2015 was 80.56, making it the most unequal country in the developed world.[18] Moreover, consistently, the wealth of the first, second, and third quintiles of the population combined—that is, the poorest 60 percent of the population—never exceeded 11 percent of the nation's total wealth. The fourth quintile of the population had a share of the nation's wealth that usually hovered around 14 percent, and the top quintile of the population had a share of national wealth that ranged from 75 percent to 87 percent. Thus, if wealth statistics are of any significance, at no point was the United States a country with anything like an egalitarian distribution of property.[19]

At only one point, in the middle decades of the twentieth century, did the United States move away from inequality generally, but historians disagree about the reasons. Shammas argues that property-law reform enabled women to have a greater share of property or to have property count as theirs in tax returns. More women also entered the labor force. For Williamson and Lindert, the "Great Compression" of midcentury was based on the waning of unemployment during the Great Depression and World War II; government transfers, in the form of either taxation or direct transfer payments; and a reduction in the prices of necessities that made up the consumer basket of poorer people. The Great Depression may also have substantially eroded the wealth of the top 1 percent of the population, from about 36.6 percent of the national wealth in 1929 to around 25 percent in 1950.[20] No matter what the cause of the Great Compression of the postwar years, inequality began increasing again in the 1980s, under pressure from both economic trends (deindustrialization and globalization) and government decision making (tax cuts for the wealthy and cuts to social and educational spending) and has now reached levels at or above those in the 1920s.[21]

In addition to showing that inequality has been a constant feature in American history, this book will also argue that inequality is not necessary for, and in fact undermines, national prosperity. The economist Simon Kutznets predicted in the 1950s that while industrialization invariably results in inequality in the short run, in the long run one can see an inverted "U-shaped" curve, as economic growth lifts all fortunes and helps to compress inequality.[22] Kuznets's supposition has not been borne out by experiences in the developed world since the 1980s.[23] In contrast, Williamson and Lindert and Thomas Piketty have shown that inequality is not a necessary condition of economic growth. The U.S. economy grew impressively even during the Great Compression of the mid-twentieth-century.[24] And there are many ways to encourage growth that do not end up promoting inequality, including infrastructure projects, public health, and education.[25]

Finally, this book will show that, at certain crucial moments in American history, there were options presented—forks in the road—that were not taken, and that might have resulted in better outcomes. Such critical turning-points include the end of the Civil War, when the government failed to consider stakeholding for freed African Americans; during World War II, when a proposal was on the table to make the nation responsible for the full employment of its citizens; during the Nixon administration, when a basic income guarantee came close to passage; and during the Reagan administration, when neoliberal promises distracted working people from deindustrialization and globalization.

This book is divided into eight chronological chapters. Chapter 1 covers the period from the American Revolution to the late 1820s. It argues that like the classical civilizations that the Founders so much admired, a virtuous American republic was predicated on the theory that all and only white men were equal citizens, but that this did not mean they were entitled to equal standing or even equal political participation. This chapter shows that what relative economic equality did pervade before the Age of Jackson was only possible due to the arrogation of Native American lands, the unfree labor of slaves, and the unpaid labor of women and children.

Chapter 2 reviews the period between the 1829 and the Civil War. Increasing demand for commercial goods impelled changes in the organization of labor that were intended to increase productivity. Rationalization of the workshop promoted a work routine in which poorly trained, unskilled workers could replace highly skilled workers who had served full apprenticeships. At the same time the probability increased that some artisans would never move from journeyman to master status, states eliminated property qualifications for white men to vote. Did "real" inequality have a political solution? The late 1820s and 1830s ushered in a new era of thought and discourse about inequality, illustrated by the ideas of the labor philosopher Thomas Skidmore, the Workingmen's Party, and the National Reform Association, responsible for the slogan "Vote Yourself a Farm!" Twenty years of lobbying culminated in the Homestead Act, one of the most radical steps toward equitable distribution of property in American history. In the South, in contrast, criticism of economic inequality was more muted because whiteness had tangible benefits that compensated to some extent for vast differences in life chances.

The transformation of 4 million enslaved people from property into largely unpropertied "free laborers" contributed greatly to increasing inequality in the last third of the twentieth century. Unlike freed slaves or serfs elsewhere, freed people in the United States were not given any kind of financial stake, due to the pervasive myth that that political equality and the "freedom of contract" would result in social and economic justice eventually. Chapter 3 shows that the end of slavery, the Panic of 1873, the Great Strike of 1877, waves of immigration in the North, and urbanization impelled a wide-ranging discussion of inequality and distribution. Thinkers like Henry George and Edward Bellamy, and organizations like the Knights of Labor and the Populist movement, exerted ideological pressure for social change and greater equality of condition.

Chapter 4 investigates the period between the turn of the century and the Great Depression, the era of the most acute disparities in income and wealth in American history. But this was also the era of some of the most impressive brainstorming about eliminating inequality. Writers like Herbert Croly and Walter Weyl advocated for the recovery of America's "national promise" through government regulation intended to help the poor develop their unique talents. Progressives, at both the state and the federal level, identified and sought to remove threats to equality of opportunity: poor public health, lack of educational facilities, child labor, and unregulated food and drugs. Settlement house workers, largely women, lived alongside the clients they served, clearly seeing them as neighbors rather than as an alien nation. World War I precipitated a conservative backlash. By the 1920s, American prosperity had become fully identified with business growth. Regulation and redistribution were off the table in favor of individual self-improvement, education, Americanization, and eventually restriction of immigration flows from poorer areas, all of which steps were theoretically intended to enable people to achieve their full potential.

During the Depression era, which is covered in Chapter 5, unprecedented economic challenges pushed issues of distribution, and equality of condition, to the forefront of politics. After four years of high unemployment, poverty, and suffering under President Herbert Hoover, the nation was ready to experiment simultaneously with banking regulation, large-scale public works employment, agricultural restrictions, and industrial codes. Activists like Francis Townsend, whose ideas shaped Social Security, and politicians and political candidates like Louisiana governor Huey Long (Share Our Wealth) and California gubernatorial candidate Upton Sinclair (End Poverty in California) pushed Franklin Delano Roosevelt to pursue a more radical Second New Deal. The Republican Party, the business community, and the Supreme Court offered their resistance. While the New Deal pioneered some of the programs that helped compress inequality as never before in the following two decades, President Truman's administration missed the opportunity to pass the Full Employment Act (1944), which would have made employment a right, and designated the government the employer of last resort.

The years between the end of World War II and the early 1970s marked what economist Paul Krugman calls the Great Compression, covered in Chapter 6. Not only was the economy growing, fueled by the expansion of manufacturing and pent-up wartime demand, but the fact that working-class and middle-class people had discretionary income to spend produced general prosperity. Relatively high tax rates on the highest incomes failed to hold down economic growth; impressive levels of unionization kept wages high. Although modern-day economists like Krugman might look on this period as an idyll, it was not beneficial for everyone. The postwar period demonstrated the impact of racism and housing segregation on prosperity. By the 1960s, a concern with "pockets of poverty" in inner cities and Appalachia revived the discourse about inequality. Despite the expenses of a war in Vietnam, Democratic administrations pursued a "War on Poverty" that led to another period of policy experimentation. Medicare and Medicaid expanded the social safety net, and a number of community action agencies sought to involve poor people in providing their own services, but the characterization of the War on Poverty as a failure helped to stigmatize the poor.

During the Nixon administration, the President's Commission on Income Maintenance recommended a basic income guarantee for low-income Americans, the Family Assistance Plan. The plan was never enacted, although the Earned Income Tax Credit had its origin in this idea. When the Family Assistance Plan stalled and died, the political will to broaden the social safety net evaporated under economic pressure. Stagflation, the oil shocks of the 1970s, and deindustrialization brought malaise to the United States. These conditions enabled widespread acceptance of an alternative theory of prosperity, discussed in Chapter 7.

Divorced from both equality of condition and equality of opportunity, Ronald Reagan's tax cuts, military spending, safety-net slashing, and "trickle-down" economics promoted the idea that the freest markets were most efficient, and the most efficient markets produced the most prosperity. Although direct subsidies to income only represented a very small percentage of the annual U.S. budget, welfare programs and the people who used them came under attack. The formerly deserving poor, mothers with children, had now become "welfare queens," and Bill Clinton, a Democratic president, collaborated with the Republican Congress to create time limits and work requirements for those on income support. While income inequality grew, working people's experiences remained divided by race.

The last chapter of this book examines the sources of the Great Recession that began in 2007, and the structural features that continue to widen the income and wealth gaps in the United States. As middle-class people fell farther behind, discontent manifested in the Occupy Wall Street movement on the left of the political spectrum, but also in the Tea Party movement on the right and the Black Lives Matter movement, a movement about class and opportunity as well as about race. During the 2016 presidential race, the Republican candidate Donald Trump advocated policies he claimed would promote prosperity for American workers, like immigration restriction and protectionism. Given the long history of inequality in the United States, and the polarization of legislative politics at every level, the prospect for reform seems dim, but proposals have included criminal justice reform, a basic income guarantee, free college education, or the government as the employer of last resort.

This volume includes a select bibliography. The complete bibliography for *Two Nations, Indivisible* can be found at the following website: https://history.nmsu.edu/two-nations-indivisible-bibliography/.

CHAPTER 1

The American Revolution and Equality

The roots of the "two nations, rich and poor," lie in the founding moment of the United States. Although the American Revolution was not a social revolution, the myth of the new state was that "all men are created equal." Like the classical civilizations that the Founders so much admired, a virtuous American republic was predicated on the theory that all (white) men were equal citizens. This did not mean they should have equal economic standing or even equal political participation, but rather that some degree of independence was necessary to participate in a democracy or a republic.[1] And as in those classical civilizations, in the United States this commitment to egalitarianism for some coexisted with slavery for others. This chapter will explore the tensions between the limited ideological commitment to equality and the social stratification of the early republic, including the way in which, in the South, even the nominal equality of whites depended on the enslavement of African Americans. It will also examine some of the challenges to the constitutional order that were based in different understandings of the degree to which the revolution promised economic well-being.

Part of the American "myth of the state" is that the American Revolution represented an important transition in the way people thought about an individual's moral worth. Many historians see the early American republic as the moment in which Americans were most united in their commitment to egalitarianism.[2] Gordon Wood, for example, argues that Americans followed the English Whig tradition by affirming a commitment to the moral and legal equality of the individual. Wood further argues that even though women and African Americans were excluded from this vision of equality, the founders' rhetoric of equality made possible the later liberation of slaves and

empowerment of women.[3] This attempt to paint the United States as excep-
tionally egalitarian is undermined by the fact that (for example) Britain eman-
cipated its slaves without reference to the American Revolution, and
American women received the right to vote no sooner than women in many
western European countries. The fact that Wood makes the argument at all
shows that the myth of American exceptionalism dies hard.

A contending school of thought, associated with the historian Arthur
F. Young, characterizes the American Revolution as incomplete. Young
emphasizes that common people, including such groups as slaves, frontiers-
men, and apprentices, had radical traditions (including religious traditions)
that predated the spread of Whig ideology; that they called for broader goals,
including economic egalitarianism; and that their critique lasted far beyond
the revolution.[4] The broadest commitment to the moral equality of the individual came at the moment that the Declaration of Independence was issued,
but the Declaration was intended primarily to equate the moral worth of
white Americans with that of white Britons, rather than to make broader
claims. When it came time to enshrine American values in the Constitution,
there was no mention of individual equality, either in the original iteration
of the Constitution or in the first 10 amendments.[5]

Historians also disagree about whether the existing economic records
show equality or inequality as the major feature in early America. Allan
Kulikoff found, for Boston, that the level of economic inequality in society
was increasing steadily from 1687 to 1830, but that the major gains of the
top 10 percent, from 46 percent to 63 percent of the total wealth, occurred
before 1771. Kulikoff further found that economic disparities were inherent
in all but the lowest-status trades, that the wealthiest men were rewarded with
public office, and that those with the highest wealth occupied the most
responsible elected offices. Boston's residential patterns were segregating, as
the poorest members of the community moved to either end of town where
the property values were lower; and a steady stream of migrants, some of
whom would have been without resources, came to the city to seek their fortunes. Wealth did tend to change for individuals over the course of the life
cycle, as young men without property gained modest competencies in middle
age, but family wealth for middling artisans tended to decrease again in old
age so that men had very little income to leave to their wives.[6]

In contrast, G. B. Warden denies that inequality was significant. He questions Kulikoff's conclusions, since the tax data for revolutionary Boston on
which Kulikoff based his findings are incomplete and overstate rather than
understate inequality. Warden claims that because the discontent that was
expressed was not formulated in terms of "class conflict," inequality was

relatively unimportant. "The failure to relate socioeconomic inequality with revolutionary political agitation suggests that the relation did not exist at all, cannot be reconstructed in the present, or has little interpretive significance other than as an unexplored assumption and peripheral implication."[7] Gordon Wood said something similar when he asserted the absence of the "horizontal solidarities of occupation and wealth with which we are familiar today."[8]

In fact, the truth lies somewhere in the middle; American society at the time of the revolution had inequality as a prominent feature, and yet the tools to critique that inequality were just being crafted. The wealthiest 10 percent of the population in 1774 owned 50 percent of the nation's wealth, but apparently this ratio was thought to be acceptable for a republic, since the top decile owned much more than that in European countries. Of course, the Founders never explained what ratio of property holders to the unpropertied, and what concentration of wealth, would have been *unacceptable* in a republic; to have done so would have required analytical tools that they lacked.[9] American writers generally argued that the economic independence conferred by property ownership was crucial to the survival of the republic. At the same time, these assumptions worked only as long as slaves and Native Americans were mentally "relegated ... to special castes, outside society."[10]

After the revolution, regions developed their own patterns of inequality. Plantations most closely approximated static European hierarchies. Like European aristocrats, wealthy planters could leverage existing social and economic advantages to gain more of the best land and confer their status onto their children. In rural areas with family farms, all family members were economic participants, enjoying at least the power that inheres in making a significant economic contribution. Despite the debate that has taken place in history journals about whether farm families were essentially proto-capitalist in their practices or whether they had other primary values besides making a profit, the social structure of the countryside remained static.[11] In larger, commercial farming areas and the larger port cities, economic power was more concentrated, and laborers occupied a spectrum from skilled artisans, down through journeymen and apprentices, to unskilled laborers, and to indentured servants and sailors who were not free to make their own contracts.

That the Founders were neither socially nor politically egalitarian is clear from both the aristocratic European lifestyles that they emulated and from the Constitution that they eventually wrote. Historian Richard Bushman emphasizes the importance to early republic elites of the notion of "gentility." Gentility was expressed through a habitus—a constellation of behaviors, possessions, and living conditions that telegraphed social station instantly in a hierarchical society. The genteel wore expensive, impractical, hard-to-launder clothing, with clean collars and cuffs, showing others instantly that they did not need to do manual labor and were wealthy enough to hire laundresses on a regular basis. They surrounded themselves with china plates, silver services, mahogany furniture, and clocks. They built their large houses on the plan of British country estates (with the exception of Thomas Jefferson, who designed Monticello himself and then had his slaves build it for him). They danced; they cultivated the arts of discrimination between fine and inferior wines, gardens, paintings, and meals; they took pride in their status as conversationalists; they had their portraits painted. For a people so nominally opposed to the "luxuriousness" of a monarchical society, they were remarkably steeped in luxury themselves.[12] Over the course of the nineteenth century, items like carpets and porcelain became more affordable, and the proper consumption of these items became a requirement for possession of respectability; in turn, wealthier Americans promoted changing fashions that made it harder for middle- and working-class Americans to keep up.[13]

Moreover, many of the Founders acknowledged that a functional republic required a division of labor between the producing and the governing classes. Only men of leisure, who could sit back and study contemporary problems, could govern wisely. As historian Andrew Shankman has pointed out, while the Founders were ready to discard hereditary positions, they were unwilling to discard the rationale for hereditary positions, which in Europe generally conferred that leisure, education, and distance.[14] British North America had been a stratified society, with patricians and plebeians who ate different food, wore different clothing, lived in different houses, and did different work or no work at all. These distinctions among people continued after the revolution and mapped onto the distribution of wealth.

SLAVERY

British North America, and then later the United States, accommodated degrees of servitude from slavery through indentured laborer and redemptioner status (people who owed labor to pay back the cost of their passage from Europe) and apprenticeship. People lived their lives not only within patriarchal families but also within patronage networks.[15] What makes such a situation egalitarian at all? Americans saw themselves as more equal than Europeans because the average American seemed more prosperous than the average European—or at least, this was the myth to which most Americans gladly clung.[16] The generalization was only even the tiniest bit true if slaves were not considered Americans of moral worth.

At the time of the American Revolution, almost one-fifth of all Americans were held in hereditary bondage, a fact that is too easily written off by scholars addressing American inequality.[17] Slavery was rhetorically charged; the fear that George III intended to enslave the North Americans by depriving them of British liberties had motivated Americans' commitment to the revolution in the first place.[18] For white colonists, enslavement meant not so much forced labor as subjection to another person's will; the vague language of the Declaration of Independence aside, in 1775 it was clear that African American independence and the independence of white rebels from the English yoke were diametrically opposed concepts. The British proclamation of November 5, 1775, proposing to free all indentured servants and patriot-owned slaves who took up the British colors made one thing clear: that white "freedom" from British subjection entailed black servitude, and black freedom entailed white "servitude."[19] Word of British intentions to free slaves spread wildly throughout the colonies, so that all through the war, slaves deserted plantations to join the British, even as late as the 1781 Battle of Yorktown.[20]

By 1776 the South had transitioned from being "a society with slaves" to "a slave society," whose legal and social underpinnings made it impossible to escape slavery without physically leaving the geographical region.[21] The even nominal equality of white Americans in the South depended not only on the unpaid labor of slaves but also on the existence of the institution of slavery. Southerners appreciated slavery not only because someone else did their hard physical labor for them but also because the institution of slavery helped them distinguish intellectually between themselves and enslaved black people. "Slave owners were sure that, if they were in the same position as their slaves, they would prefer to be killed rather than to accept enslavement."[22] The existence of slavery also made freedom have a very particular meaning for white Americans. Freedom became "negative liberty"—as the absence of external control—rather than "positive liberty," the resources to be able to make choices and carry them through. Negative liberty continued to be a handy heuristic after the revolution, too: "the continuing liberal emphasis on abstract freedom long diverted attention from the bondage of such unequal relationships as traditional marriage and total dependency on wage-earning employment."[23]

After the revolution, slaves worked not only in the fields but in every sector of human activity: they worked "in temperate highlands as well as in tropical lowland, on farms as well as plantations, in cities as well as in the countryside; they worked in fields and in shops, in manual and skilled occupations, in civilian and military life, up trees and down mines, on land and at sea."[24] Had a black workforce been unavailable, American white "equality" would have looked completely different, historian J. R. Pole argues. "In all probability a much more massive unfree or limited service would have been drafted into the plantation colonies from the ranks of white convicts and other outcasts —in which case the planters' privileges would unmistakably have rested on the labour of landless workers with small hope of advancement for themselves and their children."[25]

Plantation owners were paternalistic in their language, referring to their slaves as part of their families, but they calculated slaves as property and did not hesitate to sell them, distribute them in wills, or take any other steps that were necessary to maximize profit.[26] If slaves are counted both as wealth and as potential owners of wealth, then inequality in the entire pre-Civil-War period is even more extreme than scholars of American inequality have calculated.[27] Nor was the society in which slaves lived a monolith; rather, occupation, gender, the size of the community in which slaves lived, and geography created inequalities.[28]

The existence of slavery in a "free" country entailed a certain amount of cognitive dissonance. James L. Huston argues that from the outset, slavery conflicted with the notion of receiving the fruits of one's labor that was essential to Republicanism, and that writers including Thomas Paine and Thomas Jefferson realized this.[29] But the Founders did not let their hesitation about labor's rewards get in the way of a federal Constitution that enshrined and perpetuated slavery. And the Northern states enjoyed the benefits of a prosperous South.

AFTER THE REVOLUTION

The tumultuous 1780s called into question whatever limited commitment to economic egalitarianism the Founders would have claimed. The war took a terrible toll on some areas of the country, with crops and houses burned, cattle and horses requisitioned by both sides in the conflict, and the labor force cut drastically due to the fighting. The result was a depression from which the new republic did not emerge until the turn of the nineteenth century; per capita income fell from about $2,140 in 1774 to about $1,200 in 1790.[30]

During the 1780s, Massachusetts was convulsed by a series of constitutional protest attempts and armed uprisings. These were led by small farmers who were feeling oppressed both by the contraction of the money supply and the state's plan for collecting its debts. The burden of taxation fell most strongly on these indebted farmers, whose creditors refused to allow them to pay their debts with depreciated paper money. There was a shortage of hard currency, since most of it was flowing abroad to pay off debts that the states had contracted during the Revolutionary War; this deflation caused prices to plummet, including the prices of the crops farmers could sell. The Massachusetts General Court, with an eastern (that is, mercantile) Massachusetts bias, did nothing to relieve the economic distress, except to repeatedly exhort western farmers that attempts to close courthouses or to call county conventions of town meetings to organize protests were illegal.[31] In some counties, 25 percent of farmers were being sued for debt at a moment in time when indebtedness still meant the sale of all of one's goods and chattels and imprisonment in a debtors' prison.[32]

After years of trying to force the Massachusetts General Court to listen to their pleas, several hundred Hampshire County farmers finally arrayed under the command of Luke Day and Daniel Shays, a poor farmer and former captain in the Continental Army. The irregular troops first paraded in 1786 through the streets of Springfield, home to a federal armory. Then, in late January 1787, the Shaysites clashed with the Massachusetts militia guarding the armory. Although the militiamen were hesitant to fire directly at their neighbors, ultimately they did, and four protestors were killed. The rebellion then turned into a long retreat and chase and finally ended in February, when Shays and his troops surrendered. After the rebellion, the composition of the state government changed, and the incoming legislator and governor pardoned the participants in the rebellion, including Shays.[33]

Similar convulsions occurred in 8 of the 13 colonies. In Rhode Island, peace was restored when the legislature agreed to issue paper money that could be used for the repayment of debts.[34] British North America had made an ideological transformation from a monarchy to a republic, a state that at least nominally had its sovereignty in the people. Thus, opponents of rebellion against the state could argue that rebels were partial and self-interested, marginalizing complaints that had their roots in economic grievances.[35] Federalist elites would frame Shays—who did not represent himself in print—as a dangerous demagogue rather than as the somewhat hesitant representative of a much larger backcountry movement in favor of more directly democratic government.[36]

Shays's Rebellion is one example of the conflict over inequality in the early republic; the debate between Jeffersonian Republican William Findley of Western Pennsylvania and financier Robert Morris over the rechartering of the Bank of North America is another. The Bank of North America was a private commercial bank that became the first centralized financial institution in the country. Findley opposed the bank, arguing that such a large, powerful economic institution might destabilize the rough social and economic equality necessary for political participation in a republic. Findley supported protecting private property, but a national bank was an entity of unprecedented size.[37]

Another check to egalitarianism was the decision to replace the Articles of Confederation with a federal Constitution.[38] Federalists, supporters of the Constitution, were largely wealthy men of commerce. Antifederalists, who supported the state legislatures, were largely farmers.[39] Arguing against the ratification of the Constitution, New York's Melancton Smith warned that the document "will raise a few to the height of human greatness and wealth, while it will depress the many to the extreme of poverty and wretchedness." [40] Contrasting the sure tyranny to follow after the adoption of the Constitution with the much weaker Articles of Confederation, Smith emphasized that the Articles had protected all classes of property. Using a reference to Leviticus, Smith asked, "What is your condition? Does not every man sit under his own vine and under his own fig-tree, having none to make him afraid? Does not every one follow his calling without impediments and receive the reward of his well-earned industry?"[41]

The elite pamphlet conversation on constitutional ratification acknowledged that property was essential to political independence, but participants did not argue every man had a right to property. Virginia statesman Richard Henry Lee, in his "Letters from a Federal Farmer," noted the importance of "the equal division of lands among our people" as a way of securing good government, but he was critical of the "men in debt, who want no law, and who want a share of the property of others; these are called levelers, Shaysites, etc."[42] Lexicographer Noah Webster equated property with political power and suggested that the government should not support the protection or entail of estates from one generation to another. Webster claimed that only widespread possession of land, and the diffusion of knowledge, could guarantee freedom. "An equality of property, with a necessity of alienation, constantly operating to destroy combinations of powerful families, is the very *soul of a republic*—While this continues, the people will inevitably possess both *power* and *freedom;* when this is lost, power departs ..."[43] Webster's equation of property ownership with independence also implied that the poor, who were then flocking into the mid-Atlantic states, should not have the right to vote as long as they remained poor.[44]

Some of those poor spoke for themselves. Historians have fixed particularly on the writings of William Manning, a revolutionary war veteran and tavern keeper of modest means and education, whose tract, the "Key of Liberty," emphasized that widespread economic independence was central to the success of a republic. During the economic crisis of the 1780s, those who held the nation's public debt, especially soldiers, had sold their debt certificates for pennies on the dollar, because they feared that they would never be paid back, and it was better to get something rather than nothing. Speculators bought the debt certificates, concentrating them in only a few hands. At this point Secretary of the Treasury Alexander Hamilton, in his 1790 *Report on Public Credit,* recommended that the government assume and fully fund state debts, thus paying back those who had speculated on certificates, while their original owners would be out of luck.[45]

William Manning wrote one of his first political tracts in response to Hamilton's report, advocating that the original owners of the public debt be repaid, because they had only agreed to sell their debt certificates due to economic pressure that had been put on them by financial elites.[46] Manning later expanded his critique of society into a general political tract, "The Key of Liberty," in which he outlined prescriptions for a free society. "That government is most free that causes the greatest sum or degree of individual happiness in this world with the least national expense," Manning wrote. "The happiness of a person consisteth in eating and drinking and enjoying the good of his own labors, and feeling that his life and liberties (both civil and religious) and his property are safe and secure; and not in the abundance he possesseth, nor in expensive and national grandeur, which have a tendency to make other men miserable."[47]

Manning described society as divided between "the Few," who had an interest in maintaining inequality because their success depended on the dependence of laborers, and "the Many," who could easily be misled about their true interests if they were deprived access to education and the press.[48] He also advocated the formation of local chapters of a national body, the Laboring Society, to represent and educate working people. These aspects of Manning's thought convinced historian Alex Gourevitch to see Manning as a progenitor of nineteenth-century working-class reform movements.[49] Insisting on egalitarianism did not mean that Manning rejected progress or growth. He participated in the commercial economy, contracting to have part of a canal dug through his property, selling off pieces of land, and borrowing money from a bank. But these activities do not necessarily mean that Manning signed on to the "liberal" individualism of the market.[50] Rather, he would share a labor theory of property and an appreciation of the power conferred by wealth with many other critics of the social order over the next two centuries.[51]

Manning's vision of the proper direction for the republic can be contrasted with that of Alexander Hamilton, the author of the plan to fully reimburse war debts (and thus speculators). Hamilton supported this plan not only because the United States had a responsibility to pay its debts but also because the commercial investors who bought the debts were important to future economic growth. Hamilton's other proposals included federal assumption of existing state debts, to strengthen the central government at the expense of the states. He favored the creation of a Bank of the United States, which he hoped would, like the Bank of England, extend credit and thereby aid manufacturing. His *Report on Manufactures* emphasized that the future of the United States ought to lie in the manufacture of finished goods and so advocated industrial subsidies and protective tariffs.[52]

By the 1790s, economic conditions for American artisans were worsening. Journeymen—workers who had completed their apprenticeships but were employed by master artisans rather than owning their own shops—were beginning to see themselves as having interests different from those of their employers. They thus created their own journeymen's societies to parallel those their masters created.[53] Although elites had welcomed crowd participation in riots when it served their interests in the decades before the 1790s, once a stable and constitutional government had been formed, they expected dissent to be channeled into constitutional forms.

In the same decade, nascent political parties crystallized around the ideas of Alexander Hamilton (the Federalists) and Thomas Jefferson (the Democratic-Republicans). The Federalists, largely proponents of an alliance with Britain, criticized popular political protest. Invoking the French revolution, they referred to the Democratic-Republicans as Jacobins.[54] And it was true that the Democratic-Republicans admired the French revolutionary example, because the French revolutionaries initially professed their commitment to the equality of the individual, going much farther than the American revolutionary generation had been willing to do. The "Declaration of the Rights of Man and the Citizen" asserted that social distinctions were only acceptable if they contributed to the general good and enshrined the right to property as one of four fundamental rights.[55] Throughout the 1790s, the United States found itself caught in the midst of a 22-year war between Britain and France, both in terms of internal politics and foreign policy.

The new nation was also strained by tensions between the developed seaboard and poorer inland areas. On the western Pennsylvania frontier, speculators with surveying experience monopolized the good land; 10 percent of landowners held between 37 and 50 percent of the available land.[56] Up and down the frontier, Westerners lived lives that were completely different from anything imaginable by coastal elites; they farmed the most marginal land with the poorest tools while living crammed together with extended families in filthy cabins. They were also insecure, attacked in spectacularly gory fashion from time to time by economically embattled Native Americans, and responding with just as much brutality. While poorer farmers struggled, the Spanish, who controlled the Mississippi River, barred them from using it to ship crops to market. In a good example of poor timing, the federal government created an excise tax on whiskey, depriving western farmers who happened to have grain surpluses of an outlet for their goods (if excess grain could not be shipped downriver, at least it could be fermented and distilled, and then became a useful tool for barter in a cash-poor society). Alexander Hamilton, who was familiar only with large eastern distilleries that worked year-round, failed to see that a whiskey excise would devastate the western farmer. Moreover, the excise had always been a particularly unpopular tax, dating back to Britain in the 1720s, when opponents first argued that such a tax reached beyond trade regulation.[57]

As with Shays' Rebellion, the first actions of the Whiskey Rebels were peaceful and constitutional; westerners met in assemblies to condemn the excise tax. In some regions, they tarred and feathered excise tax collectors, preventing the tax from being collected at all. By August and September of 1794, three years after the passage of the excise, the frustrated western poor were arming, drilling, creating alternative societies for the pursuit of political aims, and erecting liberty poles, all things seen by those in the east as a threat to order and possibly to the future of the republic. President George Washington, in response, dispatched over 12,000 thousand militiamen to put down the uprising, outnumbering the rioters almost two to one.[58] As historian Alan Taylor points out, the Whiskey Rebellion was just one of many episodes in which frontier farmers attempted to impose their agrarian—and egalitarian—vision on the new republic. Ultimately, this vision triumphed, because it was taken up by Thomas Jefferson.[59]

WRITING ON INEQUALITY: THOMAS PAINE

Historians Richard Ellis and Gordon Wood both argue that the revolutionary generation really thought that with hard work, given the opportunities available in America, manly independence was assured.[60] In an era in which the continent seemed to stretch bounteously and emptily to the west, thinking about equality of end results was not important. The land could, at least in theory, serve as a "safety valve." People who might find themselves relegated to subordinate wage-earning positions could always leave the cities and go farm.

One of the few early Americans arguing that an equal process did not necessarily lead to an equal or even an acceptable result was political philosopher Thomas Paine, whose pamphlet *Common Sense* had been the catalyst for a declaration of independence from Britain in 1776. In *Agrarian Justice*, Paine made one of the first arguments in favor of government policies to promote a redistributive "stakeholder society."[61] Written when he was a representative to the National Assembly in France, *Agrarian Justice* proposed that the citizens of a nation had a natural right to resources and that governments should pay all citizens reparations to account for the usurpation of their right to an equal share of those resources.[62] Paine argued that "civilization" had costs as well as benefits. Without economic organization there was no economic growth and development, but economic development also produced "extremes of wretchedness."[63] He argued that no one born into a state of civilization should be worse off than had he been born in a state of nature.[64]

In a state of nature, Paine reasoned, every person had access to resources; over time, these resources were taken up and cultivated. But people born into an existing state of civilization could not collect the resources that were their right. To preserve the benefits of economic development while acknowledging that those without land had been treated unjustly, Paine advocated the creation of a national fund to pay each person a "stake" of 15 pounds sterling when he or she turned 21. Those over 50, and all blind people or those with physical disabilities, would be paid a pension of 10 pounds a year.[65] Paine proposed funding the pensions through a 10 percent estate tax.

Paine argued that his plan would restore economic justice and increase national prosperity. Young adults collecting a stake at age 21 would be less likely to fall into poverty in the future: "When a young couple begin the world, the difference is exceedingly great whether they begin with nothing or with fifteen pounds apiece. With this aid they could buy a cow, and implements to cultivate a few acres of land; and instead of becoming burdens upon society, which is always the case where children are produced faster than they can be fed, would be put in the way of becoming useful and profitable citizens." Paine invoked the notion of an interdependent society and a social debt; he claimed that a man "owes on every principle of justice, of gratitude, and of civilization, a part of that accumulation back again to society from whence the whole came."[66] Although Paine's redistributive taxation plan was never implemented, and *Agrarian Justice* remains one of Paine's lesser-known works, he inspired egalitarian working-class movements in both Britain and the United States.[67]

JEFFERSON AND INEQUALITY

While Alexander Hamilton's national plans promised to create cities full of factories, Thomas Jefferson famously championed widespread landownership.

As he wrote in his 1782 *Notes on the State of Virginia*, "Those who labour in the earth are the chosen people of God, if ever he had a chosen people, whose breasts he has made his peculiar deposit for substantial and genuine virtue. It is the focus in which he keeps alive that sacred fire, which otherwise might escape from the face of the earth. Corruption of morals in the mass of cultivators is a phenomenon of which no age nor nation has furnished an example."[68] Farmers could always depend on the soil to support themselves and their families without slavish dependence on wages. Mentally surveying the North American continent, and familiar with the farming capabilities of the average eighteenth-century family, Jefferson expected that the United States would have little to worry about in this regard for thousands of generations.[69] Jefferson even drafted legislation to grant each Virginia resident 75 acres of free land upon marriage.[70] The working-class land reformers described in Chapter 2 quoted Jefferson avidly; they loved his notion of "the palpable truth, that the mass of mankind has not been born with saddles on their backs, nor a favored few booted and spurred, ready to ride them legitimately, by the grace of God."[71]

But ironically, Jefferson's agrarianism did not really imply equality. To make his worldview at all consistent, Jefferson had to exclude people of African heritage from "the mass of mankind." Antislavery society founder Anthony Benezet and Thomas Paine, among others, had proposed to create an agreeable end to slavery by manumitting African Americans and giving them land beyond the boundaries of the surveyed states. As a group of enslaved African Americans had written to Massachusetts governor Thomas Hutchinson in 1773, "Grant us some part of the improved land, belonging to the province, for a settlement, that each of us may there quietly sit down under his own fig-tree, and enjoy the fruits of his own labour."[72] But Jefferson felt that "neither slaves who lacked civic identity or capacity, nor uncivilized and barbarous indigenous peoples who lacked any conception of property rights, could make legitimate claims on the land."[73]

Nor was this the only inegalitarian consequence. Because Jeffersonians believed ongoing access to more land, rather than redistribution of resources, was the best way to secure economic equity, the United States became committed to conquering more land, subjecting the lands and persons of Native Americans to perpetual threat.[74] While the British had responded to Native landownership with a 1763 declaration preventing British North American settlement west of the Appalachians, Americans had no reservations about expanding into Indian lands.[75] By the 1790s this had resulted in full-blown warfare in the Northwest Territory and an end to the pretense that expansion rested on anything other than colonialist conquest.[76]

Had the United States followed Paine's suggestions for taxation and redistribution, there would have been less perceived need to expand.[77] But as it was, the nation provided for the welfare of white families by acquiring land from Native Americans at bargain rates. In the decade beginning in 1790, the United States acquired 18,500 square miles of land from Native Americans through treaties—a price of less than two cents an acre. In the next decade, the government added an additional 153,400 acres of the Trans-Appalachian west at less than half a cent per acre.[78] Expansion westward required state intervention at every turn: in wars against the Indians, in the signing of treaties, and in the surveying of the land. Land sales generated some of the only revenue enjoyed by the federal government at this time.[79]

Ironically, given Jefferson's egalitarian intentions, the availability of vast tracts of land exacerbated inequality, as well-connected speculators bought the best lands at low prices. In Ohio between 1800 and 1820, 10 percent of male householders owned 50 percent of all of the available land, with some of the largest landowners—often, unsurprisingly, surveyors with inside information about the best investments—owning thousands of acres. Landowners generally were better off than in Europe, where a smallholder would be lucky to have 5 acres. The median American land holding was around 150 acres, and few farmers owned less than 40 acres, but many of the individuals flooding to Ohio owned no land at all.[80] Federalist speculators argued there could be no good title until the government catalogued and sold the land, and that acquiring title was the only way justly to acquire property. Squatters settled beyond the bounds of federally surveyed land, putting pressure on the government to acquire more land from the Native Americans and then to sell it in smaller parcels and for a lower price. Ultimately, historian Reeve Huston argues, the squatters and settlers were seen as a politically unstoppable force, paving the way for a policy of Indian removal by the Jackson administration.[81]

With the Panic of 1819, the bottom fell out of the land market, and those who had bought land from private owners rather than directly from the federal government found they could not renegotiate their contracts. In the new western states, debtors crusaded for replevin laws to delay the repayment of land-related debts, only to be overruled by courts that found that the sanctity of private contracts bulked larger than the general welfare.[82] President Andrew Jackson in particular opposed relief for debtors, and so the party that crystallized around him in the 1820s was much more concerned with limiting the scope of government than using the tools of government to promote equal opportunity. Although Jackson publicly accepted "distinctions in society" as completely natural, he earned support from the "common man" because he professed willingness to keep government from taking the little property owned by poor farmers and harassed working men.[83]

While life in the early American republic was not egalitarian, it was necessarily, in many senses, cooperative. Northern farm families living outside urban areas had highly interdependent relationships, both among family members and between families. While these were not egalitarian relationships either legally or practically, the participation of all family members in their gendered roles was crucial to familial success. Men planted, harvested, acquired and repaired farm tools, and participated in public activities, including militia service. Farm families depended on women to do everything from the daily chores of cooking, cleaning, fuel-gathering, and childcare; to the weekly or semiweekly tasks of baking and laundry; and the intermittent tasks of preserving meats, making butter and cheese, sewing, making soap, and gardening. Children were also involved with chores, including egg-gathering, the feeding and care of livestock, and bird-scaring.[84]

Over the first two decades of the nineteenth century, the United States experienced two interlocking revolutions that undermined this cooperation: a revolution in the nature of inland transportation, and a related "market revolution" that increased the participation of rural and inland urban people in formerly somewhat isolated market activities. Whereas before 1800 the most important American trade had issued from the five major Atlantic ports of Baltimore, New York, Philadelphia, Charleston, and Boston, shipping troubles emanating from attacks on neutral rights during the long war between Britain and France encouraged the nation to turn inward. Thus, during the war of 1812, and especially after it, with the advent of Henry Clay's "American system," an increasing emphasis on infrastructure resulted in road-building, canal-building, and the introduction of steamboat traffic on the Mississippi and other rivers crucial to trade shipment. As scholars of the early republic have pointed out, American farmers had always participated in trade of their excess produce, often through the barter system, but being interconnected with a larger national network of trade led them to scrutinize their priorities. Was the most important thing in life to be able to provide for one's family, to be relatively comfortable, to achieve, in the parlance of the time, a "competency?" Or was it to accumulate wealth and then invest in other projects?[85]

The nature of the workshop also changed. Long apprenticeships to train artisans in all of the "arts and mysteries" of their trade had been the norm in the eighteenth century. During the first two decades of the nineteenth, young men who previously would have stayed to learn a trade had opportunities to earn wages after being only partially trained. Those who took on apprentices and wanted to keep them had good reasons to hold off on actually training them until the very end of the indenture period.[86] These changes in the organization of the workplace, long predating mechanization of production, caused journeymen to form some of the first trade unions in the United States.

As this chapter has shown, despite Thomas Jefferson's airy profession in the Declaration of Independence that "all men are created equal," at no point during the early American republic was the nation committed to equality of either result or opportunity. Hierarchies of social station and social worth existed, were acknowledged, and were acted out through the possession of consumer goods. Alexander Hamilton advocated remaking Britain on American soil, and in the long run, his vision of a country with a national debt, a powerful credit-extending banking sector, and legions of waged workers seems prescient. In the short run, he was defeated by Jefferson's advocacy of an agrarian republic for white farm families. But even Jefferson's agrarian republic depended on slavery in the South and on the involuntary acquisition of land from Native Americans in the West.

Elite voices were not the only audible ones. Americans objecting to economic exploitation pushed back during the Shaysite and Whiskey Rebellions. William Manning's vision for labor organization and Thomas Paine's for taxation and redistribution were missed opportunities. But although more radical critics of economic inequality were brushed off as "levelers" or "agrarians," they were just the first of a long line of dissenters. If the inequality was continuous, so was the critique, as the next chapter will show.[87]

CHAPTER 2

Workingmen, Land, and the Age of Jackson: 1829–1865

Challenging an older historiographic tradition that claimed that the antebellum period provided great opportunities for upward mobility, the historian Edward Pessen wrote, "That antebellum Americans were ... probably better off than were most other people, is significant. Yet it does not render less inequitable the vast economic gulf separating Americans of similar age, nor does it reduce the gulf between the American ideal and the American reality."[1] Indeed, the antebellum period was a time of bewildering political and economic change in America. Infrastructure improvements impelled a market revolution, and demand for manufactured goods of all kinds increased. Changes in the organization of labor meant to streamline production made it more likely that some artisans would never move from journeyman to master. At the same time, property qualifications for suffrage were eliminated for white men, bringing poorer men into the political conversation. In the northern states, the late 1820s and 1830s ushered in a new era of thought and discourse about inequality, illustrated by the ideas of working-class philosopher Thomas Skidmore, the Working Men's Party, and the National Reform Association. The Homestead Act (1862) for which workingmen lobbied before the Civil War was a response to the allegation that land monopoly produced dependent workers.

In the South, in contrast, criticism of economic inequality was more muted, for several reasons. In the North, the critique of inequality issued from the working class, but the existence of slavery prevented large numbers of working-class migrants from moving to the South at all, since enslaved people occupied their economic niches. The number of northerners increased from 7.1 million in 1830 to 10 million in 1840 and then to more than 14 million in 1850, while the South contained fewer than 9 million people by 1850.[2] The least-well-off people in the South were enslaved, but poor white workers saw whiteness itself as property and did not see enslaved people as their allies. Slavery inflated the value of land in the South; it provided the resources that were integral to the northern textile industry; and it caused southern entrepreneurs to attract credit from both the North and international sources. As property, slaves represented about 18 percent of the wealth of the nation, and securitized mortgages on slaves were popular financial instruments among international investors before the Civil War.[3]

THE MARKET REVOLUTION

In the 30 years before the Civil War, the vast majority of Americans still lived and worked on farms, and "urban areas" were defined as concentrations of more than 2,500 people, so that even most people who lived in urban areas lived in towns rather than cities. Moreover, while new transportation opportunities like roads, canals, and later railroads brought antebellum Americans into a network that gave them access to new commercial opportunities, they were not made obsolete by factory production. In contrast with the situation in Europe, where the transformation to rational farming often meant a flood of former farm laborers from farms into factories, the availability of land meant that American farmers could keep moving westward until almost the end of the century. Until about 1880, American industry was mostly small-scale and grew in small increments and by expanding westward. Vertical integration, and firms that employed thousands of people, would really have to wait until the advent of the railroads.[4]

While antebellum Americans outside New England and the mid-Atlantic states did not, then, experience an "industrial revolution" like that of contemporary Britain, they did experience a "market revolution" that gave rural dwellers access to finished goods and caused the development of inland towns.[5] With the advent of the steamboat, freight rates on the Mississippi River fell from 6.2 cents per ton-mile upstream to 0.4 cents per ton-mile. The development of canals and railroads meant that shipping goods inland from the Eastern seaboard ports, which had been almost impossible in the eighteenth century, now took less than a week.[6] Americans could communicate with unprecedented ease due to the development of the telegraph and the steam-powered printing press.[7] The rate of growth of gross domestic product per capita doubled from 0.5 percent per year to almost 1 percent per year. At the same time, the concentration of populations in new urban areas presented problems of crowding, disease, lack of clean water, and lack of sanitation.[8]

The demand for, and possibility of producing, ever more cotton with slave labor led to the physical expansion of the United States. It also led to the increasing significance of the United States in the share of the world's cotton production. From 1791 to 1851, the cotton production of the United States expanded from 469 million bales to 2.5 billion bales, and from less than 1 percent of the world production of that staple to 67 percent. The United States supplied 99 percent of all of the raw cotton used by Great Britain's massive textile industry in 1851, and cotton represented 60 percent of American exports.[9]

The Gini coefficient of wealth inequality, which had been 0.694 in 1774, increased to 0.832 in 1860. Even incremental changes in the economy were producing significant inequality.[10] The inequality of the antebellum period is even more acute when we consider the plight of enslaved people, who are excluded from the above Gini coefficient calculation. The inequality of the antebellum period had physical effects. Over the period between 1780 and 1850, life expectancies at age 10 declined in the United States from a high of almost 56 years to a low of 48, and mean heights dropped from 5 feet 7 inches for white men to 5 feet 6 inches. These factors suggest that in the short run, market revolution changes could be detrimental. Historians have suggested that inequality of distribution, variable trade cycles, urbanization, and the ease with which diseases could travel along new trade routes may have been to blame.[11]

In his book *Democracy in America*, written after an 1831 tour of the United States, the Frenchman Alexis de Tocqueville praised American social and economic mobility.[12] Of course the second quarter of the nineteenth century saw the making of many fortunes in diverse industries. The Astor family made a fortune through fur-trading, shipping, and real estate speculation; the Lowells and Lawrences erected textile factories in New England. But these examples tell only part of the story. Barriers to entry in many fields may have been relatively low, but artisans without family money found it increasingly hard to reach "master mechanic" status.[13] Technological advances caused a divergence between the fortunes of the unskilled and those who could afford to employ, or be hired to maintain, the new technologies.[14]

Nor were the artisans the most disadvantaged. Unskilled laborers, the men who operated the dredging machines or dug the canals, faced low wages and periods of unemployment that barely kept their families out of poverty. Poor families relied on a combination of household resource pooling, scavenging, and occasional stays in almshouses to keep body and soul together.[15] Since the poor spend more of their pay on basic commodities that are less sensitive to changes in technology, the movement of prices can have an outsize impact on their relative prosperity. Before 1860, the cost of living was higher for the poor than the rich, based on the basket of goods and services that they were likely to buy.[16]

Black urban families faced some of the most daunting odds, since discrimination limited black men to fields like unskilled construction laborer, carter, and, if very lucky, barber, and relegated black women into the roles of laundress and street vendor. Racism, including the unwillingness of whites to sell property to black families, created residential segregation. Although the vast majority of black families in this period were headed by two parents and were buoyed up by participation in mutual support societies and in the church, they still skated at the edge of destitution.[17]

One of the most prominent features of modern American inequality is the stigma surrounding poverty and government assistance. Historians trace the roots of the discourse on the "deserving" poor in America to the antebellum period. Overseers of the poor—those who could grant or deny poor relief—differentiated between such worthy objects of charity as the elderly, the disabled, and industrious widows and unworthy objects: single men who were capable of work. In order to ensure that the almshouse was truly a last resort, they supported only a truly miserable and highly regimented lifestyle for their inmates. Because the undeserving poor were thought to be poor because they were immoral, even meaningless work, like working a treadwheel, was emphasized.[18]

THE POLITICAL TRANSFORMATION

Although economic inequality among white males increased in the decades before the Civil War, it was partially offset by political inclusion. During the 1820s, following the example of the six new states that entered the union, existing states changed the basis of voting from property-ownership to white, male personhood.[19] Within this changed milieu, national politics, which had settled into a one-party system between the end of the War of 1812 and the 1824 presidential election, saw revived partisanship. Banking and tariffs emerged as important issues.

While President Andrew Jackson was not the representative of the common man that his publicists made him out to be, he did very vocally oppose the recharter of the Second Bank of the United States. Jackson and his partisans thought that in the process of issuing paper money, banks made profits, whereas there were no excess profits involved in trade with hard currency. The Second Bank of the United States had been created in 1816 by government charter, thereby representing the sort of "chartered monopoly" that these men most feared. As Jackson explained when he vetoed the recharter of the Bank, he did not believe that equality of condition could ever be attained, but every man had the opportunity to benefit from the fruits of his own industry, as long as government intervention did not worsen inequalities by giving privileges to some and not to others.[20] Jackson's opponents, the Whigs, argued that the Bank benefited everyone by providing easy credit that was necessary for the expansion of the economy, but that argument did not prevail. Ironically, after the veto of the Bank's recharter, state banks that moved into the banking vacuum shifted vast fortunes to slaveholders who sought to bring new southern soil under cultivation.[21] Jackson supported tariffs, portraying them as patriotic weapons nurturing all American infant industries from competition by foreign trade. Moreover, if American industries were protected, American manufacturing workers could earn higher wages and avoid becoming impoverished like English factory workers.[22]

Newly enfranchised workingmen not only participated in presidential elections and shaped concerns about inequality at the national level, they also participated in a popular politics much closer to the ground. As historian Paul Gilje shows, the nature of rioting changed in the 1820s and 1830s from deferential crowd behavior to "collective bargaining by riot." This tactic spread from the ranks of unskilled laborers, who traditionally had little leverage, to journeymen in the skilled trades, who felt increasingly pressed between an affluent class of master craftsmen and a large pool of partly trained workers who were capable of doing the journeymen's jobs for less money. Working people in this period talked not about class but rather about productivity as indicative of social worth, since productivity illustrated a "virtuous, honest, hardworking citizenry."[23] This social critique implicitly rejected the "gentility" to which the middle and upper classes aspired. Working people used violence to protest not only against oppressive labor conditions, but also against religious minorities and African Americans. In turn, elites deputized professional police forces to put down these disturbances. Taken together, these developments show that if there had been a cross-class alliance after the American Revolution it was breaking down.[24]

Inequality came to the fore in the antebellum era not just because the economy and political structure were changing but also because for the first time, in an era of print that was cheap both to produce and consume, working people had easy access to the tools of dissemination for their ideas. English emigrant William Heighton organized the *Mechanics' Free Press* in Philadelphia in 1828 and used its space to rail against "invidious and artificial class distinctions, unnatural and unjust inequalities."[25] Newspapers like *The Working Man's Advocate* persisted for years, providing New York's labor activists with the space for editorials, explanations of their grievances, summaries of their activities, and calls for action. Labor newspapers called for equal educational opportunities for workers' children, for reductions in the length of the work-day, and for an end to the practice of imprisonment for debt, all on the grounds that these prevented working people from equal political participation and knowledge.[26] These newspapers could freely be exchanged by mail, meaning that editors copied each other's editorials and articles and helped create a national discourse.[27] As historian Arthur Young has shown, during the 1830s labor advocates began to portray the American Revolution as a people's revolution, bringing back into popular consciousness events that had been largely forgotten, like the "destruction of the tea" (renamed the Boston Tea Party).[28]

As fathers, the New York Working Men were particularly determined that their children not grow up in a society structured by inequality. Some of the labor advocates sided with socialist advocate Robert Dale Owen, who advocated state-run boarding schools. All children would be removed from their homes and raised collectively by the state in a way that would give all children equal advantages. Others were galvanized by workingman Noah Cook's proposal for the state to subsidize free public day schools for working-class children. Even the Cook faction did not necessarily oppose state-funded boarding schools.[29]

But this nascent critique of inequality and the creativity aimed at its resolution were undermined by factors that divided urban working people. By the late 1820s, the political parties, Whig and Democrat, had become ethnic proxies for native-born Americans and immigrants respectively, and on Election Day, voters literally had to fight their way to the ballot boxes amid threatening scrums.[30] African Americans, who were embraced by neither political party, asserted themselves against the re-enslavement of runaway slaves through riots. Historian Paul Gilje catalogued riots in 1819, 1826, and 1831. Much more common were race riots by white workers against African American institutions and churches, including an 1834 riot intended to purge the city of black people.[31]

ANTEBELLUM WRITERS ON INEQUALITY: THOMAS SKIDMORE

Among the New York Working Men, the man with the most thorough-going proposal for addressing inequality was Thomas Skidmore. Born in Connecticut in 1790, Skidmore began his career as a teenaged teacher in a village school. He became an itinerant educator, with positions as far south as

North Carolina, never staying in one position for long. Then, after three years spent in Wilmington, Delaware, working in the gunpowder and wire industries, he migrated to New York City. There he married and began to raise four sons before his life was cut short by cholera in 1832.[32]

In his 1829 *Rights of Man to Property!*, Skidmore described a detailed plan for distributive justice.[33] He began with the familiar premise that self-ownership and owning one's labor power are crucial elements of human freedom: "Whenever nations have ceased to exist . . . it has been because there has prevailed in them no system, or theory of government, whereby property should be as nearly equal among the people, comparatively speaking, as their stature; and yet so constructed, as that each individual should labor, as it were, *exclusively* for himself, except so far as regards contributions to the public service."[34] But Skidmore also understood that arriving at adulthood with no property except the ownership of one's own labor put one at an incredible disadvantage. A man who only owns himself is forced to deplete his own resources and sacrifice physical comfort in order to survive: "How can it be said, that I am created with an equal right to this happiness—with another, when I must purchase property of him, with labor and suffering, and when he is under no necessity to purchase the like of me at the same costly price?"[35] Skidmore denied, moreover, that a fair contract could ever exist between a poor person, who lacked a share of resources, and a wealthy person.[36]

Skidmore asserted a broad claim: that humans had an initial and prepolitical right to an equal share of resources, which could be generalized from the right to life. No one questions that a person has a right to breathe, take in light with his eyes, or occupy the space taken up by her body. Skidmore argued that the necessities that support physical existence—food, water, and shelter—are only extensions of the human body because they are the things humans need to survive.[37] Each individual is primarily focused on perpetuating his own existence; if she is deprived of those basic necessities, she can have no motivation to support the government or the economic structure.[38] Creatively, Skidmore recognized that we have responsibilities to the rising generation. People continue to be born into a world in which property has already been distributed or claimed. But a child has just as much right to resources as those who preceded and surround him, simply "in virtue of his existence, and in virtue of the existence of the property in question. They are inseparable; while one has vital life, or the other physical existence."[39]

Many of the founders were influenced by the English philosopher John Locke, who had argued that people create private property by fencing land, improving it, or otherwise mixing it with labor.[40] In contrast, Skidmore denied that labor had magical properties that conferred ownership on natural resources. He noted that because civilization is so ancient, no matter how much labor individuals perform, they are tremendously indebted to preceding generations for preparing infrastructure.[41] Moreover, since a natural right to resources does not identify any particular *tract* of land or set of resources as belonging to any particular person, taking ownership of particular tracts without everyone's consent made everyone else worse off.[42] Everyone has an equal claim, and "there can exist no power whatever to destroy equality of rights, but the power of violence and injustice."[43] All of these premises lay the groundwork for Skidmore to assert that people only have a right to their possessions during their lifetimes.

Skidmore devised a mechanism to distribute property that people could use during their lifetimes and to collect that property again after their deaths. Using the state of New York as an example, he proposed a property census. All citizens of the state would be required to register all the real and personal property in their possession (anyone holding back items from the general inventory would have to serve 14 years in prison for grand larceny). Having performed the property census, the state would issue the adult natives of the state with a dividend, or credit, corresponding to their equal portion of the value of the goods and chattels enumerated in the state. Once this dividend was credited, the state would hold an auction, at which credited citizens would purchase real and personal property. Those who were disabled or insane would also participate, represented by guardians or trustees acting on their behalf.[44] Anything so large or complex that it could not be divided up might be jointly purchased by a group of people.[45] After the auction, the value of the goods sold would be compared with the original dividend, and those who remained creditors to the state because they had not spent their original dividend would be entitled to a second dividend, called a patrimony.[46] Thus, some people in the state would have acquired property, and others a credit against the government.[47] Because those citizens reaching adulthood in every year subsequent to the initial auction had a claim on resources, Skidmore proposed that each year, the general inventory be repeated with the goods of everyone who had died in the past year. This inventory would then be divided up among those who come of age. People receiving their dividend might take it in cash or in credit to buy the goods that the state would always have on sale.[48]

This would create an initial equality; but how would it be maintained over time? Skidmore proposed that states be prohibited from recognizing and executing wills, since inheritances concentrate property within families over time. He argued that wills unfairly allow the current generation to bind future generations. "For, as individuals are equal one with another, so are generations;

and to allow a past generation to extend the operation of its laws or its wishes into the present generation, contrary to their consent, is to allow a principle which destroys the existence of equality between one generation and another."[49] While Skidmore's assertion may seem surprising, political scientist Michael Levy points out there is nothing inherent in liberalism that automatically protects the right to make bequests or gifts of property to future generations. The most important thing to ask is: what does a society value? Is it most important to guard against inequalities that prevent large numbers of people from achieving life goals or participating meaningfully in political decisions, or is it more important to protect the rights of the deceased to make bequests? At least in 1829 and in the United States, the answer to this question had not been definitively settled.[50]

Skidmore also suggested that the state provide for all children. Some parents are too poor to have any property to share with their children; some choose not to share with their children; some children are orphans. But each child has a natural right to sustenance. Skidmore suggested that the state invest some of the proceeds from its annual auctions in a state treasury to pay for each child's needs. Other members of the Working Men's Party favored state-funded boarding schools that would give even the children of the poor economic opportunity, but Skidmore was the only one to also advocate a stipend.[51] He argued that a state-assured patrimony would be much more secure than a parent's personal fortune.[52] Although Skidmore rejected any calls for poor families to regulate their fertility, on the grounds that this would interfere with their right to reproduce, he advocated not only for child benefit but also for state-funded health insurance.[53] Ultimately, he argued, each generation was entitled to the rights enjoyed by previous generations: "Those who have arrived at maturity have not done so without being in debt to a generation which has gone before them. This debt they must discharge by making payment to the generation which comes after them."[54]

Finally, Skidmore argued that property and political power were inextricably united:

> Whoever looks over the face of the world, and surveys the population of all countries; our own, as well as any and every other; will see it divided into rich and poor; into the hundred who have everything, and the million who have nothing. If, then, Mr. Jefferson, had made use of the word *property*, instead of "the pursuit of happiness," I would have agreed with him ... for I hold that man's natural right to *life* or *liberty*, is not more sacred or inalienable, than his right to property ... in the pursuit of happiness, is property of no consequence? Can anyone be as happy without property of any kind, as with it? Is even liberty and life to be preserved without it?[55]

Skidmore considered political power and property ownership as so mutu-
ally self-reinforcing that he called for the enfranchisement of Indians, African
Americans, and women so that they could use political power to protect their
property.[56] Using language similar to that of the Occupy Wall Street movement of 2011, Skidmore argued that his plan "was of the utmost benefit to
the poor and middling classes of the community, who form ninety-nine parts
in every hundred of the whole population of every country," so that "it would
be perfectly idle to oppose what so very large a majority should determine to
adopt and enforce."[57]

Was Skidmore's plan realistic? Probably not. To make his plan work,
Skidmore's New York would have had to develop a huge bureaucracy to enu-
merate all of the goods and chattels, and a place to store them. It would have
needed to maintain a state auction house and a treasury sufficient to hold the
"credits" of those who failed to spend all of their patrimony the first year.
And the bureaucracy would have had to be large and durable enough to provide annual accounting, storage, and auction services each year as people died,
their goods were confiscated by the state, and then were auctioned off to the
new group of people reaching the age of majority. Skidmore's state would
have been, by antebellum standards, mind-bogglingly large.[58] Opponents of
his plan did not dissect it in detail but rather just accused him of "agrarianism," alluding to the agrarian laws of the Gracchi of ancient Rome, who proposed to divide up land and distribute it to the people.[59]

Was Skidmore's plan significant? This is a harder question to answer. Skidmore's voice was quickly marginalized from the mainstream of the Working
Men's Party.[60] This fact has led historians to claim that his ideas about equitable distribution were unpopular with labor's rank and file. For example,
James Huston argues that the Working Men accepted the longstanding
Jeffersonian position that political equality led to economic equality unless
employers and non-producers deprived workers of their just rewards.[61] Political scientist Michael Thompson also argues that the Working Men generally
opposed state intervention.[62] On the other hand, as Paul Gilje shows, even
in New York City, some workers tore down fences that had been erected
around former commons, which he reads as an endorsement of a free-land
tradition.[63] Historian Sean Wilentz contends that Skidmore's vision captured
some of the status anxiety of the American artisan: "that something was ter-
ribly wrong in America, something unforeseen by the Founding Fathers,
something that was creating social privilege and inequality and destroying
the Republic from within, something that had to be removed."[64] Historian
J. R. Pole further emphasizes that, whatever Skidmore's direct political
influence of lack thereof, he showed that, even during the Jacksonian period,

it was possible to reference an economically egalitarian version of America's founding principles in calling for social change.[65]

The interpretations that marginalize Skidmore seem to me incorrect. First of all, Skidmore was popular enough to come within 30 votes of being elected to the New York City Council in the 1829 election, in which the Working Men comprised about a third of the electorate. Only later did *The Working Man's Advocate* back away from the call for a more equitable distribution of property, changing its banner "All children are entitled to equal education; all adults to equal property, and all mankind to equal privileges" to "All children are entitled to equal education; all adults, to equal privileges."[66]

More substantially, between 1844 and 1862, thousands of artisans, many of whom had become politicized through the Working Men's movement, lobbied Congress for "free homesteads" from the public lands. A "free homestead" is perfectly consistent with the Jeffersonian vision of small independent producers, but it requires (obviously unjust) redistribution from Native Americans who own the land to landless workers, and a massive government "welfare" program to implement.[67] James Huston has divided antebellum American political economists into "free traders," who thought abundant free land could create equal opportunity without government intervention, and protectionists, who called for government intervention like protective tariffs. The movement to obtain free land for actual settlers sits uncomfortably in the space in between. The land reformers called for large-scale government intervention in order to distribute the land. Then, the land would provide enough independence so that homesteaders could resist government control.[68]

The long history of squatting in the American West also shows that individuals eagerly asserted claims to resources. Settlers moved onto land past the surveyed boundary of the states and asserted moral claims by tilling the soil and building shelters. Some squatters banded together into claim associations both to defend each other's claims from interlopers before the land was officially sold and to keep the price of the land low once it reached auction. Squatters, portraying themselves as hardy pioneers, demanded a federal preemption law; in turn, land speculators painted them as lawless banditti. In 1841, the Preemption Act was finally passed, granting federal recognition to the squatter position.[69]

A commitment to egalitarianism can also be seen in the Anti-Rent agitation in New York's Hudson Valley, which began with the death of landlord Stephen Van Rensselaer in 1839 and lasted into the mid-1840s. The wealthy descendants of Dutch patroon landlords presided over almost-feudal leases. The leases contained obligations to landlords, restrictions on the use of leased land, and the quarter-sale (whereby a farmer selling his lease to another farmer had to remit a quarter of the purchase price to the landlord). The Anti-Renters portrayed the patroons as aristocratic monopolists and saw the solution to their problem as voting in concert in order to prevent unjust laws.[70] They called for an end to patroons' tax loopholes, for the right to have clear title to their lands, and for the right to have their goods free from confiscation for debt. But underneath all this lay their belief that only a more equitable distribution of the soil could prevent the oppression of some adult men by others. Anti-Renters' activities extended from publishing and holding public meetings to behind-the-scenes vigilante work by young men dressed up as Indians and armed with weapons and tin horns.

The existing New York political parties viewed the Anti-Renters' attack on patroons' titles as an attack on property, and the popularity of Anti-Rent caused a split in the political parties as well as in the Anti-Rent movement. Some Anti-Renters, those with more faith in the ability of capitalistic growth to promote equality, supported the liberal Whigs; others, who felt strongly that equality was impossible without access to land, gravitated toward the Democratic Party. Traced through either party line, Anti-Rent ideas contributed to the notion that a Homestead Act could aid political equality.[71]

Working people's enthusiasm for government action did have boundaries. The government that gave free homesteads to actual settlers on the public lands could also take away from the common stock by granting "the right of eminent domain, the right to build a ferry, or to dam a river, or by granting corporate charters." This system of using public resources for private gain deeply worried many working people in the Jacksonian era, and this concern, that state-sanctioned corporations were enjoying inappropriate levels of state power, would persist even after states did little for corporations beyond allowing them to charter.[72]

ANTEBELLUM WRITERS ON INEQUALITY: ORESTES BROWNSON

Like Thomas Skidmore, the writer and printer Orestes Brownson thought inequality was undermining the United States. Brownson approached the question of social class from a religious perspective. While some clerics quoted "the poor we will always have with us," Brownson believed that social divisions were both unnecessary and man-made. In his July 1840 *Boston Quarterly Review* article "The Labouring Classes," Brownson argued that without economic equality, there could be no political equality.[73] Brownson systematically considered, and then debunked, other proposed solutions for the problems of the working classes. For example, he derided universal public education, noting that "a swarm of naked and starving urchins crowded into a school-room will make little proficiency in the 'Humanities.' "[74] He denied that either religion or self-cultivation were solutions to economic inequality; the problem, he asserted, was systemic, larger than any one man. Moreover, Christianity as Jesus taught it meant concern for the poor and for social reform, for every man to sit under his own vine and fig tree, so that none could make him afraid.[75]

Like many in the Working Men's movement, Brownson called free white workers worse off than slaves, since white workers were often willing to work but could find no work and had all the responsibility for maintaining roofs over their families' heads and food in their stomachs.[76] No working man, he argued, had ever been able to lift himself from the position of mere operative to master on the wages of labor alone, without riding on the back of someone else.

Brownson blamed inequality in America on "sacerdotal corporations": elites who had monopolized power by capitalizing on the credulity of the common people. He proposed the repeal of all legislation that promoted inequality, and he called for the destruction of the banking system. Like Skidmore, Brownson argued that a man's property right only persisted during his lifetime; after that, his property reverted to the state, "to be disposed of by some equitable law."[77] Apparently this last suggestion caused great controversy, because in the reprinted edition of his article, Brownson denied having any radical intention or disrespect for private property.[78] Ultimately, Brownson became convinced that the only hope for the United States lay in a utopian Christian commonwealth.[79]

Brownson was not the only antebellum Christian with progressive thoughts about inequality in the period of the Second Great Awakening. Historian of religion Randall Balmer has recently emphasized that Jacksonian clergymen were often politically progressive and attuned to the problem of poverty. Clergy not only promoted reforms that advanced equality of opportunity, like free public education, antislavery, and rights for women, but also sometimes criticized capitalism for its embrace of greed.[80]

ROLE OF WOMEN

How did antebellum Americans justify the continued exclusion of women from the benefits of property ownership, citizenship and political participation? Single women could make contracts and serve as executors and guardians but could not vote, serve on juries, or serve in elected positions. Married women lacked political and legal equality in the antebellum period due to the existence of legal doctrines that subsumed their separate legal personalities under those of their husbands.[81]

The introduction of widespread men's wage labor outside the home helped to demarcate women's work inside the home as unpaid and therefore worth less—both less than men's work and less than the economic partnership characteristic of the colonial farm or the rural homestead. Women were encouraged to consider their contribution to the family economy unimportant, despite the fact that, particularly for urban working-class families, women's abilities to scavenge fuel and food, recycle and reuse clothing and other household items, and house rent-paying lodgers were vital.[82] Women who worked for wages were largely invisible, since their work lay outside the normative ideal; they were also paid much less than men, making female-headed households some of the poorest.[83] Occasionally, a subset of women showed that it was possible for women to exercise power without completely disrupting the order of things. In the South, for example, the widows of slaveholders wielded great economic power while simultaneously claiming to do what their late husbands would have wanted them to do, or acting for the benefit of their minor children. Such women rarely remarried, showing that there were clear benefits to be had in the widowed state.[84]

Some contemporary women, including antislavery advocates Angelina and Sarah Grimké and a Massachusetts woman writing under the pseudonym Keziah Kendall, detailed the injustices wreaked on women by the legal definition of their role. Kendall noted that marital mixing of property often left women poor and powerless. In her own case, because she wanted to marry a man who had a previous business failure, the policy had also left her permanently single. The Grimké sisters used the Bible to assert that men and women were created equal and were meant to be treated as equals. Legal decisions, not nature, created inequality.[85]

Some advocates used women's helplessness or inferior status to argue that they should have economic power. They claimed that that a wife's separate estate, brought into a marriage, ought to be protected from confiscation by a husband's creditors. Women and children lacked protection from unscrupulous or unlucky heads of families. Opponents of such legislation pointed out that couples could shelter some of their property by simply designating it as the wife's separate estate. Some even argued that granting married women property rights was the first step down the slippery slope to women's suffrage. But by 1848, nineteen states had created acts insulating married women's separate property.[86]

State constitutional conventions that met between 1820 and 1860 provide some of the most solid evidence about how contemporaries saw women's political role. One or two proponents of women's suffrage might put forth the idea, but the vast majority of male legislators immediately ruled out women's political participation on two grounds. The first was that women were adequately protected by the political participation of their husbands or fathers; and the second was that women's own moral superiority would be undermined by their participation in politics. Politics might expose women to problems and questions that would render them less womanly.[87] Of course, some women did participate in shop floor politics without becoming "unwomanned." Women textile factory workers fomented strikes in the 1830s and a created a movement to restrict the workday to 10 hours in the 1840s. But even they followed the expected life-path; 85 percent of women workers married after leaving the mills.[88]

BLACK AMERICANS, FREE AND ENSLAVED

While women were excluded from political participation on ideological grounds, free African Americans were prevented from enjoying the rights of citizenship, including voting, on the grounds of expediency. Historian Rowland Berthoff's study of state constitutional convention debates shows that before the Civil War, most politicians at such conventions did not attempt to argue that black people were biologically inferior to whites but rather that enfranchising them would cause great resentment by white voters and southern states. Many also expressed fears that African Americans would somehow come to dominate the political system or that political integration was a gateway to social integration and miscegenation. Ironically, at the same time that these conventions excluded blacks and women from political participation, they began to acknowledge the personhood of corporations.[89]

For most antebellum Americans, the exclusion of enslaved African Americans required little justification. Historian Edward Baptist emphasizes that enslaved African Americans were considered to be completely interchangeable parts in the system of Southern agricultural production no matter what skills they might possess. For example, when it served their financial calculations, plantation owners forced slaves to migrate away from their families. By the 1820s, slave traders had become professionalized, purchasing enslaved people in large numbers from the upper South and selling them to areas like Georgia and Louisiana in which there was large demand for forced labor.[90] Whether working as cotton field hands or overseeing other crops, slaves generally worked under the gang labor system, from sunup to sundown, between five and six days a week.[91] To maintain productivity, planters used physical punishment to create levels of productivity among enslaved workers that would later be unknown among free workers doing the same tasks.[92]

Economic inequality was especially severe in the antebellum South. Enslaved African Americans constituted between 30 and 40 percent of the population in 1860. If slaves are counted as wealth, then they constituted about 50 percent of Southern wealth, and most of that wealth was concentrated among the top 5 percent of white families. Seventy-five percent of white households did not own slaves. The top thousand planter families had an income almost equal to the remaining 660,000 white families in the South.[93]

But even within the great inequality that was slavery, there was further variation. Some enslaved people did participate in the market economy in their own right. In northern Virginia, enslaved people could rent out their time for a few hours on Saturday evenings or on Sundays (although this "free time" conflicted with the only opportunities that many men had to visit their families on neighboring plantations). In the Louisiana sugar-growing regions, slaves were overworked during the two- to three-month "grinding season" when the cane was processed. But when not engaged in these 18-hour workdays, they were expected to tend their own gardens and to raise chickens to sell back to the plantation owner or to local markets. In the rice fields of low-country South Carolina, enslaved people worked by the task and could stop work when the day's stint was completed. Many cultivated surpluses of food and sold crops for cash.[94]

Slaveholding fostered inequality in other ways as well. Although plantation owners sold cotton to Europe at the low prices that were possible due to slave labor, across the region people failed to plow profits back into the development of infrastructure or cities. As a result, southern states generally had unimpressive domestic markets.[95] Slaveholding also put a brake on direct investment in industry, since slaveholders had most of their capital tied up in land and slaves, although they did approve a tariff on southern manufacturing and used state funds to subsidize railroad construction.[96] But historian Steven Hahn argues that some southern whites who did not own slaves saw slavery as beneficial because it protected an older lifestyle of cultivating crops for home consumption and bartering skills for other needs.[97]

Slavery eventually acquired many layers of justification. After Nat Turner's Rebellion (1831), which culminated in the deaths of 55 whites, defending slavery seemed even more urgent. Once, slavery had been characterized as an unfortunate institution that it was too late to eliminate; later, it was defended positively as the best social system.[98] Virginian Thomas Dew described forced labor as economically progressive and pragmatic, claiming that it was important to counteract African Americans' desire for unlimited leisure.[99] South Carolina's John Calhoun denounced the notion that all men were created equal. Without inequality, there could never be progress: "The main spring of progress is the desire of individuals to better their condition ..."[100] While the northern states were home to cut-throat capitalism and to a natural war between labor and capital, Calhoun described each plantation as a microcosm of harmony between labor and capital, embodied by the person of the plantation owner.[101]

One of the most prolific anonymous editorial writers on slavery, Virginia lawyer George Fitzhugh, advocated slavery as a form of paternalistic social organization for workers. As had the New York Working Men, Fitzhugh argued that competition promoted a race to the bottom in living standards. He claimed that workers and their employers in the North were only linked by the impersonal cash nexus, and that a manual worker had almost no power compared with the man who would or would not hire him. But Fitzhugh went beyond the arguments of northern workers by arguing that dependent relationships were better because they caused an affectionate tie: between husbands and wives, parents and children, and masters and slaves.[102] He argued that in the best-case scenario, all workers would be enslaved.[103] In the north, newspaper editors went wild, printing and reprinting Fitzhugh's anonymous editorials while alleging a southern conspiracy to deprive white workers of their liberties.[104]

Historian Peter Kolchin argues that slaveholders in the United States (in contrast with the Russian serf-holders he compares them to) were able to defend slavery freely because of the free press in the United States. In fact the press was not free, as the persecution of abolitionist editors and the inability to deliver abolitionist tracts in the South showed. For southerners, slavery signified more than just economic achievement; it also signified social, racial, and political supremacy that might be lost if the slaves were freed.[105] In the South before the Civil War, then, inequality was an article of faith.

Between the late 1820s and the Civil War, transformations in infrastructure and changes in the organization of the workplace created a more integrated national market, at least in the northern states, but they did so at the expense of white urban workers whose skills were no longer protected. Enfranchised white male workers used their new political power to challenge inequality through strikes and an active Working Men's Movement, achieving part of what they asked for in the form of subsidized homesteads at the expense of Native Americans. The contribution of women and of enslaved African Americans to national productivity was largely ignored.

By the 1850s, the discourse about economic inequality was pushed aside by sectional tensions that had their roots in economic and geographic expansion. Worrying that northern states intended to regulate away slavery, depriving slaveholders of their property in humans, southern politicians responded with the threat, and then the reality, of secession.[106] The new Republican Party, the party of Lincoln, adopted the mantle of free labor, but this meant only the freedom of the individual worker to contract, no matter how little leverage the worker might have in the negotiating process. The Democratic Party embraced the concept of economic independence, but it was independence for white men only. The country could accommodate a range of economic strategies, including slavery, which protected the independence of white men in the South; and the union movement, which protected the independence of working-class white men in the North.[107]

Throughout the Civil War, glimmerings appeared at times of the importance of inequality. It was audible in the complaint that the war was a rich man's war and a poor man's fight, since slaveholders could be exempted from the southern draft, while wealthy and middle-class northerners could hire a substitute or pay a $300 commutation fee.[108] It was visible in the 1863 New York draft riots, as angry draftees set fire to African American homes, orphanages, schools, and other buildings.[109] Inequality was palpable during the war when African American Union troops were paid less than their white comrades, and later when only free blacks rather than former slaves received their back pay.[110] At the end of a four-year Civil War, while slavery had been outlawed, the deep economic inequality created by a forced labor system remained unaddressed, and, as the next chapter will show, the commitment of the reigning Republican Party to "freedom of contract" meant that it would not be addressed for the remainder of the nineteenth century.

CHAPTER 3

Free Labor and Social Darwinism: 1865–1900

W hile the Civil War ended slavery, inequality changed shape rather than disappearing. Waves of immigration to the North, urbanization, and a complete revision of the labor system among freed people in the South precipitated a wide-ranging discussion of inequality and distribution. Large-scale industrialization, the formation of vertical and horizontal trusts, and the creation of transcontinental railroads facilitated the growth of large, untaxed, individual fortunes. But financial panics in 1873 and 1893, and the Great Strike of 1877, revealed the limitations of American upward mobility and the shortcomings of a philosophy predicated on individual bootstrapping. Some Americans, like sociologist William Graham Sumner, proposed that evolutionary theory meant that intervention in the economy to help the poorest would have tragic effects for the future of the race. Other thinkers, like politician Henry George and novelist Edward Bellamy, equally believed in evolutionary progress but proposed innovative solutions to inequality like the single tax and the industrial army. Organizations like the Knights of Labor and the Populist movement exerted ideological pressure for social change and greater equality of condition, but they were fragmented by racial and ethnic tensions.

RECONSTRUCTION

The new inequality of the late nineteenth century converged on the United States from several different directions, one of which was the handling of the postwar southern economy. The Civil War left approximately 4 million enslaved African Americans nominally free but able to make very few social or economic choices. As the American land reformers had predicted, freed African Americans equated independence with landownership, and during the Civil War, the Union experimented with redistributing Confederate land to freed slaves. Radical Republicans in Congress proposed a program of dividing confiscated Confederate lands from 70,000 rebel leaders into small farms. Each family would receive up to 40 acres of land and seed money from the federal government. General William T. Sherman's Special Field Order 15, promulgated on January 16, 1865, reserved the coastal islands and former Carolina rice plantations to distribute to formerly enslaved families. The Freedmen's Bureau was empowered, beginning in March of that year, to divide the land into 40-acre plots that could be purchased after a three-year lease agreement. In the short run, 40,000 African Americans received land grants of almost 40,000 acres.[1]

Promising experiments ended due to lack of wider support in Washington for confiscation and redistribution, lest such policies make people dependent on charity.[2] By 1866, white plantation owners were allowed to re-enter their former lands and then to claim back lands that had been distributed to black families. Due to bureaucratic snafus, many black people had never received titles, which made their land tenure very easy to contest. Many who were deprived of their land grants despaired of being able to raise a crop without seed money and began to work for white planters under labor contracts; others were directly dispossessed. Historians differ about whether land reform was likely to have been successful. Roger Ransom argues that, given the shortage of credit and failure of infrastructure in the postwar South, freed blacks were very unlikely to have been successful commercial farmers even had they been granted land.[3] Moreover, black landowners with substantial land generally opposed confiscation and redistribution, instead emphasizing that all freed people had the opportunity to save their earned wages in order to buy land. The black community disagreed about whether freedmen possessed the work skills to compete in free labor markets.[4] Either way, the fact that freed slaves began their postslavery lives with nothing but the clothing on their backs, rather than receiving start-up land and livestock, had long-term consequences for American inequality. As late as 1910, white southern property ownership outstripped black property ownership by a factor of 16 to 1.[5]

Once Abraham Lincoln had been assassinated and his replacement, President Andrew Johnson, had been impeached, the momentum for Reconstruction passed to the congressional Republicans, who were much more eager to punish the South than Lincoln or Johnson had been. The Civil

War amendments—the Thirteenth, Fourteenth, and Fifteenth—eliminated involuntary servitude, established citizenship and "equal protection" under the laws, and guarded the voting process against discrimination based on race. Given the longstanding "hidden assumption" that political equality produced economic equality, giving African Americans the vote made some sense. But the radical Republicans saw the vote as mainly protecting workers from actions that might deprive them of the fruits of their labor, and assumed that the rest of the economy would function as though it were composed of individuals capable of choosing from a wide variety of labor situations.[6]

The impact of the Fourteenth Amendment was even more ironic. Its guarantee of equal protection to all "persons" ultimately facilitated the protection of business interests over those of human beings.[7] This opened the way for the Supreme Court to pare back the scope of black civil rights through the *Slaughterhouse Cases* (1873). At issue was an 1869 law, passed by Louisiana's racially integrated postwar legislature, reserving to a single slaughterhouse in New Orleans the right to slaughter all of that city's livestock (meat packers could pay the slaughterhouse to have their stock slaughtered there, so that it did not, in fact, prevent anyone from doing business). The law, intended to rectify longstanding problems of pollution in a city lacking sewers, disadvantaged some of the city's older white families who maintained their own slaughtering facilities. The Supreme Court declared the 1869 law valid, ruling that the Fourteenth Amendment did not apply to immunities and privileges granted by states, but rather only to federal ones.[8] The narrowed scope of the Fourteenth Amendment enabled both Jim Crow laws segregating public facilities and, ultimately, the 1896 doctrine that separate facilities for black and white people were acceptable as long as they were "equal."

At the same time that the Supreme Court limited African Americans' protection from state discrimination, the court expanded the Fourteenth Amendment protection of corporations as legal persons in *Santa Clara County v. Southern Pacific Rail Road* (1886): "One of the points made and discussed at length in the brief of counsel for defendants in error was that 'corporations are persons within the meaning of the Fourteenth Amendment to the Constitution of the United States.'" The Chief Justice announced, "The Court does not wish to hear argument on the question whether the provision in the Fourteenth Amendment to the Constitution which forbids a state to deny to any person within its jurisdiction the equal protection of the laws applies to these corporations. We are all of opinion that it does."[9] The finding that corporations are persons within the ambit of the Fourteenth Amendment set the stage for twenty-first century Supreme Court decisions protecting corporate religious and free-speech rights.[10]

When another of the cyclical economic panics characteristic of the U.S. economy in the nineteenth century struck in 1873, northern investors refocused their attention away from reconstruction of the South. The contested presidential election in 1876 between Rutherford B. Hayes and Samuel Tilden was settled with a compromise that left Reconstruction to the southern states and exposed the black workforce to widespread exploitation. Sharecropping became a form of slavery lacking only the name. Rural black families continued to labor as part of the plantation system until the end of the nineteenth century, some in the same cabins they had lived in while enslaved, working for the same masters, and rooted to the spot because they needed to incur debt in order to furnish tools, food, and clothing for themselves and their families. They had ingenuity and energy. As historian Jacqueline Jones points out, many families were resourceful, moving from one sharecropping situation to another to try to maximize the limited rewards that might be available: better land for a family garden, a better chimney, being closer to a school.[11] When they had an opportunity, freed people purchased farms, but few banks would lend to them. The postwar black experience showed that white employers were not the rational calculators that economic models purport them to be; as James Huston notes, for white supremacists, there were psychic rewards that accrued from discriminating against black workers.[12]

Historians thinking about counterfactuals have posed alternatives that Reconstruction governments might have chosen that might have produced a better long-term picture for equality. For example, congressional legislation could have funded the Freedmen's Bureau for a period of decades, making freed people direct wards of the federal government and thus neither taxed nor legally bound by the (discriminatory southern) states. Unfortunately, bureaucracies created in the late nineteenth century to exercise wardship over colonized people (e.g., the Bureau of Indian Affairs) had poor track records.[13]

What is clear is that the post–Civil War period saw the failure to replace a long-term system of inequality with a system more likely to grant justice. Millions of people who had involuntarily donated labor, often over the course of a lifetime, to the economic success of a nation that excluded them were morally entitled to a government program to at least partially repair the damage. Although this crossed almost no one's mind at the time, Americans could have consulted a model near at hand. In 1861, Tsar Alexander II freed the serfs of Russia. Rather than leave them proletarianized, the nation set up a program for serfs to buy the property on which they had formerly worked. The government advanced repayments to the landowners, and the serfs paid back the government over a period of more than 40 years. Without an economic foundation for prosperity, even the civil and social rights that the congressional Republicans thought they had guaranteed for the freed people failed to last. Southern states engineered methods to exclude black voters, and lynching of black people accused of committing crimes or even breaking arbitrary social rules was rampant.[14]

WORKING CLASS

Freed black people represented one vector for post–Civil War equality; industrialization, immigration, and the resulting large-scale urban poverty were others. Between 1865 and 1914, about 33 million people—most of them young and male—crossed the Atlantic to find work in the United States. These migrants were remarkably diverse, speaking a babel of languages and hailing from a number of different countries.[15] Immigrants settled in cities like New York and Chicago, which struggled with providing adequate housing, sewage, trash pickup, and public education. Historian Steven Fraser describes the transformation of the late nineteenth century:

> High death, injury, and unemployment rates; precipitous deterioration in diet as well as in the size and comforts of home; abandoned backyard vegetable gardens; common hunting grounds and fisheries privatized; urban squalor; obsolescent skills and forsaken traditions; exhausting, high-speed work routines lasting twelve hours or more unlike anything ever experienced before: a daily life cycle consisting of work, punctuated by short hours of eating and sleeping . . .[16]

Structural unemployment became possible in the late nineteenth century for the first time, not only due to industrialization, but also because the option to resort to natural resources in times of scarcity was cut off. In hard times people had been able to hunt, fish, or farm; in urban areas these options were no longer available.[17] While other countries pursued programs that buffered poor people against the worst excesses of industrial capitalism at the time, American cities limited their spending to sewer systems, street cleaning, and public health measures to make sure that the diseases and problems of poverty did not spread to wealthier neighborhoods.[18] Immigrant neighborhoods were painted as slums that both welcomed the poor and perpetuated poverty by producing offspring who were unhealthy or who refused to work.[19]

In May 1873, Austrian banks failed, partly due to the rise of American agriculture as a rival to Europe. International credit needed by banks on the American East Coast dried up.[20] In September of 1873, the American economy convulsed as financier Jay Cooke's Northern Pacific Railway project went bankrupt. Bank failures followed, and the New York Stock Exchange was temporarily shuttered. With no access to credit flows, half of the railroads in the United States went into receivership. Business generally contracted, throwing large numbers of people out of work. Simultaneously, the federal government retired Civil War paper money and demonetized silver, contracting the money supply. The Panic of 1873 caused a six-year depression, during which the United States saw for the first time a roving reserve army of the unemployed.[21]

By the 1880s, a movement toward ethnography of urban life arose in the United States, impelled largely by middle-class reformers. Pioneering police photographer Jacob Riis's *How the Other Half Lives* (1890) took middle-class observers inside the decrepit basements and overcrowded tenements that were home to many working families and the desperately poor. Other writers dressed down as "tramps" so that they could penetrate into hobo camps and shelters for the homeless and interpret that life to middle-class readers. Participant-observers reported that the long-term unemployed had developed deviant attitudes toward work. They worked seasonally, regarding periods of unemployment as "vacations"; they worked deliberately, restricting output; and they threatened to recruit respectable workingmen and, even worse, young boys into their ranks.[22]

Despite being described and objectified, working people were neither quiet nor helpless. Steve Fraser argues that, in contrast with the present, which he calls an "age of acquiescence," workers in the late nineteenth century effectively fought capital using weapons like mass strikes and boycotts.[23] The growth of the railroad industry after the Civil War spawned a large population of workers disadvantaged by the conditions of their employment. They faced dangers caused by long stretches of risky single track, understaffing, lack of safety devices, and failure by management to pay workers until they had completed a round trip. Locomotives exploded, trains crashed, and brakemen were killed manually braking trails or coupling cars by hand. In 1890 alone, 2,451 railroad worker fatalities and 22,396 injuries were reported.[24] The Panic of 1873 resulted in wage cuts in an already burdened industry. A proposal for a second set of wage cuts across several railroad companies in 1877 resulted in a three-week-long strike, and because some railroads were in receivership, courts could punish strikers for interfering with court-owned possessions.

The strike spread to cities across the country; in each city, rioting and discontentment took on a local form. In San Francisco, strikers attacked the Chinese workers who they thought were taking their jobs. In Galveston, strikers attacked African Americans. In Baltimore, the rough and the respectable alike joined forces to tear the uniforms from the backs of state militiamen brought in to break up the strike. When state militias proved ineffective, President Rutherford B. Hayes sent in federal troops. The Great Strike served as a template for many other instances of the army being used against striking workers.[25]

After the strike, many workers poured their energies into a new union movement, under the auspices of the Knights of Labor, a national organization composed of local unions. The Knights unionized white and black, male and female workers. They agitated for the eight-hour workday and an end to child labor. Terence Powderly, Grand Master Workman of the Knights, advocated widespread landownership and believed that wage earners should not be worse off than if they worked their own share of land.[26] But although they grew from the republican antimonopolist roots of the pre–Civil War trade unionists and land reformers, the Knights of Labor embraced an ideology of harmony of interests between employer and employee, largely missing the fact that it was in the interest of corporations to pay workers as little as possible.[27]

Although the Knights of Labor grew greatly, hitting a peak of around 729,000 members in 1886, southern states had substantially fewer members—only about 50,000.[28] The Knights in the South, despite the best efforts of their leaders, were divided by racism, which led to the formation of segregated assemblies and the exclusion of black Knights from southern Knights of Labor social events.[29] The Knights of Labor also targeted Chinese immigrants, who, it was alleged, were taking their jobs, were willing to work for lower wages, and were failing to assimilate into American society. The Chinese, the Knights ironically claimed, in their slavish refusal to fight back, undermined the entire category of working men, threatening the masculinity of all male workers. The union movement expended much of its energy lobbying for exclusionary legislation and occasionally turning to anti-immigrant violence.[30]

In 1886, the Knights of Labor fomented a strike wave across many industries in favor of the eight-hour day. At a massive public demonstration in early May in Chicago's Haymarket Square, someone tossed an incendiary device. Between the explosion and the melee afterward, seven policemen and three civilians were killed. The press and the police blamed foreign workers—anarchists—for the disruption. Knights leader Terence Powderly condemned the participants as dangerous radicals.[31] After the Haymarket Riot, the Knights of Labor quickly lost adherents, despite their rejection of violence or even strikes as proper negotiation techniques. Between 1885 and 1888, the membership of the Knights of Labor eroded from 729,000 to 260,000, and by the turn of the century they only numbered 20,200.[32]

As the Knights of Labor faded, the American Federation of Labor (AFL) gained ground. The Knights had espoused complete economic and political reform. In contrast, the AFL aimed to unionize only skilled, white, male, workers, mostly of northern European ancestry, and to focus on wages.[33] Arrayed in their AFL member unions, these men became a "labor aristocracy," with wage levels much higher than those of most immigrant, female, or black workers. Well-paid skilled workers constructed a complex culture that focused on masculinity, mutuality, and racial consciousness, but their prosperity depended on the exclusion of the foreign and the unskilled.[34]

While the late-nineteenth-century working class was remarkably active compared with workers at other moments in American history, it was hampered by its lack of unity. Workers were divided: among those considered "foreign," like the Chinese; workers from southern and eastern Europe, like the Italians and Jews, who were considered unskilled; and nativist American workers.[35] This immigrant influx drove down the price of urban labor, but native born Americans' prejudice against immigrant workers prevented effective unionization. Even socialism in the United States focused more on antiglobalization and anti-immigration rhetoric than on building a united working class.[36]

THE CORPORATE FORM AND POPULIST PROTEST

A final vector of inequality in the late nineteenth century was the triumph of the corporate form, facilitated by federal assistance and plenty of corruption. The United States subsidized the growth of the railroads through vast land grants, totaling 131,230,358 acres. Selling the land parcels between the checkerboard parcels granted to the railroads for double the going price raised even more money that could be funneled back into the railroads. Historian Richard White argues that the transcontinental railroads in the United States suffered from duplication of effort and poor planning, because the root purpose of their funders and builders was not actually to transport goods but rather to enrich themselves through railroad funding. They were able to do this largely through a friendly network of newspaper reporters, politicians, and businessmen. As happened with subprime mortgages during the Great Recession of 2006, railroad financiers raised funds by issuing and packaging new investment instruments, with the assets of their nonexistent companies as collateral. Investors looking to make a quick buck had no access to the insider knowledge they would have needed in order to discriminate between good investments and the investment equivalents of vaporware. Those with insider knowledge, like the organizers of the Credit Mobilier holding company, reaped rewards between $11 and $20 million in just a few years.[37]

Rather than being filtered through the U.S. government, foreign capital was invested in the railroads through private banks, which could then regulate the railroads in their own self-interest. As Richard White points out, "railroad rates affected the structure of entire industries." Wheat and cattle, timber and sheep, all had to be shipped by rail both as raw and as finished products, and the fact that only the railroads themselves understood the logic of their price structure meant that their rates seemed like unreasonable and monopolistic taxation to the people having to pay them.[38] New states gained disproportionate power due to the importance of railroads to the less-developed regions of the United States and because senators were allocated without reference to population.[39] At the same time, railroad price discrimination against small shippers sparked protest.[40]

As urban workers reacted to industrialization, so rural workers reacted to railroad corporatism. In Texas, farmers formed the Farmers' Alliance, combining ideas about agrarian self-sufficiency with the notion that credit—paper money or "greenbacks"—should be more widely available. By 1885, the Farmers' Alliance had reached 30,000 members in 49 Texas counties. By the end of the decade, farmers and workers joined together in Texas to call for the eight-hour day, a mechanics' lien law, and government ownership of the communications and transportation systems.[41] Farmers lobbied for railroad rate regulation on the grounds that the railroads were giant chartered monopolies, able to evade the laws of supply and demand.[42]

By 1892 there were 2 million members of the Farmers' Alliance and a million members of the Colored Farmers' Alliance and Cooperative. The groups combined with the residue of the Knights of Labor to produce the People's Party or Populist movement.[43] The People's Party's Omaha Platform began with an apocalyptic preamble:

The conditions which surround us best justify our co-operation; we meet in the midst of a nation brought to the verge of moral, political, and material ruin. Corruption dominates the ballot-box, the Legislatures, the Congress, and touches even the ermine of the bench. The people are demoralized; most of the States have been compelled to isolate the voters at the polling places to prevent universal intimidation and bribery. The newspapers are largely subsidized or muzzled, public opinion silenced, business prostrated, homes covered with mortgages, labor impoverished, and the land concentrating in the hands of capitalists. The urban workmen are denied the right to organize for self-protection, imported pauperized labor beats down their wages, a hireling standing army, unrecognized by our laws, is established to shoot them down, and they are rapidly degenerating into European conditions. The fruits of the toil of millions are boldly stolen to build up colossal fortunes for a few, unprecedented in the history of mankind; and the possessors of those, in turn, despise the republic and endanger liberty. From the same prolific womb of governmental injustice we breed the two great classes—tramps and millionaires.[44]

Ignatius Donnelly, the Minnesota politician and novelist who penned these words, did not realize their unfortunate timelessness. The Omaha Platform called for farmers and urban workers to unite, for nationalization of railroads and public utilities and limitation of the size of government, for free coinage of silver and expansion of the money supply, and for a graduated income tax. The Populists demanded guaranteed voter rights, term limits, and initiative and referendum. They also advocated the subtreasury system, by which farmers could contribute grain in return for negotiable instruments that they could use to pay debts. In 1892 their presidential candidate, James B. Weaver, earned the electoral votes of four states and won more than a million votes.[45]

Populism was a big-umbrella movement. Historians of Populism once characterized the movement as the last gasp of a Jeffersonian vision, with strong roots in the movement culture of the Farmers' Alliance.[46] Recent writers argue that, far from being agrarian throwbacks, Populist leaders understood that the state could be harnessed to create a better version of capitalism.[47] Among the Populists were Christian fundamentalists seeking the restoration of a moral order that had been lost, and quasi-millenarians using last-days rhetoric to characterize what was happening in the United States.[48] They were generally bound together by their commitment to more equal outcomes, although they variously put forth many ideas for how equality might be achieved.[49]

Although the Populist Party made the best third-party showing in American history to that time, the party largely dissolved when the Democratic Party adopted the most popular Populist plank, free coinage of silver. Republican William McKinley's triumph in the 1896 election over the Democrat William Jennings Bryan put an end to the ambitions of the Populists specifically, but not to the notion of government regulation generally, since McKinley's assassination enabled his vice president, the energetic reformer Theodore Roosevelt, to occupy the presidency.

PROPONENTS OF INEQUALITY

Not everyone who noticed the inequality of the postbellum period considered it a bad thing. E. L. Godkin, editor of *The Nation*, thought that poverty was an immutable fact of human existence, since people, like other animals, reproduced up to the carrying capacity of their environments. He inferred from evolutionary biology that some humans had natural advantages over others and that they constituted the "fit." Government intervention to promote equality was therefore useless, although government could help to advance the status of society's fittest by rooting out corruption, encouraging temperance, and promoting cultural uplift.[50]

To call such reasoning Social Darwinism may be misleading. The term perhaps grants more influence to Darwin's ideas than he had among American social scientists and ignores the impact of non-Darwinian ideas. Some social scientists, for example, had a neo-Lamarckian belief that the environment could have a multigenerational impact.[51] But to make a semantic argument about whether promotion of inequality ought to be called Social Darwinism misses a bigger point. Many contemporary thinkers, like the English social theorist Herbert Spencer, argued that government attempts to interfere with a functioning economy ranged from futile to bad. Sociologist and economist William Graham Sumner, author of *What Social Classes Owe to Each Other* (1883), argued that supporting the neediest members of society would undermine the social structure. For Sumner, capital was a civilizing force, the great motor of modernity. He did not call capitalists "job creators," but the phrase aptly captures his opinion. He railed against the taxation of the rich, argued that inequality had no moral component, and recommended exhorting the poor to work harder. The state was nothing but a vehicle for paupers, who were the bane of the republic, to make claims on hardworking "forgotten men."[52]

In his 1889 article, "Wealth," steel magnate Andrew Carnegie, himself an immigrant and the son of a poor Chartist, lauded wealth differentials. Only poverty gave individuals the motivation to work harder, he argued; equality of condition could only occur in conditions of material backwardness. In contrast, "inequality of environment, the concentration of business, industrial and commercial, in the hands of a few, and the law of competition between these ... [is] essential to the future progress of the race." He considered this "sometimes hard for the individual," but "it is best for the race, because it ensures the survival of the fittest in every department."[53]

For Carnegie, the United States at the end of the nineteenth century was the paragon of what was possible:

> The Socialist or Anarchist who seeks to overturn present conditions is to be regarded as attacking the foundation upon which civilization itself rests, for civilization took its start from the day that the capable, industrious workman said to his incompetent and lazy fellow, "If thou dost not sow, thou shalt not reap," and thus ended primitive Communism by separating the drones from the bees.[54]

From Carnegie's perspective, men were born more or less industrious and capable, rather than being influenced as babies by families that had more or less to offer them. There was no merit in giving "trifling amounts" to individuals, even for basic needs. "Neither the individual nor the race is improved by alms-giving. Those worthy of assistance, except in rare cases, seldom require assistance. The really valuable men of the race never do, except in cases of accident or sudden change."

Even as he cast aspersions on the poor, however, Carnegie argued that the wealthy had a responsibility to their less-fortunate fellow men. Having acquired their fortunes by their assiduity and intelligence, the wealthy ought to spend the majority of their money to improve the lot of their fellows in ways they saw fit. "The man of wealth thus becoming the mere agent and trustee for his poorer brethren, bringing to their service his superior wisdom, experience, and ability to administer, doing for them better than they would or could do for themselves." Carnegie himself endowed many public libraries and recommended that other wealthy men provide art galleries and parks, but he never addressed whether, in a nation with universal male suffrage, it was appropriate to endorse an economic system that assumed that wealthy people were morally superior or that poorer people were incapable of making their own decisions about their lives.

PROPONENTS OF EQUALITY

Carnegie had one thing in common with nineteenth-century proponents of equality: the notion that he was inextricably connected to other Americans in "society" and had some responsibility to others. Social thinkers in both Britain and the United States in the 1880s promoted the notion that no one was a social atom, that people ought to be knit to each other with certain rights and responsibilities by virtue of being co-citizens, and that the state had a role to play in nurturing accomplishment and education to make this possible.[55] The Social Gospel movement, which emerged simultaneously from the churches and from the grassroots, provided a religious grounding for such policies by emphasizing that the Bible promoted neighborly uplift and care for the poor.[56]

Some writers, such as muckraking journalist Henry Demarest Lloyd, identified monopolies and corruption as the enemies of society. In *Wealth Against Commonwealth* (1894), Lloyd despaired because Americans' attempts to institute municipal services like streetcars and gasworks were "sung to sleep with the lullaby about government best, government least."[57] Lloyd painstakingly chronicled the emergence of crony capitalism, false corporate entities, differential pricing, and rebates in the railroad and oil industries, all presided over by a sham regulatory system. But in the end he did not blame the corporations but rather the men behind them. "The real actors are men; the real instrument, the control of their fellows by wealth, and the mainspring of the evil is the morals and economics which cipher that brothers produce wealth when they are only cheating each other out of their birthrights."[58] Corporate capitalism eroded American morality.[59]

Lloyd noted that the United States was a political, but not an economic, democracy. To become an economic democracy, the country needed to acknowledge the demands of society, not just those of the individual. "The happiness, self-interest, or individuality of the whole is not more sacred than that of each, but it is greater," Lloyd wrote.[60] For Lloyd, the solution was not regulation, which he called just "the agitations of the Gracchi, evidencing the wrong, but not rising to the cure." Rather, he sought industrial liberty through widespread cooperative industry. He anticipated that being stakeholders in a larger enterprise would help workers to make cultural progress.[61] And, centrally, he pointed out that there was more than one way to build complex industrialism in the late nineteenth century, and other countries were able to do it in ways that did not necessarily and permanently sacrifice the public to the corporations.[62]

By the end of the nineteenth century, some regulation was in place, transcontinental railroads capitulating because they thought they could control the regulation to their benefit.[63] The Interstate Commerce Commission (1887) was intended to prevent railroads from engaging in the monopolistic practices from which they had benefited over the previous 15 years. The Sherman Anti-Trust Act (1890) targeted combinations in restraint of trade, although it was used more often to suppress unions than to dismantle corporate trusts (individuals involved in unions were seen as conspiring together, whereas the individuals who made up the fictive personhood of the corporation were viewed by the courts as comprising a single person).[64]

The changes of the late nineteenth century gave rise to economic protest literature that called into question American exceptionalism.[65] In 1896, Charles Barzilai Spahr, who held a Ph.D. from Columbia University and edited a magazine called *The Outlook*, wrote *An Essay on the Present Distribution of Wealth in the United States*, systematically evaluating economic inequality in the United States. Spahr found that the area of greatest inequality had moved from the American South, where before the Civil War the divergence between plantation owners and slaves had been the greatest, to urban areas, where property was very unequally distributed. Using returns from New York and Massachusetts to draw conclusions for the rest of the country, Spahr estimated that seven-eighths of the people owned just one-eighth of the national wealth, and that the top 1 percent of families owned more wealth collectively than did the lower 99 percent.[66]

Spahr went on to attempt to compare American incomes with European incomes, a difficult task since the United States at that moment lacked any income tax. His figures were impressionistic, inferred from a combination of rental costs and the average fraction of people's incomes that went to pay rent. But he concluded that the average laborer's family earned no more than $300 a year in rural areas and $500 in towns, and that "one percent of our families receive nearly one-fourth of the national income, while fifty percent receive barely one fifth."[67] Spahr argued that U.S. tax policy exacerbated this disparity. When taxes paid at the point of sale were added to property taxes, "The wealthiest class is taxed less than one per cent on its property, while the mass of the people are taxed more than four per cent on theirs. In this way the separation of classes is accelerated by the hand of the state."[68] Spahr favored a progressive property tax that more equitably spread the tax burden.

In a second work entitled *America's Working People* (1900), Spahr expanded his critique, fleshing out the statistics into individual stories. In the factories of the industrial North, married women and teenagers labored, but men in their early forties were considered too old to be hired. In the South, white mill workers were systematically underpaid, yet unwilling to bring in unions because their willingness to accept lower pay was their one competitive advantage.[69] Spahr described African Americans in the South as disfranchised, systematically excluded from mill work, paid less than whites on a dual labor system, subject to lynching, and offered fewer months of education each year.[70] Pennsylvania coal miners were forced to shop at company stores and to systematically overpay for the gunpowder that they had to furnish for their own underground blasting.[71] Pittsburgh steel workers were subjected to 12-hour days and to a punishing lack of free speech about working conditions.[72]

While Spahr described the prevailing inequality, other writers, including Edward Bellamy and Henry George, proposed far-reaching reforms. Born in Philadelphia in 1839, Henry George was a nineteenth-century working-class renaissance man, who plowed through a series of jobs, including seaman, before landing in San Francisco as a penniless journalistic hopeful. After a formative visit to New York City, where he observed the slums, George began to involve himself in journalism and in California politics. In 1871, he wrote a short tract on land policy that eventually was expanded into *Progress and Poverty: An Inquiry into the Causes of Industrial Depressions and of Increase of Want with Increase of Wealth* (1879). George's tract was hugely popular and led him to speaking tours of the British Isles and Australia.[73] He ran for mayor of New York City at the height of popularity of the Knights of Labor, but lost the election despite their support, possibly because he had taken an unpopular stance on those arrested in the Haymarket riots. The next year, in a run for secretary of state of New York, he fared even worse. He ultimately died without holding elective office, but his ideas were well known.[74]

As Thomas Paine had in *Agrarian Justice*, Henry George proceeded from the premise that no man in late-nineteenth-century America should be worse off than he would have been in a state of nature. In fact, he thought the lower classes in Britain and the United States had worse access to resources than did Tierra del Fuegans or Australian aborigines.[75] As Thomas Skidmore had, George believed that every person had a natural right to the soil, which could be inferred from God's design of man as a rational creature. Just as God had created the universe to follow natural physical laws, so, George proposed, there were natural social laws. The existence of poverty in a land of plenty proved that people were attempting to subvert God's plan by monopolizing the land and other natural resources. Land monopoly was a particularly abhorrent theft that undermined man's very nature:

> The ownership of land is the great fundamental fact which ultimately determines the social, the political, and consequently the intellectual and moral condition of a people. And it must be so. For the land is the habitation of man, the storehouse upon which he must draw for all his needs, the material to which his labor must be applied for the supply of all his desires . . . On the land we are born, from it we live, to it we return again—children of the soil as truly as the blade of grass or the flower of the field. Take away from man all that belongs to land, and he is but a disembodied spirit.[76]

As it was, landowners, through rent, took payment away from both labor and capital. The more complicated the economy became, and the more labor was debased, the less an individual was able to do anything for himself outside of the existing system. "The primeval curse comes to be looked upon as a boon, and men think, and talk, and clamor, and legislate, as though monotonous manual labor in itself were a good and not an evil, an end and not a means."[77]

In *Progress and Poverty* George considered, and discarded, six different solutions for the inequality he saw around him, including cutting government expenditures, better education, unionization, cooperative production, or even a more general distribution of land. The last, he suggested, would raise standards of living generally but do nothing for those who had to live by factory labor rather than farming. Moreover, it would result in a huge bureaucracy.[78] George's policy choice was a steep tax on the unearned rent from land.[79] He expected his single tax on land to yield several benefits. The tax revenue could be put toward relief of social ills. George also expected that taxation would lead people to sell off any unproductive land they were holding. Finally, it would build a sense of social solidarity that had gone missing in a highly strati-fied society: "It is not the taxes that he is conscious of paying that gives a man a stake in the country, an interest in its government; it is the consciousness of feel-ing that he is an integral part of the community; that its prosperity is his prosper-ity, and its disgrace his shame."[80]

George considered his land tax to be part of a greater plan for national uplift.[81] He hoped to see "public baths, museums, libraries, gardens, lecture rooms, music and dancing halls, theaters, universities, technical schools" as well as municipal utilities and the funding of scientific basic research.[82] While Godkin and Carnegie alleged that poverty is an important spur to personal industry, George countered that "the work which improves the condition of mankind, the work which extends knowledge and increases power, and enriches literature, and elevates thought, is not done to secure a living ... it is the work of men who perform it for their own sake, and not that they may get more to eat or drink, or wear, or display. In a state of society where want was abolished, work of this sort would be enormously increased."[83] Ulti-mately, George warned, the United States was at a turning point. As urban political corruption showed, economic inequality eroded the political process, but the political system might still be rescued.[84]

Henry George's ideas found support throughout the English-speaking world. He was hailed in Ireland and Scotland, where land possession was a live issue. In the South, the black newspaperman and former slave T. Thomas Fortune enthusiastically embraced Henry George's ideas, arguing that the conflict between tenant farmer and landowner was based on class rather than race.[85] In contrast with those who had disagreed with Skidmore, those who disagreed with George tended not to call him a socialist or a communist. George's critics argued that his taxation plan was misdirected since he sought to tax land but not other natural resources.[86] George also had a critic on the left, the radical Victor Drury, who espoused the confiscation and collectiviza-tion of land and was popular with some members of the Knights of Labor.[87]

Like Henry George, the novelist Edward Bellamy formulated a plan for reform of American equality whose popularity crossed over from the written word into a social movement. Born in Chicopee, Massachusetts, in 1850, Bellamy worked as a journalist for the *Springfield Union* before becoming a novelist. His 1889 novel *Looking Backward* was the third-best-selling American book of the nineteenth century, selling more than a million copies, over a hundred thousand of those within the first two years after publica-tion.[88] In *Looking Backward*, Bellamy described an ideal society that, in contrast with the United States in the late nineteenth century, did not embrace greed as a central motivating characteristic. Bellamy's utopia balanced economic productivity and personal prosperity—all citizens would be required to invest their time and effort in the state but would be rewarded with provision for their needs.[89]

The novel's protagonist, Julian West, lives a life of wealth and entitlement in Boston in 1887. Plagued by insomnia, he has his servant hypnotize him to sleep. While he sleeps, West's house catches on fire and the servant dies; with no one to revive him from hypnosis, West continues in a state of suspended animation. When he is awakened in the year 2000, miraculously not having aged a day, West finds that Boston society—paralyzed by the "labor problem" when he went to sleep—has been completely transformed. Dr. Leete, Julian West's tour guide through the future, explains that during the intervening period, Americans have fashioned an entirely new economic system. It was not based on a Skidmorite division of resources, even though that might have been the most fair option: "The restoration of the old system with the subdivision of capital, if it were possible, might indeed bring back a greater equality of conditions, with more individual dignity and freedom, but it would be at the price of poverty and the arrest of material progress."[90] Rather, in response to rising inequality and concentration of wealth and power, the government had nationalized all, becoming the single employer: "the epoch of trusts had ended in the Great Trust. In a word, the people of the United States concluded to conduct their own business, just as one-hundred years before they had assumed the conduct of their own government."[91]

In the Boston of Bellamy's year 2000, everyone aged 18 to 45 participated in an industrial army, required to "contribute his quota of industrial or intellectual services to the maintenance of the nation."[92] Because everyone was an industrial conscript, patriotism motivated all to work hard.[93] For the first three years of their army service, all men and women worked as common laborers; then they chose a career or one was chosen for them. In order to make all trades equally attractive, in Bellamy's utopia, people working at more unpleasant tasks had shorter workdays. "The principle is that no man's work ought to be, on the whole, harder for him than any other man's for him, the workers themselves to be the judges." If a trade were so arduous that it had to be done in ten-minute shifts, then that would be the length of the workday.[94]

In return for their participation, all in Bellamy's utopia, including the disabled, the mentally impaired, and children, were given a government "credit card" loaded with the same number of dollars.[95] The credit accrued to every person as a matter of right, regardless of his or her ability to work. As a critic of Bellamy explained, "Every person is free to spend his income as he pleases;

but *it is the same for all,* the sole basis on which it is awarded being the fact that the person is a human being."[96] In the novel, Julian West points out to Dr. Leete that if all are given the same government credit, then the more physically or intellectually gifted might do twice as much work as the less gifted for the same pay. Leete has an interesting answer: "The amount of effort alone is pertinent to the question of desert [worthiness]. All men who do their best do the same. A man's endowments, however godlike, merely fix the measure of his duty."[97] With differential wages removed from among the factors able to motivate people to work, the society of Bellamy's utopia depended on other factors. "With us, diligence in the national service is the sole and certain way to public repute, social distinction, and official power. The value of a man's services to society fixes his rank in it."[98]

In one sense, Bellamy's plan narrowed the freedom of its participants, since anyone who opted not to contribute his labor to the large corporation that was the United States would, in Bellamy's own words, "be left with no possible way to provide for his existence. He would have excluded himself from the world, cut himself off from his kind, in a word, committed suicide."[99] Conceived another way, however, Bellamy's plan offered much more freedom. Education in Bellamy's fictional future Boston was fully subsidized, enabling children from any background to choose any available trade or profession. No one entered the workforce before the age of 21. And while "retirement" was not even a concept, much less a possibility, for most Americans in the 1880s, in Bellamy's utopia everyone retired from the industrial army at the age of 45 and then pursued any avocation, or none.

Like Henry George, Bellamy argued that repetitive manual work was not necessarily the most meaningful part of anyone's existence.[100] Also like Henry George, Bellamy described as the largest problem America faced the failure of the rich to acknowledge that rich and poor were part of a common cause, and that the wealth of the current generation had been built on the backs of the generation before them. Bellamy called his unique ideology "Nationalism," to differentiate it from socialism, and it was hugely popular with sectors of the American public.[101] Nationalist clubs began to be formed as soon as the book was published, and the movement soon had two magazines and a monthly newspaper, *The Nationalist.*

EXPERIMENTS IN EQUALITY AND RELIEF OF THE POOR

Writers like Henry George and Edward Bellamy were joined in the last two decades of the nineteenth century by settlement-house founders like Jane

Addams, who promoted equality through social and moral uplift. A graduate of Rockford Seminary and long dedicated to the notion of somehow bettering humanity, Addams was inspired by the example of London's Toynbee Hall settlement house to create her own modern settlement in Chicago.[102] Toynbee Hall, a building in London's poor East End, had been founded with the idea that the poor could be socially uplifted if cultured people lived nearby, interacted with them, and served as their example.[103] Addams founded her project, Hull House, in 1889 in Chicago's noisome Nineteenth Ward. Hull House offered its immigrant clients children's clubs, a kindergarten, a place for people to gather with the others who spoke the same language, and even the "Working People's Social Science Club," with lectures on economic and sociological topics. Addams and her coworkers learned much from their clients and ultimately became lobbyists for labor reform. One Hull House worker, Florence Kelley, even became the first inspector to enforce Illinois's new Workshop and Factory Act.[104]

Although individual settlement houses tended not to cross the color line, there were settlement houses for the black community. Reverdy Ransom, an African Methodist Episcopal minister, founded the Chicago Institutional Church and Social Settlement in 1900. As Wendy Deichmann describes, "Organized as a residential city mission, it featured an auditorium, dining room, kitchen, and gymnasium. Programs included men's and women's clubs, childcare, concerts, classes and lectures." Ransom eventually helped to found the National Association for the Advancement of Colored People (NAACP).[105]

PANIC OF 1893

Settlement houses joined a constellation of institutions for conveying poor relief, ranging from almshouses, which had existed since the late eighteenth century, to orphanages, wayfarers' homes, police station "lodging rooms" where the homeless could seek shelter, public hospitals, and dispensaries. The logic of nineteenth-century poor relief was that care should be institutional—that is, available in a large, easily recognizable public building—and be accompanied by a large dose of moral instruction and possibly some involuntary labor. If institutionalized poor relief was limited and discriminatory on the basis of race and gender, at least it had the benefit of being easy to navigate, since there was no overarching bureaucracy.[106]

In 1893, these institutions for relief of the poor found themselves tested as the U.S. economy plunged into another of its periodic depressions. Historian Louise Knight notes that about 600 banks and 15,000 businesses, representing

$550 million in liabilities, had failed, and one-fourth of the nation's railway infrastructure was in receivership.[107] By 1894, over 4 million Americans were unemployed, and the only responses were local and piecemeal, conducted by municipalities that offered a subsistence wage for a couple of days of public work. Tramps took to the nation's rail system, looking for jobs that did not exist.[108] When the economy failed to revive quickly, Jacob Sechler Coxey, a quarry owner who had begun his work-life in a steel-rolling mill, took action. Forced to lay off workers as the economic depression deepened, Coxey, who was a member of the People's Party, advocated a stimulus plan: bond-funded, government-supervised public improvements, including good roads. He announced that he would lead industrial armies from the West and Midwest to march on Washington to demand relief or jobs, as a sort of human petition.

Coxey and his colleagues received much scathing press coverage.[109] "The American tramp is the product of indiscriminate almsgiving," claimed the editor of the Portland *Oregonian*, "organized and inclined to demand rather than supplicate relief from want and salvation from work."[110] The Coxeyites noted that they were starving in a land of plenty despite willingness to work. The issue was unjust distribution rather than moral worth.[111]

The largest "industrial armies" appeared in the West. Western Coxeyites demanded the revival of silver coinage, because the demonetization of silver had resulted in mines being shut down and former mining communities becoming completely deserted. In Montana, a group of Coxey devotees stole a train, and then when they were apprehended and barred from the rails, built a flotilla of boats to travel down the Missouri River, a sort of "Coxey's Navy." They traveled more than 2,000 miles before one of their leaders absconded with their entire treasury.[112] Coxeyites in Oregon also attempted to steal a train; Attorney General Richard Olney foiled their plans by using federal troops to protect the trains because the transcontinental lines were in federal receivership.[113] Coxey's own Massillon, Ohio, contingent of only a few hundred protesters reached the nation's capitol in May 1894, singing songs set to the tune of popular folk songs:

> There's a deep and growing murmur
> Going up through all the land
> From millions who are suffering
> Beneath Oppression's hand
> No charity, but justice
> Do the working poor demand
> And justice they will gain.[114]

While Attorney General Olney filed injunctions to keep Coxey's Army from important buildings, these protests showed that, pushed far enough by inequality, the American poor could take direct action. Coxey himself lived until 1951, long enough to claim that his demands had been the basis for Roosevelt's New Deal. The marches of the Coxeyites occurred simultaneously with a nationwide boycott of Pullman cars by railroad workers, in sympathy with workers at the Pullman factory. Because the Pullman strike brought home the consequences of industrial discontent to so many people who were not themselves workers, it caused class polarization.[115] Once again, strikers were met with military force.[116]

The late nineteenth century set many of the patterns for modern economic American inequality. The failure to deal with the economic legacy of slavery with reparations or an economic stake meant continued disadvantage for African Americans. The concentration of poor immigrants into urban enclaves perpetuated poverty and divided the labor movement, as native-born Americans blamed immigrants for driving down the labor market. The Supreme Court helped to perpetuate racial inequality with decisions that made the Jim Crow laws possible, while simultaneously protecting corporations as fictive legal persons.

Historian Sean Wilentz asserts that in the post–Civil War period, the United States saw an ideological paradigm shift; monopolies and corporations were naturalized, seen only as the outgrowth of "objective market forces."[117] In turn, corporations converted manual labor into unskilled labor, rough equality into hierarchy, and individualism into conformity.[118] Although Americans before the 1880s had not equated business size with efficiency, it became clear by the 1880s that enormous corporations benefited from economies of scale and so were efficient, and efficiency replaced fairness as the intrinsic value.

In the late nineteenth century, a series of attempts to reform American inequality hit a concrete pylon. Farmers and workers combined into the Populist Party, but its successes were short-lived. Although thinkers like Henry George and Edward Bellamy had tantalizing suggestions about major restructuring that might be undertaken, they remained just tantalizing suggestions. Experiments with settlement houses were promising but small scale. Workers and others combining to assert rights, or to strike, were met with troops or even hanged as anarchists. Somewhat ironically, an anarchist's bullet killed President William McKinley at the state fair in Buffalo, New York, in 1901, ushering in an era of reform by bringing to the presidency a Republican willing to use big government to promote the national good.

CHAPTER 4

Liberalism in the Age of Monopoly: 1900–1929

The period between the turn of the century and the Great Depression saw some of the most acute disparities in income and wealth in American history. By the 1920s the United States had adopted the mantra that whatever benefited businesses was good for the country as a whole, an assertion made again in the 1980s and 1990s.[1] American capitalism had changed in the late nineteenth century with the formation of large corporations and trusts, the sharpening of class relations, and the transformation of the United States into a consumer society. The results were now obvious, and sociologists began to describe the impact of increasing inequality.[2] Government actions addressed inequality not through redistribution but rather through steps intended to enable people to achieve their full potential. Called Progressivism in the United States and Liberalism in Great Britain, this new theory of government proposed that government could contribute to the common good.[3]

The Progressives combined a concern for social uplift with the same attitude of cultural superiority that animated late-nineteenth-century colonial adventures.[4] Progressives had two main concerns: to protect personal opportunity from being squeezed out by corporate growth, and to assimilate waves of immigrants coming to the United States.[5] At both the state and the federal level, Progressives sought to remove threats to equality of opportunity: threats in the form of illness and poor public health, lack of educational facilities, child labor, and unregulated food and drugs. They worked to expand the stock of public goods, which, as historian Daniel Rodgers describes, included "public forests and conservation lands, national parks and public playgrounds, much more extensive municipal services, [and] comprehensive

public schools."[6] Progressives at all levels were committed to the belief that
the state had an important role to play in bolstering positive freedom.[7]

At the same time, Progressives hammered on the theme of American
exceptionalism; the United States, they asserted, did not need or want redistribution or socialism to achieve more equal outcomes. In Britain, Liberal
and Conservative governments began to construct a welfare state between
1900 and 1929, with some of the first old-age pensions and support for
women and children. In the United States, this did not happen, for several
reasons. In the West, the U.S. military had successfully confined Native Americans to reservations, opening up land for white settlers and decreasing the
need for a strong government presence. These western settlers distrusted
government and banks and had little patience for the new immigrant working
class. Regional divisions helped to keep U.S. government spending to a minimum compared with other countries, so that by 1913, the United States was
spending only 0.5 percent of its $5 trillion gross domestic product on social
programs.[8] The fact that many social welfare reformers were women, and that
women remained disenfranchised until 1920, also helped to limit reform.[9]

TWO NATIONS AND THE PROGRESSIVE RESPONSE

Economically speaking, the early decades of the twentieth century marked
a zenith in American inequality, based on wage and wealth levels and on
prices. Inequality was most noticeable in urban areas like New York and
Chicago, where visitors were shocked by the contrasts between rich and poor
neighborhoods and the divergent life chances of wealthy and poor children.
The relative price of food increased greatly, so that white urban laborers saw
their cost of living increase 22 percent over 18 years. But inequality was not
limited to the cities; farm families saw a rise in their cost of living of 41 percent
between 1896 and 1916.[10]

Poor urban dwellers often lived in crowded tenements, some rooms of
which had neither windows nor airflow. Lax legal regulation left tenants
responsible for making improvements; code violations and unhealthy living
conditions were rampant.[11] Many poor city residents, including children,
worked from home, assembling items like boxes or paper flowers, sewing
shirts, or scavenging fuel and castoffs from the streets. Because many cities
franchised out what we might consider to be essential public services, the provision of goods like trash pickup and transportation was spotty in poor neighborhoods.[12] Social crime was often essential to survival: domestic workers
stole food from their employers, miners took coal from coal trains, and people
whose power or water had been shut off found ways to pirate utilities.[13]

By the 1960s, social critics were blaming economic inequality on the decline of the two-parent family. But for many working-class families between 1900 and 1929, family relationships were instrumental and economic, based on the ability of each family member to contribute to the greater family economy and to compensate for otherwise unlivable wages. Working-class wives saved the family money through home production, generated cash through taking in boarders or lodgers, did other people's laundry, periodically pawned goods, and economized. Children contributed their wages to the family economy as soon as they were old enough to work (or before that, if a parent could forge the necessary paperwork). Extended families stretched their resources by crowding into single homes or apartments.[14] Over the course of the twentieth century, the opportunities for married women to contribute to the family economy without going out to work dwindled; "among disadvantaged working-class families ... male employment became less secure, and the decline in household production left a gap in the family budget that was less easily filled."[15]

Muckraking journalists exposed many of the shortcomings of American life. Some were more concerned with political corruption than with corporate corruption, but some, including journalists Upton Sinclair and Charles Edward Russell, became avowed socialists after learning about the conditions of the urban poor.[16] In 1912, the Commission on Industrial Relations convened to study the problem of American unskilled workers, noting the psychological setbacks caused by seasonal unemployment.[17] Progressives also studied the plight of working women; the Russell Sage Foundation's studies show that women in factories worked long hours, and that women's and children's work at home was completely unregulated. The *Report on Conditions of Women and Child Wage-Earners in the United States*, funded and authorized by Congress and produced between 1910 and 1913, ran to 19 volumes.[18]

While during the late nineteenth century the main reformist voices railed against monopolies because they saw them as government-created special interests, twentieth-century Progressives grudgingly acknowledged that corporations were here to stay. Attacking the existence of the corporate form was increasingly interpreted as cranky or not realistic within a market economy.[19] Progressives instead sought to "bound the realm of price and commerce" by limiting clearly oppressive work contracts, stopping the use of fraudulent advertising claims, and preventing the sale of food or medicine that was clearly detrimental to public health. Progressives argued that the federal government had a responsibility to regulate the corporations for the benefit of consumers.[20]

Muckraking elicited responses at the local, state, and federal levels, and although reformers might not have characterized themselves as belonging to a coherent reform movement, they did share ways of talking about the social ills that the United States then faced. At the local level, for example, progressive superintendents of schools redesigned curricula around individual student interests and needs and moved away from rote learning, with the notion that their mandate now included socializing students for "happy living in a democracy."[21]

At the state level, progressive governors like Robert LaFollette of Wisconsin agitated for direct primaries in the hopes of stamping out political corruption, and enlisted academics at state universities to provide policy guidance.[22] Some state courts supported economic regulations that protected health, safety, and welfare. Courts ruled in workers' favor to eliminate payment in scrip, to establish safety standards in dangerous workplaces, and to provide for workers' compensation for workplace injuries. States interpreted the legislative "police power" to ensure welfare more expansively than did the Supreme Court.[23]

President Theodore Roosevelt expanded the federal government's purview in the first decade of the twentieth century. For Roosevelt, monopolies and inequalities of wealth threatened to undermine society itself by depriving individuals of the human dignity that they needed in order to be political participants, and he noted that no corporation was guaranteed the right to vote. "The men and women who are broken by the hard strain of modern industry, and are driven lower and ever lower until they accept wages which will not allow them to be decently fed and clothed or comfortably housed, cannot render to the community the services which should be demanded of all American citizens."[24] For Roosevelt, any country in which the right to property was unregulated wrongly prioritized property above people. Roosevelt argued that, by battling slavery, the Union had rejected this set of priorities in the Civil War. "We grudge no man a fortune in civil life if it is honorably obtained and well used. It is not even enough that it should have been gained without doing damage to the community. We should permit it to be gained only so long as the gaining represents benefit to the community."[25]

Roosevelt believed that only an energetic national government could accomplish these crucial goals: "I do not ask for overcentralization, but I do ask that we work in a spirit of broad and far-reaching nationalism when we work for what concerns are people as a whole ... where the whole American people are interested, that interest can be guarded effectively only by the national government."[26] He called for workers' compensation laws, safety regulations in the workplace, the regulation of women and children's labor, a minimum wage sufficient to support a family, and hours of labor that afforded workers some leisure. During his presidency, the Department of

Labor, the Bureau of Mines, the Department of Commerce, and the Department of Agriculture were created. These new agencies generated statistics that could support regulation.[27] Roosevelt was a trust-buster, but he differentiated between good trusts, which concentrated power but provided necessary services at reasonable rates, and bad trusts, which harmed the public by charging unreasonably high prices while reducing competition. The Bureau of Corporations (1903–1914), set up by Theodore Roosevelt to serve as a corporate watchdog, investigated conditions in industries including "beef, tobacco, petroleum, lumber, cotton, water power, steel [and] sugar, investigating not only for working conditions but also for trust-like behavior." The Department of Justice could use that information to prosecute corporations under the Sherman Anti-Trust Act.[28]

The one institutional stumbling block to Progressivism in this period was the Supreme Court. The Court blocked most economic intervention by narrowly circumscribing the degree to which the federal government had the right to regulate commerce, the justices taking it upon themselves to "prick out" the boundaries of acceptable regulation in every piece of legislation.[29] In *Lochner v. New York* (1905), a majority of justices struck down a law that set maximum hours for bakers' work days; they argued that such a law would deprive workers of the freedom of contract. In his dissent, Justice Oliver Wendell Holmes argued that the Supreme Court was grafting a particular economic theory onto the Constitution. He asserted that the majority of Americans disagreed about making freedom of contract the only legal value, and that it was their right to legislatively alter free markets, as had already been done with (for example) laws against usury and Sunday trading.[30]

Roosevelt's "New Nationalism" was so dependent on his leadership that it all but died out once he left office. His hand-picked successor, one-term president William Howard Taft, promised in his inaugural address to continue Roosevelt's Progressive policies. But with his own party split between a progressive and a conservative wing, Taft disappointed Roosevelt by following the conservatives. He dismissed Roosevelt's cabinet secretaries, differed from Roosevelt on the issue of environmental conservation, and failed to recognize that some trusts served the public interest.[31] Taft's record caused Roosevelt to run against Taft for the Republican nomination. Although Roosevelt won a majority of votes cast in state primaries, he was outmaneuvered by party bosses at the national convention, and he and his supporters bolted from the convention and called for a Progressive Party convention instead.[32]

When Taft, running as the Republican nominee, and Roosevelt, a Progressive Party nominee, split the Republican vote, Democrat Woodrow Wilson was elected—only the second member of the Democratic Party to hold the office since the Civil War. In his pursuit of election in 1912, Woodrow Wilson gave speeches that sketched out an America in decline, ruled over by shadowy and monopolistic industrial forces that had sold out the Jeffersonian vision. But like other Democrats of his period, Wilson was attuned to the notion of states' rights.[33] This commitment limited his willingness to use the federal government to intervene economically. The Federal Trade Commission (FTC) created during his administration was empowered to issue cease-and-desist orders to companies that made false claims, but the FTC usually did not exercise its power. The Clayton Anti-Trust Act (1914) was intended to clarify the Sherman Anti-Trust Act but failed to benefit labor.[34] By the time World War I broke out, national progressivism had sputtered to a halt.

UNION UPRISING

During the Progressive era, working people unionized avidly. They had good reasons to agitate for change. Workers encountered dangerous and unfenced machinery; even when safety measures were available, employers could claim that installing them was too expensive. Employers claimed that workplace injuries were due to worker negligence or failure to master the English language. Workers labored long hours, in uncomfortable postures, without sufficient meal breaks or bathroom breaks. Mechanical engineer Frederick Winslow Taylor's innovation of "scientific management" introduced time–motion studies intended to find the "one best way" of performing every factory task; Taylorism made production efficient but deprived the worker of all autonomy of movement on pain of fines or dismissal.[35] And most depressingly, the cost of adapting physically to the workplace was shifted onto the worker; there was no regulation to compel most workplaces to restrict work hours, provide rest and meal breaks, or install safety devices.[36]

By 1920, more than 5 million Americans belonged to labor unions, as contrasted with fewer than 500,000 only 20 years previously.[37] Even during this moment of relative labor unrest, however, the workforce remained divided between men and women, between native-born and immigrant workers, and between the white workers and the black workers who were often used to break strikes.[38] The American Federation of Labor emerged as the major overarching entity organizing male skilled workers. The AFL (founded 1886), was led by cigar-maker Samuel Gompers, an advocate of "pure and simple" unionism. Originally composed of 13 national craft unions, the federation used the strike weapon but avoided any political involvement, like running candidates for office. By charging high dues and not making the unionization of women or new immigrants a priority, the AFL became almost exclusively white, skilled, and male.[39]

But the first two decades of the twentieth century also saw the emergence of the Industrial Workers of the World (IWW, or "Wobblies"), "one big Union" dedicated to organizing men and women, white and black, skilled and unskilled. The IWW rejected AFL gradualism. They favored such direct actions as work slowdowns, working "to rule" (following all of the rules and regulations tends to slow the pace of work), and sabotage if necessary. Members of the IWW worked toward the elimination of the capitalist state, which they thought to be incompatible with democracy.[40] They also campaigned in favor of free speech, suing state and local governments, and their radicalism left them open to state repression.[41]

In New York, New Jersey, and Massachusetts, garment workers' unions, supported by the Socialist Party, mounted great strikes under the aegis of the Women's Trade Union League (WTUL).[42] White, male craft union leaders asserted that employees could negotiate fair contracts with their employers; women employees, who were paid less as a matter of course, did not agree.[43] The WTUL supported "protective legislation" that used assumptions about women's greater physical weakness or their importance as mothers to target women for shorter hours and for minimum wages. Protective legislation established entities like wages boards and arbitration tribunals and supported the appointment of female factory inspectors, interposing the power of the state between employer and employee.[44] The sacrifice of 146 women to industrial excess in the 1911 Triangle Shirtwaist Factory fire showed just how necessary these protections were. The employers of these young, immigrant workers had locked the exit doors of the building in order to deter theft, so that women had a choice between flinging themselves from the ninth-floor windows of the ten-story Asch building or burning to death.[45]

Democrats and Republicans attempted to appeal to workers by claiming that their platforms promoted economic prosperity for all. But in the first few decades of the twentieth century, third parties also emerged, deploying a more critical language of class. Voters' options ranged from the Progressive Party to the Socialist Party, the Farmer-Labor Party, and the Workers' Party. Rather than seek revolution, the Socialist Party, which nominated Eugene V. Debs for president in 1912, pursued legislation that benefited workers, like child labor legislation and workers' compensation, and the strategy of collective bargaining.[46] The Socialist Party also advocated for votes for women, who could see that the state might serve to assist rather than to hinder them. Socialist parties elected 12,000 candidates to office in 340 cities in 1912, and

Eugene Debs attracted 6 percent of the popular vote. Once in office, Socialist city officers addressed crucial working-class issues like sanitation, zoning, and improvement of squalid working-class neighborhoods.[47] But their reach was limited, because despite their gradualism, they were met with antisocialist hysteria that culminated in the first Red Scare of the late 1910s. The Espionage Act and Sedition Act criminalized antiwar efforts and speech critical of the government; Debs was jailed.[48] Ultimately, third-party voting died out, constricting the options of Americans concerned with inequality to whatever the most progressive policy of the Democratic Party happened to be.[49]

Some of this pressure did culminate in reform—particularly in the shape of protective legislation for women. States set maximum working hours for women or prohibited them from working at night. A test of that general principle came with the Supreme Court case of *Muller v. Oregon*; the Court ruled that legislation limiting women's hours of labor was constitutional largely because the state had a public interest in women's role as reproducers. The Court had decided against maximum-hour laws for men in *Lochner v. New York* (1905), showing that the willingness to regulate women's hours rested on a different principle.[50]

Labor historian Alice Kessler-Harris argues that the Supreme Court was willing to countenance protective legislation for women because justices identified women workers as lesser economic beings. Throughout the nineteenth century, women's waged work had always been seen as ancillary to men's and in some sense as hindering men's ability to earn a full "family wage." To the extent that women were interpreted as working only for "pin money," their claim to equality was undermined. But in the twentieth century, being willing and able to work was a prerequisite for full economic citizenship. Protective legislation envisioned women first as mothers—no matter what the intentions of any particular woman on the score of motherhood—and kept them out of certain fields entirely. At the same time, protective legislation did not extend to some really onerous work, like farm work or domestic labor.[51]

Protective legislation did not extend to the minimum wage, either *Adkins vs. Children's Hospital* (1923) struck down as unconstitutional a law that legislated a minimum wage for women. For the Court, the fact that women had achieved *formal* equality—the right to vote—was sufficient; *substantive* equality, especially economically, was not within the purview of the state to regulate.[52] Unfortunately, this was the same reasoning that had condemned most freedmen to sharecropping and low-wage jobs after the Civil War.

Protective legislation also had difficulty reaching child workers. A majority of states regulated child labor, but inspections were insufficient and, as a

result, lawbreaking was rampant.[53] Congress attempted to impose a federal
ban on child labor by regulating the interstate carriage of manufactures created by children in factories. In *Hammer v. Dagenhart* (1918), the Court
acknowledged the societal benefit of eliminating child labor but accused
Congress of overreach and insisted that each state regulate as it saw fit.[54]
Child labor was not federally regulated until the 1930s and still remains
incompletely regulated, a situation that clearly impedes equal life chances for
those forced to labor as young children.[55]

VOLUNTARY PROGRESSIVISM

Economic inequality came under fire not only from the government and
from workers who themselves were experiencing the impact of inequality,
but also from a host of charitable organizations. The Charity Organization
Society and the Salvation Army, both dating from the nineteenth century,
only distributed relief to the "deserving poor": those struck down by the illness or death of a male breadwinner, the very old, and orphans. As a result,
only a small number of families qualified for relief, and only after prying
examination into their living conditions and personal habits. New York phi-
lanthropists delighted in showy cross-class events like Christmas dinners, providing publicity for themselves but only limited help for the poor. The lack of
a social safety net, and the great divide between the upper ten and the lower
ten thousand, meant that wealthy people were constantly bombarded with
begging letters from the poor, sick, and disabled.[56]

Into this vacuum stepped women active in the settlement house movement
to build community centers in urban areas, live alongside the poor, and provide
them with role models and tangible social services. Animated by Social Gospel
beliefs that Christian salvation required not only faith but also emulating
Christ's life by doing good work, these highly educated middle-class women
made some of the pioneering contributions to the sociology of inequality.[57]
Mary Eliza MacDowell, who had trained at Chicago's Hull House settlement,
directed a settlement among the eastern European immigrants of the Chicago
stockyards, including "day nurseries, English classes, garbage disposal, and a
neighborhood playground while unionizing stockyard workers and agitating
for the vote for women in municipal elections." Other new social-service organizations, often led by women, provided new immigrants with English classes,
cooking and child care classes, and other Americanization programs. Immigrant
communities also developed their own such organizations.[58]

Settlement-house workers believed that citizens had social as well as political responsibilities to others.[59] The settlement-house founder and labor

reformer Jane Addams's *Democracy and Social Ethics*, published in 1902, argued that democracy could only succeed if people built social relationships outside their own class—a position that involves recognizing that not everyone is "middle class," as Americans like to claim.[60] Lillian Wald, founder of New York City's Henry Street Settlement, knew that her poorer neighbors were people like herself, with the same ambitions and hopes for their children. Her willingness to listen to their needs led to creative solutions. She founded a home nursing service for people who were ill but could not afford to go to a hospital due to lack of child care. Schoolchildren who lived in tenements did not thrive in school because they had neither quiet nor room to work in their crowded apartments; Wald prevailed on the New York City school board to create open study rooms in school buildings for them to use.[61]

Anna Julia Cooper, a supporter of the Colored Social Settlement (1902), wrote, "The Social Settlement, with its home life, its neighborhood visiting, its clubs, classes and personal service is endeavoring to bring higher ideals of life and character to many who are largely cut off from good influences and opportunities; to stimulate ambition, raise moral standards, strengthen character and develop capacity for self-help."[62] Admittedly, Cooper's rhetoric is similar to that of functionaries in the British Empire who saw the people in the areas they colonized as lesser beings. Social settlement founder also tended to reject explanations of social inequality that might cause class conflict. But colonialist and conservative as they may have been, settlement workers proved their empathy for, and commitment to, the populations they served.[63]

In addition to founding settlement houses, middle-class reformist women promoted "child hygiene" as a way to equalize life chances for the poor. They took on such targets as unclean water and adulterated milk, crowded public school classrooms, and lack of sanitation in urban areas—all out of a sense of maternal responsibility for young children.[64] Progressives held "Better Baby Contests" to show immigrant families that with the right nurturing, clean homes, and access to pure food, poor children could be prizewinning stock. The emphasis on keeping families together resulted in the invention of the "mothers' pension." Contemporaries felt that even in a single-parent home, it was best for a parent to stay home and care for children. Rather than see single parents putting their children into "half-orphanages" because they could not afford to support them, states, beginning with Illinois, supplemented mothers' income.[65] Income supplementation was limited to female heads of household or those with completely incapacitated husbands, and it expired when children reached their mid-teens and were old enough to go to work. Additionally, recipients of mothers' pensions had to conform to whatever social norms were dictated by state oversight boards: families could not take in male boarders, for example, and purchased clothes and food were expected to be adequate but not luxurious.[66] Still, Progressives were willing to support impoverished mothers to stay home and care for their children.

Not every project undertaken by the Progressives holds up to moral scrutiny over a century later. Fearing racial "degeneration," Progressive reformers emphasized the need to build healthy bodies through active play, supervised by authorities who would ward off gang activity.[67] As experts proposed that poverty could be inherited, the concern for racial hygiene extended to eugenic strategies to prevent the "unfit" from reproducing.[68] Birth control advocate Margaret Sanger, one of the most committed to spreading information about contraception, was sympathetic to the plight of poor women but also believed that large poor families harmed society generally.[69] The concern for social "uplift" even extended to programs to sterilize those with mental disabilities or supposedly hereditary degeneracy.

While many voluntary Progressive projects were undertaken by women, the "social center" movement was an exception. Edward Ward, a Social Gospel minister and professor, spearheaded a movement intended to increase direct popular participation in politics. Public schools became social centers for discussions, staying open after the hours of classes for presentations and debates by "civic clubs." According to the historian Kevin Mattson, participation in the movement strengthened democracy by showing participants of all social classes that they could express political opinions and disagreement cogently, and that their opinions on policy mattered. Civic clubs were co-opted by the existing political parties and used as fora for the promotion of lockstep nationalism during World War I, but they provide a model for constructive grassroots political discussion that is rare in the age of the Internet.[70]

PROGRESSIVE WRITERS ON INEQUALITY

In contrast to prior generations of American writers on inequality, Progressive-era authors were more convinced that conditions had objectively worsened for workers, but also more optimistic about the prospect of solving the problem of inequality. Progressive writers on inequality touted the state as the entity best able to care for people's needs. As the Progressive economist Richard Ely wrote, "We regard the state as an educational and ethical agency whose positive aid is an indispensable condition of human progress."[71]

Herbert Croly was one of these advocates of using the state to advance human promise. Croly was the editor of an agricultural newspaper who went on to found *The New Republic* magazine. He published *The Promise of*

American Life (1909), an immensely influential text calling for economic equality.[72] Croly noted that "the traditional American confidence in individual freedom has resulted in a morally and socially undesirable distribution of wealth."[73] He traced harmful inequality to conflicting views about the proper role of government that persisted from the 1790s, when Treasury Secretary Alexander Hamilton and Secretary of State Thomas Jefferson had disagreed ideologically. According to Croly, Hamilton had had an idea of the national good, whereas Jefferson's party promoted "national drift"—abundant resources meant there was no need for government intervention in the economy. Croly showed that Andrew Jackson's administration also illustrated the ideal of abundance: "The Western Democrat devoutly believed that an approximately equal division of the good things of life would result from the possession by all American citizens of equal legal rights and similar economic opportunities. But the importance of this result in their whole point of view was concealed by the fact that they expected to reach it by wholly negative means—that is, by leaving the individual alone."[74]

As post–Civil War industrialization increased both the risk of failure for firms and the barriers to market entry, successful firms began to do everything they could to protect their interests. They evaded supervision largely due to Americans' preference for local regulation if there was to be any regulation at all. Fabulous and untouchable fortunes had been amassed: "The rich men and the big corporations have become too wealthy and powerful for their official standing in American life. They have not obeyed the laws. They have attempted to control the official makers, administrators, and expounders of the law ... while their work has been constructive from an economic and industrial standpoint, it has made for political disruption and social disintegration."[75] Clearly, the Jeffersonian "negative freedom"—the freedom to be left alone by government—could not ensure equal opportunity in an era of greatly concentrated economic power.

For Croly, the United States had a unique "national promise" that could only be realized through government intervention. He admired Theodore Roosevelt's National Progressivism and described Roosevelt as combining a Hamiltonian "big picture" with the desire to allow Americans to achieve their individual potential.[76] But Croly went a step further than Roosevelt by advocating taxation and redistribution. He argued that without this redistribution, the very liberty on which the United States was founded was in danger.[77] As Paine and Skidmore had done in the nineteenth century, Croly attacked inherited wealth. He favored a substantial tax on the largest inheritances (although not as substantial as the tax that Paine had proposed in *Agrarian Justice*).[78] He also favored unionization in all trades other than agriculture, and recognition of the collective bargaining rights of labor unions. He hoped that, once organized, workers would create contracts with a wage floor and maximum hours.[79] In a second book, *Progressive Democracy*, published in 1914, Croly expanded his recommendations to include industrial democracy through union syndicalism—a reaction to the way in which Progressive reforms like workers' compensation had provided some reforms but not gained independence in the workplace for workers.[80]

Many writers on American inequality, both in the Progressive era and today, emphasize the potential of education to equalize opportunity—but Croly felt that this suggestion was both unhelpful and insincere. Without a plan to improve the nation through "experimental collective action aimed at the realization of the collective purpose," the "books, subsidies, resolutions, lectures [and] congresses" aimed at reforming education would be piecemeal.[81] Only national efforts could free individuals from chasing the goal of amassing the most cash; the most beneficial society would instead promote individual intellectual and social development and the honing of each person's unique gifts.[82] Croly's views on education echoed those of the philosopher John Dewey, who argued that bringing out the best individual talents was crucial to fostering democracy. There could be no such thing as a standardized education, because any education that treated children like widgets, predestined for roles in a technocratic system, would stifle individual development and creativity.[83]

Like Croly, Walter Weyl, author of *The New Democracy* (1912), criticized the distribution of power and the impact of the "plutocracy" on political life. Weyl believed that the promise of American life had never been fulfilled, even during the antebellum period, due to the existence of slavery. The "availability" of land in the West not only temporarily disguised the conflict between democracy and liberal individualism but also resulted in "a scarred and wasted continent" that "showed signs of a century of rape."[84] While temporarily abundant resources distracted Americans into believing that Jeffersonian individualistic freedom was the root of all good things, trusts and the railroads snuck to the center of the American economy. Individual mortgages were bundled and sold, individual capitals securitized and monetized. The little investor thus had no idea what was going on. "Our plutocracy, based on the trust's position in industry and the trust magnate's position within the trust, is composed, to a great extent, of strong, unscrupulous, far-seeing and ultra-individualistic persons, who secured hold of our national monopolized business while we as a nation were dreaming of competitive beatitudes," Weyl chaffed.[85]

Weyl's plutocrats sought to shrink government and argued that taxation was theft. "The plutocracy preaches individual liberty, the glorious fruits of free contract, the doctrine of the influence of good men, the survival of the fittest in business, an untrammeled individualism ... It believes that while government is wise enough to put us in jail, it is not honest enough to be intrusted with our money or our business."[86] Moreover, the wealthy were able to dominate newspapers with their message, with only the upstart medium of the reformist magazine hammering against their party line.[87]

Weyl called for a revolution: harnessing government and the economy to allow for the freedom and development of all individuals. In fact, the revolution of which he spoke was already underway: "one group in the community strives to end the exploitation of child labor. Other groups seek to extend and improve education, to combat tuberculosis, to reform housing conditions, to secure direct primaries, to obtain the referendum, to punish force and fraud at the polls, to secure governmental inspection of foods ..."[88] For Weyl, this constellation of efforts and regulations constituted an optimistic Progressive movement dedicated to social democracy; he had no way of knowing that the year his work was published marked the zenith of Progressive success and the beginning of its downward slide.

THE GREAT MIGRATION AND THE BLACK EXPERIENCE

Slavery's legacy did not disappear just because the calendar indicated a new century had arrived. While white Progressive reformers sought social justice, racial divisions remained and were deepened by racialist beliefs. Some Progressive reformers working in the black community, through institutions like the National Association of Colored Women, had to cede control of their movements to white women or to work with very limited funding. The end result of this was twofold: an emphasis on social uplift that came from within the black community, and exasperation with white Progressivism.[89]

Some Progressives, like Theodore Roosevelt, believed that the potential for democracy was, at least in part, racial—that Anglo-Americans possessed more of the genius for self-government than anyone else. "Scientific racism" proposed a hierarchy of the races, with the white Anglo-Saxon at the top and other, "less advanced" cultures lower in the hierarchy. Africans and Aboriginal peoples were considered to be at the bottom of the hierarchy, but other nonwhite people were also held to be inferior. The Progressive period thus saw limitations on immigration from places like China (the Exclusion Act of 1882) and Japan (the Gentlemen's Agreement of 1908), and by the 1920s, successive Immigration Acts that drastically cut back permissible immigration from southern and eastern Europe. Circumscribing and privileging whiteness in this way meant that African Americans, even in the North, continued to be considered second-class citizens.[90]

African American leaders disagreed about the best path to prosperity for the black community. Since the 1880s, a vanguard of black intellectuals led by the theologian Alexander Crummell had called for racial uplift through higher education.[91] William Edward Burghardt DuBois, born after the abolition of slavery, was a talented young scholar. The first black American to earn a Ph.D., DuBois conducted an academic study of black poverty in Philadelphia. Published in 1899 as *The Philadelphia Negro*, it was the first of a series of statistically based studies intended to underpin urban social reform.[92] DuBois took up Crummell's flag in the twentieth century and espoused the education of talented young black people in the liberal arts so that they might provide "race leadership."

In contrast, well-known educator Booker T. Washington rejected DuBois's calls for higher education of the "talented tenth" of the black community. Instead, he favored incremental advancement for African Americans, one tiny step at a time, through hard work and painstaking economic gains. Born a slave in 1856, Washington at age 16 had sought out the Hampton Institute, a charitable organization set up to provide the rudiments of education and a good dose of moralizing to former slaves. After working as a teacher and making the right connections, he became principal of the Tuskegee Institute, raising a huge endowment for "industrial education" of formerly enslaved men and women. In his 1895 "Atlanta Compromise" speech, Washington emphasized that black Americans were willing to work hard, learn the habits of thrift and industry, and make no political or social demands on the white community. In turn, he urged white employers to "cast down your buckets where you are" by hiring black employees. Washington was no enemy to social hierarchy:

> Our greatest danger is that in the great leap from slavery to freedom we may overlook the fact that the masses of us are to live by the productions of our hands, and fail to keep in mind that we shall prosper in proportion as we learn to dignify and clarify common labour and put brains and skill into the common occupations of life ... It is at the bottom of life we must begin, and not at the top. Nor shall should we permit our grievances to overshadow our opportunities.[93]

Washington famously accommodated white racism by offering that "In all things that are purely social we can be as separate as the fingers, yet, one as the hand in all things essential to mutual progress."[94]

Washington's nonconfrontational strategy, with its emphasis on personal responsibility and the professed willingness of black Americans to be socially and economically inferior to whites, appealed to white Americans. He became the gatekeeper for public and private funds being funneled to black uplift and was an advisor to presidents. The publication of his autobiography, *Up from Slavery*, in 1901 helped to cement his popularity, since it not only followed the Horatio Alger story of success based on personal tenacity, but also did so without antagonizing southern whites over the slave past. Like DuBois, Washington placed a premium on respectability and "civilization," suggesting that he could not escape from the frame of Anglo-Saxon superiority either.[95]

For 10 years after Washington's Atlanta speech, DuBois and Washington remained cordial; Washington even offered DuBois a teaching job at Tuskegee on three separate occasions. But the two men finally fell out publicly in 1904. The passage of "Jim Crow" laws that segregated schools, transportation, bathrooms, and other public amenities, and state laws that restricted African Americans from voting, showed that Washington's Atlanta Compromise was not helping the black community.[96] Moreover, a wave of lynchings throughout the South illustrated the dangers of having an entire race of people considered to be civilly inferior.[97] DuBois helped to found the National Association for the Advancement of Colored People (NAACP) in 1909, with the intention of combatting lynching with legal weapons.

Political scientist Michael Thompson has recently criticized Dubois for insisting that political and educational rights and the cultivation of a black elite should be prior to, or in a sense, independent of, economic uplift. Thompson argues that Booker T. Washington's emphasis on economic empowerment through thousands of freed slaves pulling themselves up by their bootstraps was "more right" than DuBois's program. But DuBois predicted what actually occurred in the twentieth century. As African Americans offered their services in the labor market, that market was not racially neutral. African Americans remained poor, and ultimately, poverty itself became equated with race.[98]

The *Chicago Defender* was another strong voice in favor of black Progressivism in this period. Its editor, Robert Abbott, favored such policies as women's traditional role in the home, compulsory school attendance, the building of parks and playgrounds in urban neighborhoods, and prohibition of moral vices like alcoholism and prostitution. While many white Progressives advocated for political reforms like the direct primary and recall and initiative, the *Chicago Defender* touted the overarching importance of economic strength.[99]

As DuBois and Washington and Abbott debated the future of the black community in the press, African American families took matters into their own hands. They dispersed their households to survive. Husbands became migrant workers, picking crops throughout the South, while wives stayed in other states, raised the children, and worked as domestics in white households. Finally, to escape the combination of family separation and relegation to ill-paid rural employment, many families moved to the North. This came to be called the Great Migration: 400,000 African Americans migrated north before World War I, then 1.5 million between 1914 and 1940, and then an additional 5 million by 1970.[100]

Preliminary research on the impact of migration shows that, compared with nonmigrants, those African Americans who did migrate to the North experienced real economic gains. Those who left the South were more likely to become literate than those who stayed behind, and much more likely to move into higher-paid work than agricultural labor.[101] Of course, migration was not a perfect solution. Although northern states lacked Jim Crow laws, many public amenities were informally segregated. Some restaurants refused service to African Americans. Black workers were often the last hired and the first fired in higher-paying jobs. They were used as strikebreakers, which precipitated race riots.[102] The black urban poor used community resourcefulness to survive. An illegal sector including theft, prostitution, and vibrant numbers games prospered in some northern cities, "anticipating the emergence of the contemporary underground economy."[103]

Recognizing that African Americans in the North faced economic segregation, DuBois advocated economic cooperation. As editor of the NAACP's magazine, *The Crisis*, he advised black Americans to create and patronize businesses catering almost exclusively to the black community.[104] Similarly, Marcus Garvey, founder of the popular United Negro Improvement Association, advocated black separatism, entrepreneurialism, and ultimately, migration to Africa.[105]

PROGRESSIVISM, "AMERICANISM," AND THE FIRST WORLD WAR

World War I produced the first impressive contraction of inequality in the twentieth century. As men joined the war effort and left the domestic labor market, the wages for unskilled labor rose. Higher-skilled and white-collar workers with longer contracts that were less responsive to inflation found that their pay did not keep up. At the same time, the government experimented with price controls, rent control, and excess-profits taxes.[106] Ironically, however, even as actual inequality temporarily decreased, Americans backed away from the discussions about the importance of fostering equality.

During World War I, the government reached out to the AFL while at the same time cracking down on the IWW, which was branded as subversive. The National War Labor Board recognized the legality of collective bargaining and encouraged mediation in order to avoid strikes during wartime. At the same time, because speech against the war was criminalized, Socialist leader Eugene V. Debs was imprisoned. Debs, one of the founders of the Socialist Party in America, raised one of the few voices during and after the war against the notion that what was best for business was best for American workers. "America is now at the parting of the roads. If the outraging of political liberty and concentration of economic power into the hands of the few is permitted to go on, it can have only one consequence, the reduction of the country to a state of absolute capitalist despotism." The Socialist party platform called for nationalization of all essential industries, banks, and insurance companies with the goal of humane employment rather than profit generation. It also called for full "civil, political, industrial and educational rights" for black workers.[107]

The jailing of Debs was just the first step in the effective suppression of voices in favor of greater economic equalization. After the Bolshevik revolution in Russia, American fears precipitated a Red Scare in which any discussion of social equality was treated like the first step toward Soviet-style chaos. Attorney General A. Mitchell Palmer, whose house was firebombed by an unknown assailant, railed, "Because a disreputable alien—Leon Bronstein, the man who calls himself Trotsky—can inaugurate a reign of terror from his throne room in the Kremlin; because this lowest of all types known to New York can sleep in the Czar's bed, while hundreds of thousands in Russia are without food or shelter, should Americans be swayed by such doctrines?"[108] The Red Scare not only put discussion of economic inequality completely off limits, it also called into question such mainstays of the economic system as simple "bread and butter" unionism. John L. Lewis, the president of the United Mine Workers, objected that by bargaining collectively, workers were seeking nothing more than what employers sought. Just as today politicians note that American prosperity rests on the existence of a middle class with disposable income, so, Lewis said, "the purchasing power of the American masses is the pivot upon which our whole economic system turns."[109] The National Union of Manufacturers in return produced anti-labor literature and called for the open shop, in which collective bargaining was impossible because workers could choose not to become members of the union.[110]

During the 1920s, American workers were encouraged to identify themselves fully with American business enterprise, on the theory that economic expansion benefited everyone. Harvard economist Thomas Nixon Carver predicted that everyone would become a capitalist, "owner or part owner of some of the instruments of production called capital," not through confiscation but rather through hard work.[111] Job-linked perquisites had existed from the beginning of American industrialization, but the variety and scope of such offerings grew during the 1920s, helping workers to lose interest in unions. In addition to company housing and company stores, larger factories—those with several hundred workers—branched out to provide on-site lunches, recreational facilities, and employee representation plans, in which employees could provide advice on the operation of the plant. Employers introduced pensions for long service, paid vacations for production workers, group life insurance, and citizenship classes. These programs were often more show than substance; one historian estimates that they did not amount to more than 2 percent of the average company's wage bill. Still, they provided good publicity for business and helped to forge a tie between employer and employee that was stronger than the ties workers had with each other.[112]

The Ford Motor Company offered a very generous $5 per day wage to employees who were willing to demonstrate to home inspectors that they were following the expectations of normative middle-class domesticity: eating American food, not living with large extended families, not drinking and carousing.[113] Ford and many other companies during the 1920s became more stringent in their hiring, instituting personnel departments and attempting to use more skilled, higher-wage workers to boost productivity.[114] Whether the constellation of perquisites that historians call "welfare capitalism" was an attempt by employers to beat back unionism or whether it just happened to coincide with a decline in unionism, by the end of the 1920s, unions had lost much of their strength. On the other hand, while workers embraced capitalism, they were also now trained to expect employers to offer certain benefits.[115]

After the short compression of World War I, income inequality increased during the 1920s until American workers were unable to afford many of the products that they worked to produce. The top-earning 1 percent of Americans in the late 1920s possessed 23.9 percent of total income, the highest percentage between 1913 and 2013. At the same time, because workers were encouraged to identify American prosperity with business growth, there was no discussion of taxation and redistribution, or of raising wage rates. President Calvin Coolidge railed against regulation on the grounds that not only was it expensive and injurious to business but also that "the present generation of business almost universally throughout its responsible organization and management has shown every disposition to correct its own abuses with as little intervention of the government as possible."[116] Julian Barnes, the president of the United States Chamber of Commerce, disparaged the lack of "fair play" when "special sections of our people, numerically strong . . . levy, through unequal and unwise taxation, and in a spirit of envy and resentment, an unfair burden, against those other groups more fortunate than themselves."[117] Of course, the notion that capitalism was always benevolent and self-regulating was tested on Thursday,

October 24, 1929, as the great stock market crash that marked the beginning of
the Great Depression began.

In contrast with many other periods in American history, the first 15 years
of the twentieth century saw some of the most sustained criticisms of
American inequality, aided by an energetic presidency and an active, muckraking press. Of course, as journalist E. J. Dionne has pointed out, the Progressives had flaws. Some of them were content to marginalize the poor from
participating in politics in the name of cleaning up corruption. Others favored
institutions that would exert a large amount of control over poor and
immigrant families on the assumption that the poor lacked parenting skills.
Except for the African American Progressives, the movement itself was
laissez-faire on racial issues, which resulted in continued social and economic
inequality for black Americans. But to focus on these things is to forget the
extent to which Progressivism was aimed at curbing the excesses of the market-
place. Progressivism used the tools of government, including free public education and improvements in public health and infrastructure, to provide
individuals with the "positive liberty" that they needed in order to achieve their
life plans.[118] During the 1920s, much of the ground gained by Progressives was
lost. The Red Scare of the late teens and early 1920s, and the emphasis on
"Americanism" and business prosperity during that decade, shut down the critique of American inequality. As the next chapter will show, the Great Depression encouraged politicians to experiment with employing government
programs and resources to address inequality on a larger scale.

CHAPTER 5

Challenge from the Left: 1929–1945

W hile the end of the 1920s, just before the stock market crashed, was famously one of the most unequal moments in American history, that all changed with the advent of the Great Depression. The period between 1929 and the 1950s marks an anomaly in the persistent history of American inequality: a "historical aberration," or as Jefferson Cowie and Nick Salvatore term it, "the long exception," as the rich and the poor moved toward each other.[1] Objectively, diminished inequality manifested itself in many ways: the average income of the richest quintile of Americans dropped from 15.5 times to 9 times that of the lowest quintile by 1951, and the inequality of wages and infrastructure between North and South decreased. Government spending during the 1930s helped to promote greater equality, since the government was able to use more of the services of the working poor than was the private sector. Because these government programs were financed through progressive taxation (tax withholding on wages did not start until 1943), government expenditure had a double effect, increasing the income of the poor and decreasing that of the wealthy.[2]

It is important to note, however, that within the general movement toward greater economic equality, other inequities persisted or even worsened. The Depression period coincided with immigration restriction, including the deportation of large numbers of Mexican and Mexican American workers. This decision may have raised wages for white workers by creating a scarcity of labor, but it relegated Mexican American workers, who had always been paid less under the dual-wage system, to a lower status.[3] Moreover, although Franklin Delano Roosevelt's party controlled both houses of Congress by 1933, securing passage of his New Deal programs required him to compromise with southern Democrats who were determined that the programs preserve white supremacy and a racial dual-wage system. As a result, some New Deal programs operated in ways that disadvantaged black workers or excluded them from benefits entirely. The Depression period thus continued the American government's tradition of refusing to confront the economic legacy of slavery.

Although the Progressives of previous decades had been troubled by the impact of inequality, the economic stagnation of the 1930s pushed the issues of distribution, and equality of condition, to the forefront of politics. Activists like doctor Francis Townsend, whose ideas shaped Social Security, and politicians and political candidates like Louisiana governor and senator Huey Long (Share Our Wealth) and novelist and progressive activist Upton Sinclair (End Poverty in California) challenged Franklin Delano Roosevelt's New Deal from the left.

While Republicans attempted to portray Roosevelt as a raging Marxist, the New Deal was in fact notable for policy moderation. Roosevelt's New Deal reversed the laissez-faire course that Herbert Hoover followed but ended up saving capitalism with methods that had long been in the American wheelhouse. The New Deal combined "emergency relief, farm aid, social security, conservation, banking and securities reform [and] fair labor standards," but as historian John Tipple pointed out, all of these initiatives, even the Tennessee Valley Authority, a huge government dam system, strengthened rather than undermined a private-industry economy. Farm income and prices rose and labor unions gained members again under the auspices of the Committee for Industrial Organization.[4] Finally, at the end of the Depression, full employment during World War II pushed the call for equality aside.

THE DEPRESSION UNDER HOOVER

Historians have pointed to a wide array of causes for the Great Depression, some of which are linked to inequality. In the longer term, poorly paid factory workers could not afford to buy the goods they produced, and inventories of consumer goods languished in warehouses. In the short run, stock market investors pushed stock prices higher by speculating "on the margin," borrowing up to 90 percent of the cost of stocks with a plan to pay back the banks after a supposedly inevitable stock price increase. When the stock market crashed, they were bankrupted. Internationally, nations imposed trade barriers against each other that resulted in rounds of retributive tariffs. Rounds of currency depreciation followed, as each country struggled to right its trade imbalance. Central banks in the largest countries used their interest rate policies to keep inordinately large levels of gold reserves, and the Bank of England, which had before World War I been able to step in as the lender of last resort, was no longer able to do so.[5] It is clear that an international event of the magnitude of a worldwide economic depression has many intersecting causes.

In the United States, the Depression was important not only because it slashed the wealth and capital income of the rich but also because it forced the consideration of new policies for grappling with inequality. The first three years of the Depression coincided with the single presidential term of Herbert Hoover, whose name became synonymous with the shanty towns—Hoovervilles—built out of scrap lumber and cloth that popped up in American major cities on his watch. To be fair, the economy had experienced panics about every 20 years during the nineteenth century; the government had never responded with massive spending programs, and the country had recovered. Hoover and his cabinet expected that the 1929 panic would be no different.

In the wake of the stock market crash, Hoover's Secretary of the Treasury, Andrew Mellon, described the crash as beneficial, enabling the economy to purge uncompetitive workers, businesses, and banks. Hoover and his cabinet opposed intervention, fearing that government "relief would itself become an instrument of patronage and the means of creating a totalitarian state," as well as undermining American individualism and creating dependency.[6] He at first attempted to stoke the economy by issuing optimistic statements that the economy would right itself. He requested, and was granted by Congress, corporate and personal tax cuts. Hoover also requested that unions hold the line on wage increase requests, that employers not cut their payrolls, and that state governors consider undertaking infrastructure projects.[7] But Hoover was neither willing nor able to compel businesses to hire workers, nor states to spend money, and even the economist John Maynard Keynes had not, by Hoover's term in office, fully developed his theory that government spending could "prime the pump" for economic recovery.[8]

Although businesses could not be compelled, workers could. Beginning in 1931, Hoover's Secretary of Labor, William Doak, responded to unemployment by seeking out migrants without a legal immigration status through a series of government-sponsored raids on low-wage industries. Southern California witnessed large-scale government-managed "repatriations" of Mexican-born immigrants and their American-born children who, leaving without documents attesting to their citizenship status, subsequently had difficulty returning. Combined with hostile conditions that promoted "self-deportation," the raids resulted in the departure of about a million workers from the labor force, approximately 60 percent of whom were U.S. citizens.

The U.S. government's plans neatly piggybacked on those of the Mexican government, which was at that time touting its economic growth and advertising the potential of agricultural colonies. But repatriated Mexicans were resented by those who had stayed through the turbulent years of the Mexican Revolution, and they found themselves plunged into deeper poverty and with diminished prospects.[9]

These attempts to manage the labor supply were insufficient as the crisis broadened. The same year that deportations began, the Depression spread to Europe. Britain, historically the financial powerhouse of Europe but crippled by World War I debts, departed from the gold standard. The Austrian central bank failed. By 1932, Hoover attempted to reverse his earlier emphasis on tax cuts by raising the estate tax and personal income taxes, and supporting banks and corporations through the Reconstruction Finance Corporation, but he still balked at providing direct relief to the unemployed. Finally, in the summer of 1932, Hoover signed legislation that funded mortgage loans and allocated billions of dollars in loans to localities to build public works. In a tribute to the emptiness of Hoover's approach, that summer also saw the violent expulsion from Washington, DC, of the "Bonus Army," destitute World War I veterans attempting to collect early on a government-promised bonus.[10]

Between 1929 and 1933, official unemployment rates increased from 3 percent to 25 percent, but in some cities, unemployment was as high as 80 percent. Of those who were employed, about one-third were part-time workers.[11] The nature of unemployment was different, too, as those who became unemployed remained unemployed for ever-longer periods of time, and even the employed suffered wage reductions. The volunteer and church organizations that had supported workers through hard times before went bankrupt.[12] By 1934, over 40 percent of people with home mortgages had defaulted.[13] These statistics, as impressive as they are, fail to capture the extent of the human suffering; the historian Studs Terkel unearthed stories of Dust Bowl refugees, of families subsisting on cast-off food, and of families huddled together under blankets all day because they had no heating fuel.[14] Unsurprisingly, when Hoover ran for re-election in 1932, he was badly beaten by Franklin Delano Roosevelt. The Democrats gained 101 seats in the House of Representatives and 12 seats in the Senate, and Roosevelt carried the electoral votes of 42 of the 48 states.[15]

THE NEW DEAL

Although born into a wealthy family, Roosevelt was characterized by people who knew him as having a "first-class temperament" and the ability to empathize with others, perhaps because of the polio that had changed his life in 1919. He could connect with people who were suffering economically—reaching out to them with his Fireside Chats over the radio and with inspired turns of phrase like the "fear itself" line of his first inaugural address. In the realm of symbolic politics, the promise of a repeal of Prohibition and the choice of "Happy Days Are Here Again" for a campaign song helped boost the national mood.[16]

Roosevelt energetically applied himself to the problems of the Great Depression in the first hundred days of his administration. Many hardworking Americans had lost their savings during runs on banks that caused small-town banks to fail. As people hid their money under their mattresses, the circulating money supply fell by a third, and the deflation made the Depression worse.[17] As soon as he was inaugurated, Roosevelt declared a bank holiday to stave off further bank failures. To avoid some of the financial problems that had led up to the Great Crash, the Federal Deposit Insurance Corporation (FDIC) and the Securities and Exchange Commission (SEC) were empowered to regulate savings bank deposits and the disclosures of public corporations, respectively. Some in Roosevelt's cabinet advocated more radical plans, like bank nationalization or the establishment of post-office savings banks, which would allow small depositors to earn interest by depositing their funds at the post office. The Glass-Steagall Act, which prohibited commercial banks from engaging in speculative investments, served to regulate the nation's financial institutions well for the next six decades until its 1999 repeal.[18]

Roosevelt also instituted reforms to address concerns about corporate greed. While Hoover had not been concerned with income inequality, Roosevelt's administration embedded rules in the Reconstruction Finance Corporation to regulate executive compensation. The Reconstruction Finance Corporation was pumping federal money into such enterprises as railroads, insurance companies, and banks, but only in the case of insurance companies was an absolute ceiling on executive compensation agreed on (of $17,500). Some railroad executives made $100,000 or more per year in 1933 dollars, but cutting their pay was off the table.[19]

The New Deal also included regulation of business. The National Industrial Recovery Act (NIRA), passed in June 1933, facilitated the creation of industry-wide and industry-generated codes regulating prices and wages. NIRA explicitly allowed workers to unionize and bargain collectively, generally granted a minimum wage of 35 to 40 cents an hour, and—to spread the work—specified a maximum workweek of 35 hours. Stores participating in NIRA displayed a placard with the patriotic blue eagle.[20] By January 1935, codes existed in 775 different industries. Although in 1935 the Supreme

Court declared NIRA unconstitutional, further legislation was passed to explicitly recognize the union right of collective bargaining.[21]

Under Roosevelt, the government took a more innovative approach to relief of the unemployed than Hoover had been willing to attempt. The Federal Emergency Relief Administration (FERA) gave block grants directly to states to distribute for relief. FERA also established cooperative farms and rural industries for relief recipients—mostly young families—who wanted to stay in rural areas. The National Industrial Recovery Act also dealt with unemployment by moving some of the urban population back to the land, just as the National Reformers had recommended in the 1840s. Ultimately, these programs were merged into the Resettlement Administration and then the Farm Security Administration, and included not only cooperative communities but also planned suburban settlements.[22]

Relief also meant having the government directly employ millions of people, setting an example for future administrations that government-sponsored public service was possible and beneficial.[23] The Public Works Administration (PWA), later renamed the Works Progress Administration (WPA), employed 8 million people and spent over $10 billion on roads, bridges, post offices, stadiums, and airports.[24] It employed writers, artists, actors, musicians, and historians in the largest government-funded cultural project in the history of the United States. The interviews that historians conducted with former slaves have been a cornerstone of historical research on slavery since their publication, helping to counteract an interpretation of slavery that included almost no African American voices. Many PWA and WPA jobs were unskilled, provided no training, and preferred manual to mechanical labor, leading to jokes that the WPA stood for "We Piddle Around."[25] Criticism notwithstanding, these jobs helped people gain confidence and have a productive role in society.[26]

Another government jobs program, the Civilian Conservation Corps (CCC), employed more than 3 million American men ages 18–23 during the nine years of its existence. CCC men lived in national and state parks; built roads, trails, barracks, and campsites; and planted forests. Moreover, since CCC jobs were often located in remote areas, businesses benefited from workers who needed food, fuel, supplies, and recreational activities.[27] When the Bonus Army marchers who had posed such a public-relations nightmare for Herbert Hoover came back to Washington two more times in 1933 and 1934, Roosevelt suspended the normal CCC age regulations to propitiate 25,000 of those marchers with jobs. The CCC also hired black workers, who constituted 10 percent of the total number of those employed, but with just a few exceptions, they lived in segregated camps.[28]

While many of the New Deal public works initiatives were minor construction projects that could be brought online quickly, the Tennessee Valley Authority (TVA) was the largest and most ambitious project that the government undertook. The TVA pumped more than $20 billion into the Tennessee Valley, constructing dams on the Tennessee River across seven states. The dams were intended both to engineer the water flow and to provide electricity to underserved areas. The project increased per-capita income in those states compared with the country as a whole, from 44 percent of the national average in 1929 to 61 percent in 1952.[29] The TVA brought power at a lower cost to the end consumer, allowing the South to modernize and manufacture.[30] It also prevented erosion and raised local wage rates. The Rural Electrification Administration, established in 1935, loaned money to rural utility cooperatives to expand electrification. In areas new to electricity, agricultural productivity boomed.[31]

NEW DEAL INEQUALITY

Although the Democratic Party controlled both houses of Congress, in order to get legislation through, Roosevelt often found it necessary to cater to southern Democrats who were eager to perpetuate white supremacy. Even in the North, party machines minimized the impact of black voters.[32] As a result, racial discrimination was not effectively targeted by the New Deal.[33] The Agricultural Adjustment Administration (AAA) provides one example. The AAA raised prices for farm goods by providing subsidies to farmers for not growing crops, but this program was targeted at larger planters. Although they were directed to maintain pre-Depression employment levels, farm owners used the occasion of farm subsidies to push largely black sharecroppers into wage labor or unemployment.[34] In Arkansas, angry tenant farmers, black and white, organized into the Southern Tenant Farmers Union, taking on the New Deal with the backing of the Socialist Party before eventually being crushed.[35]

Other New Deal programs also disadvantaged black workers. Although workers received the acknowledged right to collectively bargain, American Federation of Labor craft unions often excluded the relatively small percentage of skilled black workers in the workforce. Neither NAACP leaders nor A. Phillip Randolph of the Brotherhood of Sleeping Car Porters could motivate Congress to bar trade union discrimination against black workers.[36] The Fair Labor Standards Act excluded a majority of women and African American workers from eligibility for old-age pensions. Southern politicians argued that agricultural and domestic workers needed the incentive of poverty to perform some kinds of low-waged work.[37]

A few voices in Roosevelt's circle were committed to racial justice. First Lady Eleanor Roosevelt, WPA administrator Harry Hopkins, Secretary of the Interior Harold Ickes, and, particularly, Secretary of Labor Frances Perkins were especially concerned with problems of African American unemployment. Perkins added black employees to civil service positions, compelled the Bureau of Labor Statistics to undertake a study of black unemployment, and established a Division of Negro Labor to advise her, appointing Lawrence Oxley, himself African American, at its head. Perkins also successfully fought back against the (southern) states that refused to comply with the equal-opportunity hiring directions of the CCC, and unsuccessfully fought to have Social Security include the occupational categories overwhelmingly occupied by African Americans.[38]

Lawrence Oxley was a member of Roosevelt's so-called "Black Cabinet," an informal group of African American advisors, also including Mary McLeod Bethune, the economist Robert Weaver (who would hold an actual cabinet post in the Johnson administration), and former Fisk University Dean Ambrose Caliver. Mary McLeod Bethune, director of the National Youth Administration (NYA) Division of Negro Affairs, reflected the ambivalence of the Roosevelt administration toward equal opportunity; she was folksy and nonthreatening in front of white audiences and accepted the segregation of black youth as a quid pro quo for their employment. On the other hand, she advocated for black state directors of black NYA activities (although she tolerated the payment of disproportionately low salaries).[39] Like McLeod Bethune, the New Deal adjusted to the South's ongoing commitment to white supremacy.

BEYOND THE NEW DEAL

The New Deal was an experiment in the use of government tools to solve economic problems, but Roosevelt encountered pressure from more radical suggestions for redistribution of income. Some who called for change pointed to technological unemployment; in the modern economy, some lost jobs were just not coming back, as the tractor could do a job faster than the hoe. Others argued that economic growth was hindered by lack of economic distribution.[40] For example, the philosopher John Dewey headed the People's Lobby, one of many groups to argue that the Great Depression had been caused by underconsumption as workers could not afford to purchase consumer goods. His group advocated old age pensions, unemployment insurance, nationalization of railroads and other basic industries, progressive income taxes, and socialization of rentals of land. Like modern critics of neoliberalism, Dewey would later claim that supposedly "free market" economics was structured by rules that benefited economic elites.[41]

The Technocracy movement, founded in 1932 by Howard Scott of Columbia University, favored Soviet-style central planning. Economists and engineers, working together, would control factory output and supply chains.[42] Scott proposed a North American economic union among Canada, Mexico, and the United States, in which all citizens would perform four hours of work, four days a week, between the ages of 25 and 45, and would receive "energy certificates" entitling them to an equal share of the country's resources in return.[43]

Because the Depression struck the elderly with particular force, many proposals targeted their well-being. The United States lacked any system of federal old-age provision, and only 28 states supported the elderly poor at all. In California, one-third of the electorate, and about a quarter of the population, was older than 50. That state became a node of experimentation with pension plans.[44] Dr. Francis Townsend, a resident of Long Beach, California, was 67 years old when he was laid off from his job with the city health department. After a lifetime of work, he had no money for retirement. In a letter to the editor of his local newspaper, Townsend proposed that all elderly people and the severely disabled be awarded a $200-per-month pension. He argued that such a pension would replace charitable institutions and welfare, remove older people from the labor market, and, because it necessarily had to be spent immediately, prime the pump of the economy. Those who had already worked to make America great could spend their golden years in "scientific, artistic, and socialistic attainments."[45] His letters sparked so much interest that his plan spawned over 7,000 Townsend Clubs across the country, with several million members. Townsend and his followers got a bill introduced into Congress in 1935 that would have provided each senior with a $200 pension. Although it was defeated during the legislative process, the bill contributed to the creation of Social Security.[46]

Upton Sinclair also criticized the New Deal for not going far enough. Author of *The Jungle,* that famous exposé of Chicago's meatpacking industry and its impact on immigrant lives, Sinclair had run for the U.S. Senate twice. He also ran for governor of California twice in the 1920s as a Socialist party candidate. As part of a new gubernatorial campaign in 1933, Sinclair published a short novel, *I, Governor of California, and How I Ended Poverty: A Story of the Future.* In it, he advocated state-supported cooperative land colonies and industrial workshops for the unemployed, which would eventually become fully democratic and autonomous collectives. His vision included libraries, cultural centers, movie houses and lecture halls.[47] In Sinclair's vision, people with disabilities, the elderly, and widows with dependent children would receive pensions of $50 per month. He proposed funding this EPIC (End Poverty in California) project through property taxes on large homes, steep inheritance taxes on large fortunes, transaction taxes on stocks, and excess profits taxes on the highest incomes. He also proposed repealing the regressive sales tax and suggested that a new California Authority for Money (CAM) issue scrip, creating a second system of circulating currency atop the existing one.

Sinclair hoped his EPIC campaign would cause progressive Republicans to register as Democrats and that it would unite teachers, labor unionists, and civil servants.[48] He anticipated that corporations would be the staunchest opponents:

> We have to answer every lie before it is invented. We have to make the people understand our present social system, in which a privileged few control the sources of wealth and exploit the labor of the many. Those few control all the channels of publicity and information, and the crisis which we Americans confront at the present day is precisely this, that the people, who are supposed to use their votes to protect themselves, are kept in ignorance and do not know how to make use of their rights.[49]

Sinclair proposed educating the public and improving on Roosevelt's fireside chats with the "Governor's Gold-fish Bowl." This would be a public forum, open to the media, for any Californian to ask the governor any question.[50]

Ultimately, Sinclair anticipated that private industry would wither away when faced with the enormous financial success of the cooperatives. In essence, Sinclair's EPIC proposed slow-motion socialism, achieved without violence. Upton Sinclair clubs formed around the state in response to these proposals. His supporters included the destitute elderly, young people who were involved in starting some of the state's first producers' cooperatives, and members of local unemployed councils. Sinclair's was a true grassroots campaign, since he accepted no large campaign donations and all of his political work was performed by volunteers. As he had anticipated, California business owners raised money, including forced donations from their own employees, to torpedo Sinclair's campaign.

Although Sinclair captured the Democratic primary nomination in a heavily divided field, he was defeated during the election by the Republican incumbent, Frank Merriam, who had endorsed Townsend's pension idea. Despite Sinclair's electoral loss, the EPIC movement had an impact. Democrats, who held almost no higher offices in California in 1932, gained a majority of legislative seats. As a result, California provided pensions to the elderly and disabled and instituted a state income tax, and its Republican governor became a New Deal supporter.[51]

California radio personality Robert Noble initiated one of the more colorful campaigns for a state safety net. Named the California Life Pension movement, his project was nicknamed the "Ham and Eggs movement," after the cry "We must have our ham and eggs!" Noble advocated a state pension for every unemployed California resident over the age of 50, to be paid in scrip and distributed weekly. Each dollar's worth of scrip carried a built-in incentive to be spent quickly, since postage stamps had to be affixed to the scrip every week to maintain its status as currency. The scrip could be used for taxes and other payments to the state and, its promoters hoped, for other retail uses. Noble's Ham and Eggs movement accelerated once a Los Angeles advertising agency took up the cause, regaling the public with grisly stories of Californians who had killed themselves rather than starve to death with no source of income.

The Ham and Eggs plan was based on the theory that the economy was suffering from overproduction, and all that was needed was some demand-side stimulus, which California's elderly would provide.[52] The movement's leaders collected the signatures of about 25 percent of the state's registered voters in favor of a ballot initiative in 1937. Business groups mobilized against Proposition 25, the Retirement Life Payments Act. They argued that requiring the state to accept worthless scrip in lieu of payments would bankrupt the state, and that wealthy people would buy up the scrip for cents on the dollar and then use it to pay their taxes. Even Irving Fisher, the Yale economist whose ideas had given Noble the basis for his plan, warned that $30 in scrip paid weekly to all older people in California would swamp the currency then in circulation in the state.[53]

The Ham and Eggs movement fought back, fueled with penny-a-day dues payments by its participants, which funded speakers, public-address-system trucks, and pamphlets with titles like *Life Begins at Fifty*. In its first appearance on the ballot in 1938, the Ham and Eggs proposal was defeated by only 255,329 votes out of more than 2.5 million cast. A second bill followed with a stronger economic footing for the scrip (funded by an income tax), tighter organization, and even more signatures (over a million). The bill would have set up a State Board of Economics, with representatives from all of the important Californian industries, to balance supply and demand for goods. The bill was defeated at the polls in a 1939 special election, this time only garnering one-third of the vote cast, even though almost 83 percent of eligible voters voted.[54] While the Ham and Eggs plan was a failure, it did have an impact on mainstream politicians, who were forced to recommend raising California's existing old-age pension rates.[55]

Townsend, Dewey, Sinclair, and "Ham and Eggs" all challenged the conservatism of the New Deal, but the challenge that Roosevelt took the most seriously came from Huey Long, Louisiana's governor and then senator. Louisiana had long trailed behind even other southern states in such measures as highway construction, education, and standard of living. When Long came to power in 1928, he levied a series of taxes and then used the funds to accomplish highly visible and popular projects, like highway construction and state-provided textbooks.[56] Long's corruption was legendary and included bullying and bribery of fellow legislators. He also opposed more meaningful reforms, like minimum-wage laws and the regulation of child labor within the state.[57]

Having aspirations to the presidency, in 1934 Senator Long inaugurated a "Share-Our-Wealth" campaign for Louisiana. Appropriating the line "every man a king" from Democratic presidential candidate William Jennings Bryan's 1896 "Cross of Gold" speech, Long promised people homes, cars, radios, a guaranteed annual income, free college education, pensions for the elderly and for veterans, and a project intended to deal with the Dust Bowl.[58] Economists attacked Long's plan, arguing that confiscation and redistribution would end growth and that there were not enough wealthy individuals in the state of Louisiana to make redistribution produce the sorts of numbers he was promising for income and assets. Despite these warnings, Share-Our-Wealth clubs proliferated in Louisiana and then spread outside the state. Outside Louisiana, politicians used Long's cachet to invigorate their own political campaigns.[59] For his part, Roosevelt responded to Huey Long by having Louisiana leaders investigated for tax fraud. Long's populist challenge to the New Deal ended on September 10, 1935, when he was assassinated by an angry state resident.[60]

The neopopulism of Townsend, Long, Sinclair, and others does seem to have pushed Roosevelt to the left.[61] Fearing that Long might split the Democratic vote and allow a Republican to emerge victorious, Roosevelt commissioned a public opinion poll to gauge the extent of his support.[62] Also, "Second New Deal" proposals included such major reforms as Senator Robert Wagner's bill intended to protect the rights of labor, and the Social Security Act.[63] While some of these ideas had been in the works before the challenge from the left, Roosevelt also unexpectedly (and unsuccessfully) asked Congress for a supertax on the largest incomes and for higher taxes on corporate profits. The federal government also targeted relief dollars to Long supporters, hoping to redirect their support to FDR.[64]

OPPOSITION TO THE NEW DEAL

While the Left was united in the importance of addressing inequality during the Depression, the conservative end of the political spectrum was split. The popular "radio priest" Father Charles Coughlin appealed to working people. Although he was an early supporter of the New Deal, Coughlin was convinced that the Depression had its roots in the banking industry, and so he opposed any attempt by the Roosevelt administration to bail out the banks. His National Union for Social Justice (composed of his radio program and the people who wrote letters to him) channeled the anger of those who had not been reached effectively by New Deal programs. By 1936, however, he had effectively marginalized himself by praising both the Nazis and expansionist Japan.[65]

Idaho senator William Borah led the congressional opposition to the New Deal. A self-appointed tribune of the small businessman, Borah opposed NIRA because small producers would not be able to stay in business by underselling businesses that had larger overheads. Borah, a Teddy Roosevelt Republican, used the language of antimonopoly but equated federal bureaucracy with corporate monopoly. For him, both were evils that adversely impacted small businesses. Borah's crusade against NIRA was helpful in the short run; it pushed the Roosevelt administration to audit the program, and they discovered that in eight industries, large corporations were fixing prices to the detriment of the consumer. Ultimately, the Supreme Court followed Borah's reasoning when they invalidated NIRA codes through their ruling in *Schechter Poultry Corp. v. U.S.* (1935), the case of a small poultry seller who refused to follow the codes in his industry.[66]

The Supreme Court was Roosevelt's most powerful opposition during the 1930s. The Court found many elements of the New Deal unconstitutional, including NIRA (1935) and the Agricultural Adjustment Administration (1936).[67] After winning the 1936 presidential election by a landslide, Roosevelt proposed to help the Supreme Court "clear its backlogged dockets" by appointing one associate justice for every justice over the age of 70 then sitting on the Court. Had that step been taken, the older, conservative jurists on the Court would have been outweighed by supporters of the New Deal. Roosevelt was accused of seeking to "pack the court."[68] In the short run, the Supreme Court seemed to rein in its opposition to Roosevelt's programs, although historians, political scientists, and legal scholars continue to disagree about whether the shift in jurisprudence was part of a long, slow adjustment in the way the Court assessed its own role, or a reaction to political pressure.[69]

The American Bar Association also criticized the New Deal, claiming that the "alphabet soup" of agencies had produced an unprecedented expansion of government power. Roscoe Pound, dean of Harvard Law School from 1916 to 1936, had been a crusader for sociologically based judicial decisions during the Progressive era. Pound wrote an influential report in 1939 criticizing the New Deal's use of administrative tribunals, arguing that they were immune to the law. Pound warned that the United States was trending in the direction of the Soviet Union, where the law was whatever the administration declared it to be in any given moment.[70] Republicans in general shared some of Pound's fears; in a 1936 Gallup poll, 83 percent of Republicans surveyed said they thought that the acts and policies of the Roosevelt administration might lead to dictatorship.[71]

NEW DEAL MISSED OPPORTUNITIES

While the New Deal transformed the role of government and addressed economic inequality to an extent never before seen in the United States, there were some missed opportunities. National health insurance—some program that would compel individuals to purchase insurance—came up for discussion. Congressional advocates argued that health insurance would produce healthier workers, who could in turn be more productive. Labor unions, which were initially opposed, had evolved to support compulsory insurance. Proponents of national health insurance likened it to other forms of compulsion for the common good, including public education and the payment of property taxes. But the American Medical Association blocked any initiatives by claiming that any compulsory insurance would harm the doctor–patient relationship, promote hypochondria and moral weakness, or resemble socialism.[72]

Another missed opportunity was the extension of the minimum wage. While Roosevelt reached out to his labor constituency through the Fair Labor Standards Act, which recognized the right to unionize and created the National Labor Relations Board, labor unions and Democratic politicians were divided on the advisability of a minimum wage.[73] The AFL favored collective bargaining between (its mostly skilled, male) employees and their employers. The Congress of Industrial Organizations (CIO), which was more inclusive, endorsed a minimum wage because it offered a starting point for collective bargaining rather than a ceiling.[74] The Democratic Party was divided because the labor market in the United States was segmented. Southern workers earned lower wages, lowering the cost of production in the South and promoting southern competitiveness. For example, in North Carolina, farmers objected to the introduction of federal jobs because they interfered with their ability to hire black farm laborers and domestic workers at prevailing (low) wages. The state ultimately canceled federal projects during harvest periods and linked federal wage rates to local agricultural wages.[75] To come to an agreement with southern politicians on the minimum wage, Roosevelt agreed to exempt companies and farms that traded within individual states from paying that wage. Adjusting the minimum wage required an act of Congress rather than being indexed to prices. As a result of the restrictions put on the minimum wage during the Depression, the minimum wage failed to keep up with the cost of living throughout the twentieth century and into the twenty-first.[76]

Why did New Deal reforms not set a lasting momentum in favor of equality? Some historians emphasize that most of those involved in crafting the New Deal were not radicals or really members of the antimonopoly tradition at all, but rather were searching for a pragmatic solution to the problems of one specific economic depression.[77] Additionally, the federal government was more influenced by liberal ideas than were state governments, so few politicians rode Roosevelt's coattails at the state level, although Governor Frank Murphy of Michigan (1937–1939), who sent the National Guard to protect autoworkers during a historic sit-down strike in Flint, was an exception. As political scientist Margaret Weir explains, many state and metropolitan governments were never convinced that the New Deal was a good idea. In that sense, the New Deal had never fully triumphed, so what happened after the 1930s cannot be called a backing away. One of the initiatives which belonged to state and local governments was zoning, leading to the development of segregated suburbs that eventually became Republican enclaves.[78]

WORLD WAR II AND INEQUALITY

It is a commonplace opinion that World War II actually pulled the United States out of the Great Depression, that substantial economic growth occurred during the war, and that wartime provided a better standard of living for American workers. Some economic historians deny that the war had these consequences. Historian J. R. Vernon argues that government spending did not end the Depression, but rather, tight monetary and fiscal policies increased investor confidence.[79] Historian Robert Higgs argues that the war should not be seen as raising the general standard of living, since 22 percent of the (male) labor force was mobilized into the military—many by conscription. Being drafted took away male workers' freedom of choice, forcing them into low-paid employment as soldiers. They were replaced by teenagers, retired workers, women, and members of minority groups.

This sent the overall unemployment rate to 1.4 percent, but, Higgs argued, resulted in less comfort and happiness overall.

Economist Simon Kuznets pointed out that during World War II, much was spent on war materiel and that war goods do not improve the well-being of Americans, but rather, in moments of existential crisis, make it possible for well-being to exist at all. Kuznets argued that many military products should not even be counted as part of the gross national product (GNP), and of course, to exclude military products from GNP would show a shrinking American productivity during wartime. Paul Evans added that in a command economy like that of the wartime period, rationing and price controls deform markets and cause inefficiency and productivity losses.[80]

Economic historians like these, who challenge the historical commonplaces about World War II, make sound arguments about statistics, but they ignore an important argument about perceptions. During World War II, people said that they were better off, suggesting that perceptions of fair distribution contribute to happiness. The stock market declined, eating into the unearned income of the wealthy.[81] Unemployment was no longer the worry it had been during the Depression years. People in the workforce were working for higher wages than ever before, and with production of consumer durables curtailed, they were saving more than ever before. World War II accelerated the disappearance of inequality, as war work paid better wages and to a larger, more diverse, number of people. For example, the number of unemployed workers in wartime Detroit shrank from 135,000 to 4,000.[82] Civilian female employment increased from 12 million in 1942 to almost 20 million in 1945, and while the effects were temporary for women workers in manufacturing, those with white-collar jobs were more likely to stay in the labor market even after the war had ended.[83] The real wage rate increased 33 percent between 1941 and 1944.[84]

Wartime industries, scrutinized by the Fair Employment Practices Commission, were not allowed to discriminate on the basis of race. The rules that the commission enacted enabled firms to plausibly argue to white workers, who might otherwise have gone on strike, that they had no choice but to integrate the workforce. Black workers migrated north and west as better-paying jobs opened up to them, and they gained relative to white workers.[85] Even a long-term study of white, middle-class men indicates that many benefited from their wartime service in the long run—particularly those who were military officers, physicians, lawyers, or scientists.[86] Economically, then, World War II was an important part of the Great Compression.

On the other hand, once again, benefits were unequally distributed, as the war produced the internment of over 100,000 Japanese Americans. After the bombing of Pearl Harbor, the same WPA that helped the unemployed during the worst of the Depression built internment camps and processed internees.[87] Racism against people of Japanese origin was rife; laws made first-generation Japanese immigrants ineligible for citizenship or for landholding in many states. Returned missionaries, public-school teachers, college professors and students, socialists, and Quakers were some of the few groups who opposed internment. They pointed out the similarities between concentrating Japanese Americans in horse stables and desolate desert barracks and Nazi removal policies. Unfortunately, given the virulence of anti-Japanese racism during the war, their views were largely ignored.[88] The Japanese and Japanese Americans lost their farms, businesses, houses, jobs, and opportunities for work experiences that suited them as individuals. Twenty-five years after internment, those who had been interned were still experiencing annual incomes 9 to 13 percent lower than those Japanese Americans (in Hawaii and outside the evacuation area) who were not interned.[89]

RIGHT TO FULL EMPLOYMENT

Full employment had become so important that by 1944, Roosevelt proposed a second, "economic Bill of Rights," in his State of the Union message. He hoped to guarantee Americans full employment at a living wage, medical care, and a social safety net—the same kinds of reforms called for in Britain's Beveridge Report two years before.[90] It is worth quoting Roosevelt at some length:

> We have come to a clear realization of the fact that true individual freedom cannot exist without economic security and independence. "Necessitous men are not free men." People who are hungry and out of a job are the stuff of which dictatorships are made.
>
> In our day these economic truths have become accepted as self-evident. We have accepted, so to speak, a second Bill of Rights ...
>
> Among these are:
>
> The right to a useful and remunerative job in the industries or shops or farms or mines of the Nation;
>
> The right to earn enough to provide adequate food and clothing and recreation;
>
> The right of every farmer to raise and sell his products at a return which will give him and his family a decent living;
>
> The right of every businessman, large and small, to trade in an atmosphere of freedom from unfair competition and domination by monopolies at home and abroad;

The right of every family to a decent home;

The right to adequate medical care and the opportunity to achieve and enjoy good health;

The right to adequate protection from the economic fears of old age, sickness, accident and unemployment;

The right to a good education.

All of these rights spell security. And after this war is won we must be prepared to move forward, in the implementation of these rights, to new goals of human happiness and well-being.[91]

The Full Employment Act, introduced in 1945 by senators James Murray (D-Montana) and Robert Wagner (D-NY), presupposed that those who were willing to work had a human right to do so—not just because of the economic benefits of work but also because being able to find a job told a human being that he or she was valuable.[92] The bill would have created a partnership between the federal government, whose job it would be to calculate the size of the labor force for the coming year, and private industry, which would be encouraged, through targeted investment, to make jobs available for all who wanted to work. If the private sector could not create enough jobs, the federal government would fill in the gap with public-works employment. The bill passed handily in the Senate but was defeated in the House.[93]

Although both parties had expressed a commitment to full employment, the National Association of Manufacturers and the U.S. Chamber of Commerce lobbied against the 1945 bill. They claimed that the bill unprecedentedly interfered with entrepreneurship, that the United States was heading in the direction of totalitarianism, and that economic forecasting was too crude to ensure success. In committee, there was also much debate about the extent to which employment could be an actionable right—even for women, who were still expected to stay home and take care of their families if they could afford to do so—and to what extent it was just a worthy goal.[94] When the 1945 act failed to pass, the notion of government-guaranteed full employment would have to wait until 1978 to be seriously pursued again.

As this chapter has shown, the stock market crash and imploding economy of the early 1930s showed that an economy that valorized unlimited business growth without considering distributive justice was doomed. Hoover and the economy both floundered until Roosevelt's victory and inauguration. Roosevelt introduced important regulation through the Securities and Exchange Commission, the Federal Deposit Insurance Corporation, and the Glass-Steagall Act. The federal government also assumed responsibility for relief and reform through major Keynesian spending programs, NIRA, the CCC, the AAA, and the TVA, among others; created the first national minimum wage; and began to construct a social safety net with social security. As had happened during Woodrow Wilson's administration, the New Deal programs reflected the racial discrimination and political power of southern Democrats.[95] This would set the stage for poverty and race to be linked concepts in subsequent decades.

As the Progressive era had done, the New Deal era produced a vibrant discourse about the impact of inequality. This time, the discourse was linked to concrete prescriptions for government spending and old-age pensions, and the challenge from the Left pushed the Roosevelt administration to expand its plans. Whether or not World War II lifted the country out of the Depression or whether the country had already emerged, the war accelerated the trends for full employment and compression of inequality. The Depression and wartime periods forged widespread agreement among all parties that the best way to end poverty was through economic growth, consumerism, and regulation of the economy to guarantee fundamental fairness.[96] Postwar prosperity enabled political leaders to focus on those still living in pockets of poverty, a trend examined in the next chapter.

CHAPTER 6

The Great Compression and the War on Poverty: 1945–1979

The years between 1945 and the late 1960s saw unprecedented compression between the wealthy and the poor. It was fueled by high taxes on upper incomes, healthy American industries with high wages for blue-collar work, demographic growth, and an expanding managerial sector. The union movement flourished, and 35 percent of the workforce was unionized in 1954—the highest percentage in American history.[1] The GI bill greatly expanded access to a college education. Returns from a college education actually slightly decreased, helping to compress inequality further.[2] Between 1945 and 1973, the economy grew at the impressive rate of 3.42 percent. Although this growth rate slowed after 1973 as the price of energy (and thus the price of production) dramatically increased, by 1979, U.S. annual production was three times what it had been in 1948.[3]

At the same time that inequality was decreasing, Cold War politics constrained the development of the American welfare state. As the United States and the Soviet Union adopted Cold War stances, even those Americans who had favored some degree of central planning during the 1930s, and particularly during World War II, backed off. Now it was widely believed that government intervention in the economy led to totalitarianism, and that economic freedom was a necessary condition for political freedom.[4] Single-payer health insurance and public pensions were rejected in favor of employer-provided benefits. But later, as American industries downsized or moved overseas in the 1970s, health care and retirement would be jeopardized.[5]

As inequality decreased and the economy grew, prosperous America could afford political concern for "pockets of poverty" in inner cities and Appalachia. Books like *The Other America* (1962) and *Night Comes to the*

Cumberlands (1963), and television exposés by journalist Edward R. Murrow and others, raised consciousness about poor living standards. Public awareness led to the "War on Poverty," Medicare and Medicaid, and the creation of a President's Commission on Income Maintenance. Despite the demands put on the U.S. budget by the Vietnam War, the "War on Poverty" continued during the Nixon administration, which attempted a basic income guarantee for low-income Americans: the Family Assistance Plan. Although the plan was never enacted, the Earned Income Tax Credit (1975), a tax refund for low-income working families, had its origin in this idea.[6]

During the 1970s, philosophers as well as politicians struggled with ideas of fairness. The philosophers John Rawls's *A Theory of Justice* (1971) and Robert Nozick's *Anarchy, State, and Utopia* (1974) set out important interpretations of fair property-holding and distribution that have influenced divergent policies to this day. By the late 1970s, prosperity was lagging under the pressure of two oil shocks, unprecedented combined inflation and unemployment, and increasing American deindustrialization. The population shifted, following military bases and factories to southern states where unions were weaker or nonexistent and workers could be paid less. In the Rust Belt, the automobile factories that drove American prosperity furloughed workers.[7] In the midst of this malaise, new voices began to blame the economic slowdown on Keynesian economics, taxation, and government economic regulation. Ultimately, neoliberals abandoned the War on Poverty and claimed that economic growth on their terms would benefit everyone.

POSTWAR PROSPERITY

The notion that people had a right to gainful employment died with Roosevelt. In 1946, Congress passed an Employment Act committing the federal government to maximizing employment, production, and purchasing power "in a manner calculated to foster and promote free competitive enterprise and the general welfare."[8] Unlike the act that had failed to pass in 1945, this 1946 act strove for "maximum employment" rather than full employment, thus paving the way for a postwar consensus that varying degrees of unemployment were acceptable.[9] The President's Council of Economic Advisers (CEA), created by the act, advised successive presidents on policy, but none of the CEA chairmen prioritized government-guaranteed full employment.[10] The Republican victory over both houses of Congress in 1946, and Truman's Cold War military buildup further decreased concern with employment.[11] As Cold War ideological divisions hardened into anti-communist hysteria, the degree of central planning that Roosevelt's notions required may have seemed more Soviet than American to many. In any case, the question of a right to full employment was banished for the time being.

Over Truman's veto, Congress passed the Taft-Hartley Act (1947). The act made union boycotts and sympathy strikes illegal and banned the closed shop (in which all workers were required to belong to the union). The act also made it more difficult for unions to become established in industries by allowing employers to speak to employees against unionization, enabling states to pass right-to-work laws, and making it easier to decertify existing unions. The act also required union leaders to indicate that they had never been Communist Party members.[12] The Taft-Hartley Act, and opposition to unions by the business community and Republicans generally, caused union leaders to make a fateful choice. President Truman had hoped to expand Social Security and to create a government-funded health system like those that existed in Europe. Instead of lobbying for socialized medicine, leaders of the biggest unions, including the miners' and auto workers' unions, courted favor with their members by focusing on employer-provided fringe benefits. The unions were successful in gaining fringe benefits—"by 1954 three-quarters of union members, over eleven million workers, were covered by a health plan or pension through collective bargaining, up from one-eighth of union members in 1948."[13] Widespread fringe-benefit availability for union jobs meant that politically powerful unionized workers lacked the incentive to lobby for pensions and health care at the federal level.

RACIAL DISPARITIES

Poverty statistics improved during the postwar period. Poor white workers migrated from Appalachia to Midwestern cities, gaining access to higher-paid factory jobs.[14] African Americans continued to migrate from the poor South to the higher-paying North, where factory jobs were available. Black workers moved from earning 41 cents on the dollar compared to white workers to 58 cents between 1945 and 1963.[15] Only southern blacks failed to make gains.[16]

At the same time, as Figure 6.1 shows, rising incomes disguised continued inequality. Racial discrimination in employment continued, with African Americans either not hired at all or targeted for unskilled jobs that paid a "racial wage." Entry to union apprenticeship programs, and hiring in many industries, were based on relationships and word of mouth, systematically excluding minority applicants.[17] African American workers were hired after white workers, and because most union contracts used a seniority system, black workers were also disproportionately disadvantaged during layoffs. Finally, their jobs were some of the first eliminated as firms automated production and then moved their production out of the cities into whiter suburban areas.[18]

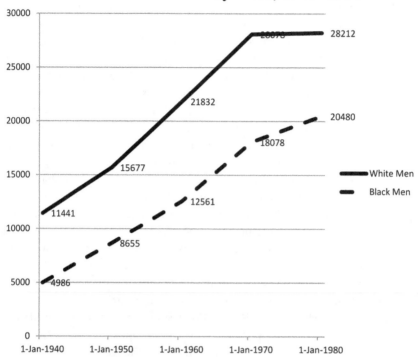

Figure 6.1

Mean Male Income by Race, 1940–1980. (James P. Smith and Finish R. Welch, "Black Economic Progress After Myrdal," *Journal of Economic Literature* vol. 27 no. 2 (1989): 519–564, at 521.)

Even in the relatively prosperous North, housing segregation pitted workers against each other. Federal government policies made mortgages on older homes or homes bought by black buyers more expensive and harder to insure. Restrictive covenants and social norms among real estate agents blocked African American movement into "white areas." Blue-collar white workers who had their own modest homes saw any black movement into these neighborhoods as detrimental to their property values.[19] Even when African Americans could get their mortgages guaranteed by the federal government, as with GI Bill–entitled veterans, banks were reluctant to extend credit.

The upwardly mobile black middle class pushed the boundaries of urban settlement, leaving behind the poorest black people concentrated in areas that then became neglected ghettoes. The construction of highways, and "urban renewal" without replacement of destroyed housing, left formerly prosperous black neighborhoods disconnected and devastated; evicted residents had nowhere to live. Public housing was also racially segregated, and needy white families were placed into public housing more rapidly than were black families.[20]

The drive for racial equality in the 1950s focused on the legal and social realms rather than the economic realm. Court decisions like *Brown vs. Board of Education of Topeka, Kansas* (1954), which mandated school desegregation, undermined the idea that separate facilities could ever be equal. A series of decisions by the Warren and Burger Supreme Courts broadened the notion of legal equality.[21] But the few programs available in the 1950s to address employment portrayed the unemployed as lacking "human capital." It was assumed that with sufficient training or the inculcation of work skills, the unemployed would naturally be hired as the economy grew. Programs like that of Detroit's Urban League introduced token highly qualified black workers into white-collar and managerial positions at the expense of thousands of working-class African Americans, who then became thought of as relatively unemployable.[22]

DELINEATING THE PROBLEM IN THE 1960s

Prosperity during the 1950s was bounded by geography and economic sectors as well as by race. Agricultural mechanization meant that large numbers of farm workers were only needed at harvest time. This forced workers to migrate to be able to live, and meant that they would be unemployed for portions of the year and living in grinding poverty most of the time. Housing for migratory workers was substandard, educational opportunities for their children almost nonexistent, and farm laborers lacked minimum wages and other federal protections. A 1960 Presidential Committee on Migratory Labor recommended reform of farm labor, including eligibility for the minimum wage.[23]

On the night after Thanksgiving in 1960, the well-respected journalist Edward R. Murrow raised public awareness of farmworkers' problems with an hour-long documentary program, *Harvest of Shame*. It had taken nine months to film and traced the journeys of various migrant families through that year's harvest. *Harvest of Shame* showed men, women, and children—the vast majority of whom were African American—who were treated little better than slaves, deprived of sanitary conditions and health care, packed into trucks standing up to be taken to the fields. The program also illustrated the contempt that some employers had for their employees. As Florida farmer Howard Jones was quoted as saying, "They eat today and they don't think about tomorrow . . . but they are happier than we are. They are the happiest race of people on earth."[24] Charles Schuman, president of the National Farm Bureau, argued that farm laborers were otherwise unemployable, so it was better for them to earn a pittance rather than be idle. He boasted that only farm employers provided the "perquisite" of housing to their employees, an incalculable benefit.[25]

Harvest of Shame left some of the burden of interpretation to the viewer. Some of the farm laborers had very large families to feed, a fact displayed without comment or context. Thirty-four-year-old "Mrs. Dobey," a white woman with nine children, could only buy her family one gallon of milk a week; 29-year-old Aline King left her nine-year-old son to watch three toddlers in a squalid camp shack while she picked beans in the field for a dollar a day. When interviewed, King said that she had been working in the fields since the age of eight and had 14 children. Murrow and show producer Fred Friendly gave little sense of what might concretely be done to improve the living conditions of the migrants or the educational prospects of their children, gesturing vaguely in the direction of farmworkers' unions while at the same time acknowledging the extreme imbalance of power between the migrants and their farm employers.

Harvest of Shame was part of a larger discourse about hidden poverty and the costs of economic inequality that emerged in the late Eisenhower administration and then grew louder in the 1960s. In 1962, the historian Gabriel Kolko published *Wealth and Power in America*. The economist Simon Kuznets had claimed that income in the United States necessarily would become more evenly distributed over time. Kolko attacked Kuznets with a statistical analysis demonstrating that Americans in fact had a remarkable lack of upward mobility. Kolko pointed out that large numbers of Americans could not afford medical expenses nor even to replace their clothing. He argued that the flagship social support program, Social Security, had been originally underfunded with the "Victorian virtue of thrift" in mind; it was meant to provide a substandard lifestyle. Kolko showed that the number of households headed by women (paid less than men) was increasing. Families that benefited by women's income as second wage-earners tended to already be above the poverty line.[26]

If mobility was decreasing, what was keeping Americans afloat? Kolko pointed to developments that have become even more crucial since 1962; Americans wishing to enjoy a middle-class lifestyle held down multiple jobs and used credit to buy things they could not afford.[27] Kolko argued that for many families, financial disaster was just an illness away; many low- and middle-income families put off going to the doctor and just lived with their illnesses.[28] Although he did not prescribe any particular change, Kolko argued that social science analysis, in its optimism about endless economic growth, had tended to miss these issues, and they could only come into focus through a hard look at the actual budgets of working people.

While Kolko's book focused on the United States as a whole, Kentucky lawyer Harry Caudill targeted Appalachian poverty in his *Night Comes to the Cumberlands* (1963). Caudill's book was a paean to the white Appalachian settlers; brave, earthy, fighting folk who had unjustly lived in poverty since the eighteenth century. "A million Americans in the Southern Appalachians live today in conditions of squalor, ignorance and ill health which could scarcely be equaled in Europe or Japan, or perhaps, in parts of mainland Asia," Caudill wrote.[29] Caudill's book is notable for its casual racism: unlike the "simple savage" Native Americans against whom these hardy frontier mountaineers fought to take the land, and unlike the black "dope fiend" railroad laborers who had been responsible for white families becoming addicted to narcotics, southern Appalachian dwellers were hardworking folks who deserved a hand up.[30] Caudill described how Appalachian whites had been taken advantage of by eastern capitalists looking for mineral rights. Then coal companies came in and paid miners with scrip that could only be redeemed at company stores, and refused to pay taxes to fund infrastructure and schools.[31] The Appalachian areas Caudill chronicled became a special focus of John F. Kennedy and Lyndon Johnson's War on Poverty.

Like *Night Comes to the Cumberlands*, political theorist Michael Harrington's book *The Other America* (1963) took white, middle-class Americans on a well-written, accessible virtual tour of places they had ostensibly never been, due to the increasing housing segregation of the post–World War II period. He described the hollows of Appalachia in wintertime, the tenements of Harlem, and the isolating apartments of the elderly who were too poor to have telephones. Harrington showed that the poor were disproportionately elderly and disproportionately stationary, stuck in economically floundering communities by ties of family, by having purchased houses, and by having been trained for economically obsolete occupations. Poor people were the most likely to have the worst jobs, but at the same time to have trouble holding on to even those jobs, through child-care issues or illnesses for which they had no medical care.[32] Harrington criticized some of the cultural manifestations of poverty—the happy-go-lucky attitudes he said he saw in Harlem, for example. But he chalked these up to the pernicious impact of poverty and racism; "If all the laws were framed to provide equal opportunity, a majority of the Negroes would not be able to take full advantage of the change. There would still be a vast, silent, and automatic system directed against men and women of color," he wrote.[33]

Not everyone agreed that the causes of African American poverty were environmental rather than internal. Senator Daniel Patrick Moynihan's report *The Negro Family: The Case for National Action* (1965) sparked a debate about the social pathologies of the new "urban underclass." The report, which at least in part blamed female-led families, single mothers, and welfare dependency for black urban poverty, produced an uproar because it was viewed as both patronizing and incorrect. Moynihan hoped that following his prescriptions would lead to a greater focus on providing jobs for African American men and increase the number of families with two parents, but his ideas were lost in the controversy over affixing blame.[34]

WAR ON POVERTY

The discourse on inequality in the 1960s coincided with, and encouraged, major government efforts to counter its effects. Inspired by his brother and campaign manager Robert Kennedy, presidential candidate John F. Kennedy drew attention to Appalachian poverty with a tour of West Virginia in 1960. This was the beginning of a presidential concern with inequality that lasted a decade. Although he had little time in office to address inequality, Kennedy presided over an expansion of the minimum wage in 1961.[35] Robert Kennedy headed the President's Committee on Juvenile Delinquency, which came to the conclusion that youth deviance was due to lack of opportunity; Robert Kennedy pushed for a domestic Peace Corps that would address both youth unemployment and deprivation simultaneously. Finally, shortly before his death, John F. Kennedy established the President's Appalachian Regional Commission, intended to expand infrastructure in Appalachia and promote economic growth.[36]

When the office of the presidency was suddenly thrust upon him in 1963, Lyndon Johnson took up Kennedy's antipoverty crusade.[37] A brief moment of congressional unity in the wake of Kennedy's assassination resulted in the passage of the Civil Rights Bill of 1964, showing Johnson that he might be able to get legislation passed.[38] After a tour of the most blighted areas of Appalachia and the rural Midwest with his wife Lady Bird, Lyndon Johnson declared war on poverty in his first State of the Union address:

> The war against poverty will not be won here in Washington. It must be won in the field, in every private home, in every public office, from the courthouse to the White House ... Very often a lack of jobs and money is not the cause of poverty, but the symptom. The cause may lie deeper—in our failure to give our fellow citizens a fair chance to develop their own capacities, in a lack of education

and training, in a lack of medical care and housing, in a lack of decent communities in which to live and bring up their children.[39]

Although Johnson's Council of Economic Advisors acknowledged that it would be possible to eliminate poverty with a one-time government income transfer of $11 billion, redistribution on that scale was not contemplated. The reigning ideology at the time was that the poor simply lacked certain skills. It was believed programs imparting those skills would increase the efficiency and productivity of the poor and benefit the economy as a whole.[40]

With the passage of the Economic Opportunity Act of 1964, Johnson created the Office of Economic Opportunity (OEO) under the executive branch and appointed Sargent Shriver as its director, empowered to allocate federal resources to local and state entities. The OEO coordinated a whole spectrum of programs, including Job Corps, Head Start, and Upward Bound. Research by the OEO in 1964 showed that 34.3 million Americans had a family income of less than $3,000 a year, and 60 percent of those lived in rural areas or in small cities.[41] While OEO monies targeted urban areas with more than 150,000 residents at first, over the period between 1966 and 1968, rural and urban funding levels began to converge.[42]

By 1968, $2.65 billion in OEO funding was distributed through more than a thousand Community Action Agencies, which were collaborations between local government, local businesses, and the recipients of services.[43] These organizations linked the federal government directly with the needs of the localities, vaulting over state governments and over social workers, who had traditionally been the gatekeepers for welfare provision. The extent to which Community Action Agencies succeeded in combatting poverty thus varied from one city, town, or county to the next. In some states, like Mississippi, the poor actually participated in designing local programs. In other areas, like Mayor Richard Daley's Chicago, federal funds were diverted to reward political supporters.

The Office of Equal Opportunity became a racial flashpoint. Sociologist Jill Quadagno argues that while the community action model was too underfunded to actually make any dent in economic inequality it did, at least to some small degree, increase opportunities for black men and women to participate politically.[44] The community action model sowed distrust among some white people, since it was aimed at empowering the poor, and many of the poor were members of minority groups. The introduction of community organizers into poor neighborhoods to sign elders up for Medicaid or publicize available government jobs rankled, especially in the South.[45] The OEO was also criticized because Director of the Office of Equal Opportunity

Sargent Shriver could decide which states would receive funding; he withheld funds from southern states that flouted civil rights.[46]

Despite its controversial profile, the OEO was not the only important element of the War on Poverty. Johnson's administration also addressed medical expenses as a cause of poverty with the establishment of Medicare for the elderly and Medicaid for the poor. Despite polls that indicated 63 percent of Americans supported Medicare and Medicaid, Johnson signed the legislation over the objections of the American Medical Association, which raised the same concerns it had during the 1930s. Ultimately, federal expenditure on health, education, and welfare tripled.[47] Finally, Congress and the Johnson administration in 1966 also expanded the scope of the minimum wage so that for the first time it applied to workers in industries doing more than $250,000 in business and to agricultural workers.[48]

ASSESSING THE WAR ON POVERTY

Objectively, the War on Poverty was a success in the short run. The poverty rate in the United States declined from 19 percent in 1964 to its lowest point ever, 11 percent, in 1973.[49] But while some of these programs were successful, they cost more than the public was willing to pay.[50] The maximum tax rate for the highest earners was dropped from 91 percent to 70 percent, placing more of the burden of both the War on Poverty and the Vietnam War on the middle class.[51]

Johnson's Great Society programs were also undermined by persistent racial divisions in the American working class. Many white union workers insisted on racial privileges, like keeping their suburban neighborhoods free of black workers, and preventing school integration made possible by busing.[52] White working-class men who had no fortunes to leave to their sons considered it their prerogative to favor them for apprenticeship opportunities and resented government programs that reserved apprenticeships for African Americans.[53] Large urban community action agencies were accused of corruption. In July 1967, rioting broke out in Detroit over police arrests surrounding an unlicensed bar, and then continued over five days, resulting in over 7,000 arrests, 43 deaths, and the burning of more than 2,500 buildings. The rioting was widely attributed to discontent with industrial relocations, housing segregation, and unemployment, and communicated to onlookers that the United States contained two nations, peaceful and violent. Riots also occurred in Chicago (1968) and Newark (1967), leading opponents of War on Poverty programs to allege that the federal government was funding black nationalist organizations.[54]

While some critics of the Great Society resented it for reasons related to race, others criticized it as an example of government overreach. Historians Lilian and Oscar Handlin, for example, claim that the Great Society was a fundamentally misguided project. They argue that because the United States contains a tension between an equitable, democratic political system and acceptance of the inequities of the free enterprise system, any attempt to foster social improvement impinges on someone's free enterprise liberties. The Handlins and other critics of the Great Society hearkened back to the antebellum language of "producer" and "nonproducer," except that this time the nonproducers were the unemployed and underemployed poor rather than the idle rich.[55] They characterized an urban "underclass" as depraved and the cities as sites of human rights violations worse than any around the globe.[56]

For the Handlins, the growth of the federal bureaucracy from almost 2 million employees in 1950 to almost 3 million in 1970 was prima facie evidence that the Great Society failed.[57] But the Handlins failed to realize that in an (irrationally) discriminatory job market, government employment was some of the only rewarding employment available for minority groups. Members of white ethnic groups—Irish, Italians, Russian Jews—who migrated to the United States at the turn of the twentieth century had helped less-skilled and less-educated co-ethnics climb the ladder in the industries they controlled and in which they came to be overrepresented. African Americans, particularly college-educated women, did not have these same advantages. The expansion of the War on Poverty thus had a double effect: it targeted poverty and provided employment for members of disproportionately poor groups.[58]

Harry Caudill, author of *Night Comes to the Cumberlands*, bemoaned the failure of Johnson's Great Society to bring permanent economic growth to southern Appalachia. He concluded that Appalachian poverty there was genetic; that the most intelligent Appalachians had long since left the area and taken factory jobs in faraway cities. A 1974 plan to conduct intelligence testing of children in three Appalachian counties, to see whether mandatory sterilization of the unfit should be recommended, was never put into action due to lack of funds.[59] Libertarian political scientist Charles Murray argued that the Great Society was a net negative, and that poverty rates were declining in the postwar period not because of anything the government did but rather because the economy was growing. According to Murray, while poverty rates fell from 33 percent in 1949 to 28 percent by 1952, to 22 percent under Eisenhower and 18 percent by 1964, by the 1970s the Great Society caused these improvements to halt. Murray also claimed that falling labor force participation and marriage rates among the poorest black and white workers were signs of cultural decay fueled by the availability of various forms of income support.[60]

Economists Martha Bailey and Nicholas Duquette argue that the War on Poverty failed because the programs were, in a sense, too purely targeted; federal funds were not used strategically to build support for Democrats, as had been the case during the New Deal. Rather, political rewards accounted for less than 1 percent of the allocation, with the rest allocated for America's poorest, most of whom were nonwhite. White Americans reacted negatively to the empowerment of nonwhite Americans and the attempt to address economic inequalities that disproportionately impacted them. As a result, even though the New Deal's long-term achievements are less impressive than those of the War on Poverty, the former is remembered as having been a success, and the latter as a failure.[61]

NIXON ADMINISTRATION

Lyndon Johnson's foreign policy failures in Vietnam encouraged him not to run for re-election in 1968. Into that breach stepped Robert Kennedy, who had been a crusader against inequality since the beginning of the decade. Kennedy had been uniquely skeptical that economic growth alone could address poverty without attention to distribution issues, or that job training sufficed when there were no jobs in a region. He favored a combination of tax incentives to entice companies to depressed areas, and federally funded public works jobs to take up any slack. Kennedy's assassination in June at the height of his popularity represented not only a tragedy for the nation but also a missed opportunity to creatively address inequality.[62]

After the debacle of the 1968 Democratic Party convention, Richard Nixon was elected, but a change in the political party in power did not bring the Great Society to a screeching halt. Nixon saw welfare reform as a central priority, as the problems with welfare were then legion. Throughout the 1960s, states and localities had narrowed welfare eligibility by excluding recipients who had babies out of wedlock or who did not meet residency requirements. State welfare rules also made it impossible for male-headed families to collect welfare benefits. Politicians complained that these rules caused poor families to break up rather than be denied benefits. The welfare system then in place, Aid to Families with Dependent Children (AFDC), reduced benefits corresponding to every dollar in earned income, completely removing any incentive to work. When welfare was new, social norms had insisted that mothers of small children stay home to take care of them, but as mothers of young children entered the labor force, expectations shifted.[63] To make things worse, people whose incomes were sufficiently low sometimes earned less than those on welfare and also were not able to take advantage of the full tax exemption to which they were entitled.[64] Finally, wide differentials in welfare payments between states led to arguments that people from some states were migrating to others just to collect benefits.[65]

As early as 1966, the economist James Tobin had pointed out these problems. He argued that the human-capital theory of poverty would not sufficiently address poverty in the short run and that redistribution of some kind was necessary to prevent poverty from having a multigenerational impact. "If a decent standard of living is guaranteed, why should anyone work to get it or to acquire the ability to earn it on his own? For centuries this cynicism about human nature has been the excuse by which the affluent have relieved their individual and collective consciences and pocketbooks of the burden of their less fortunate brethren," he wrote.[66] Tobin called for a basic income guarantee for all Americans in the form of a negative income tax. "This would not carry the stigma of charity or relief; it would be a right of national citizenship symmetrical to the obligation to pay taxes."[67] Tobin's suggestion was echoed by the Kerner Commission, otherwise known as the National Advisory Commission on Civil Disorders. The commission alleged that the repeated rioting in urban areas was due to insufficient welfare funding, which was excluding some people and keeping others below a decent standard of living. It called for a "negative income tax"—a guaranteed payment that the working poor could take as a tax rebate. The negative income tax gained popularity, eventually being endorsed by over a thousand academic economists and a second commission, the President's Commission on Income Maintenance Programs.[68]

In 1969, Nixon proposed such a negative income tax in the form of the Family Assistance Plan (FAP), which was intended to replace AFDC.[69] The FAP guaranteed each family an annual income of $1,600 and $800 worth of food stamps, in exchange for the requirement that all recipients apply for work. Working families would receive a sliding scale of benefits. While assistance levels proposed for the FAP were low compared with prevailing welfare levels in northern states, 70 percent of southern black rural families would have qualified for at least some level of benefit.[70]

Unfortunately, the FAP was attacked from both the Left and the Right. Conservatives railed against adding an additional 13 million people to the welfare rolls and worried that female heads of families would no longer have an incentive to take low-paying jobs.[71] Supporters of the poor argued that the FAP was punitive, that no family could live on $1,600, and that the compulsion to work was a form of involuntary servitude.[72] The labor movement opposed the bill, fearing that it would flood the market with low-wage laborers or even encourage large numbers of people to work at wages below the minimum.[73] Members of the National Welfare Rights Organization argued that welfare was a human right and that no moral stigma of dependency should be attached.[74] The NWRO countered with its own proposal for a $5,500 per year basic income guarantee, which would have cost $71 billion rather than the $4.4 billion estimated for FAP.[75] While the Family Assistance Plan passed the House in April 1970 by a large margin, the Senate Finance Committee rejected the legislation after input from welfare recipients themselves.

In 1971, the Nixon administration's proxies reintroduced FAP legislation, proposing a higher level of basic assistance. Again, FAP passed the House only to be defeated in the Senate.[76] Afterward, studies found that senators opposing the bill were particularly responsive to opposition to the FAP by southern whites. Raising the incomes of poor, rural blacks would have represented a financial injection into southern economies that benefited everyone, but the desire to wield the economic power of poverty against African Americans died hard.[77]

Welfare provisions were expanded in other ways in the 1970s through the food stamp program, Medicaid enrollments, and the introduction of the Earned Income Tax Credit, a tax rebate for low-income families. But the failure of the FAP was a major missed opportunity. One of the more tragic elements of the FAP's failure was that it was tied to the provision of large-scale child care for the working poor; when the FAP was defeated, so was the child care provision. The discourse around the proposal demonstrated that conservatives feared the government was overreaching and that federalized child care threatened the sanctity of the family.[78] By the mid-1970s, the residual poverty that remained was largely concentrated in states that had set lower standards for themselves for helping the poor, and the programs were funded by more generous states. Unsurprisingly, residents of wealthier states resented the differential.

WELFARE REFORM IN THE CARTER ADMINISTRATION

As economic conditions in the United States worsened throughout the 1970s, resentment of welfare expenditure grew. Former California governor Ronald Reagan, running in the 1976 Republican presidential primary, hit on a winning formula by transforming one particular welfare recipient,

47-year-old Linda Taylor, into the embodiment of everything that was wrong with government aid. Reagan never mentioned Taylor's name on the campaign trail but always invoked a litany of her crimes: "She has 80 names, 30 addresses, 12 social security cards and is collecting veterans' benefits on four nonexistent deceased husbands." And, he claimed, she drove a Cadillac limousine. Even as Reagan inveighed against "welfare queens," the *New York Times* produced evidence that the alleged fraud was much less impressive than Reagan claimed ($8,000 rather than $150,000). The audiences invited to his citizen press conferences, however, were more impressed by the claims than by the fact checking.[79] Pressure grew to "reform" welfare in ways that benefited the taxpayer rather than the welfare recipient.

Jimmy Carter promised welfare reform would be a part of his first year of office. He proposed a Program for Better Jobs and Income (PBJI), a hastily constructed plan combining a basic income guarantee with the provision of government jobs. The PBJI proposal recommended two tiers of income support: one for people who, due to disabilities or family responsibilities, were not expected to work, and a second tier for those from whom work would be required. Carter's plan made federal employment projects available in public health, the environment, recreation, and education for those in the second tier.[80] While the PBJI contained many of the same ideological underpinnings and work incentives as Nixon's FAP, it included a proposal to expand welfare spending by an additional $2 billion. Not only was this proposed spending increase controversial, but Carter administration insiders also warned that the program would be massively concentrated in a few poor southern states that had traditionally done little to address poverty.[81] Despite having Democratic majorities in both the House and the Senate, Carter was unable to cultivate good relationships with key legislators, and PBJI was killed in committee.[82]

The Carter administration also seriously grappled with the notion of government-guaranteed full employment. The Humphrey-Hawkins Full Employment Act of 1978, originally drafted in 1974, would have compelled the federal government to provide jobs for *all* who wanted to work, whether or not the private sector demanded their needs or talents. Willing workers could sue the government if it failed to find them jobs. The bill called for a government department to conduct both employment and production surveys and then generate necessary jobs, whether in the public or the private sector.[83]

Like Nixon's FAP, the Humphrey-Hawkins Bill was attacked from the left and the right. At first, the bill lacked union support; union members tended to be better off than unemployed workers and may have feared the impact of hundreds of thousands of new job-seekers flooding the market. Also, although the law was the brainchild of an African American economist, Robert Browne, and an African American politician, Augustus Hawkins, the bill received little support from the black community, which prioritized eliminating private-sector discrimination over increasing federal jobs.[84] Michael Harrington, the author of *The Other America*, argued against the Humphrey-Hawkins bill, stating that the government was taking a line that was much too pro-corporate and that there was little evidence that subsidizing private greed produced good results. Oil company subsidies had produced environmental degradation instead of energy independence; even transit subsidies had merely given white middle-class people an opportunity to leave cities for suburbs. Harrington called for the nationalization of oil and rail, federal chartering of corporations, national banking, and the nationalization of all defense contractors. "To achieve socially useful full employment, we must be prepared to take steps to democratically plan and control some of the major investment decisions in this country," he wrote.[85] But the call for something like democratic socialism was ignored.

After the oil crisis and stagflation of the mid-1970s resulted in an increase in unemployment, unions finally began to support the Humphrey-Hawkins bill. Signed into law in October 1978, the act set low targets for unemployment (4 percent) and inflation (3 percent). But once the bill was passed, the lack of an enforcement mechanism allowed its provisions to be ignored.[86]

Economic disaster would kill Carter's hopes for a second term. When Carter took office in January 1977, the unemployment rate had stood at 7.5 percent and inflation was below 5 percent, but Carter was not sure which problem to prioritize, and he had advisors on both sides of the issue. After the PBJI failed and the Humphrey-Hawkins Act became (completely ignored) law, Carter turned to address inflation. A second oil crisis hit the United States in 1979, driving the inflation rate over 13 percent. Carter responded by retrenching, cutting spending in many areas of the federal budget with the exception of defense. As the economy slowed, the deficit grew, panicking Wall Street investors, but having made his commitment to attacking inflation rather than unemployment, Carter had to support the Federal Reserve as it used monetary policy to slow the economy even further. With 1980 an election year, a recession year, and a year that promised no end to the crisis of Americans held hostage in Iran, Carter was easily defeated by a resurgent Ronald Reagan.[87]

WRITING ABOUT INEQUALITY IN THE 1970s

The modern academic debate about distributive justice emerged in the 1970s. In 1971, Harvard philosopher John Rawls published *A Theory of*

Justice, a groundbreaking book that continues to be hugely influential as philosophers and policymakers consider, in the abstract, what fairness means.[88] Rawls argued that property ownership is only possible in liberal societies because we are interdependent and cooperative in ways that secure a right to property. Those who have no property are seriously disadvantaged in several ways. First, they are unable to be equal participants in society, because they lack the basic necessities that confer human dignity: clothes, shelter, food, and safety. Second, people with no property, while nominally free to make choices, are not free to carry out any plans for their lives. When extremes of inequality are present, any sense of community that allows us to see each other as morally equivalent and worthy of respect is likely to be absent.[89]

Rawls noted that, in developed nations, much of the difference in wealth and income between the most advantaged and the least advantaged stems from factors over which individuals have no control. Nobody chooses the parents to whom they are born, the talents and aptitudes that they have or lack, or the strength of their immune system, for example. He maintained that political entities have a responsibility to correct for these fundamental sources of unfairness. Rawls argued that measures that promoted unequal outcomes were only acceptable to the degree that they gave the most benefit to the least well off. Rawls called this rule the "difference principle." He justified his theory of distribution with a thought experiment about what he called the "original position." In the original position, a person has no information about their talents, needs, or sources of privilege. They are "behind the veil of ignorance." Rawls claimed that a person behind the veil of ignorance will always choose the system of distribution that benefits the least fortunate, just in case they end up being one of the least fortunate.[90] He considered this to be proof of the ethical superiority of the difference principle.

Rawls's *Theory of Justice* has been almost unparalleled in its impact on modern political philosophy, with both critics and proponents being required to grapple with its contents.[91] For example, Columbia University professor Charles Frankel chastised Rawls for seeking equal outcomes rather than equal opportunity. He argued that Rawls's difference principle hinders excellence, because the individual struggle to overcome disadvantage has meaning: "Obviously, it is harder to develop one's abilities in an inner city slum, and obviously, social justice calls for the remedying of such conditions of poverty. But quite large numbers of people with superior characters come out of inner-city slums, and Scarsdale has been known to produce its quota of feckless types."[92]

Another of Rawls's critics, Robert Nozick, set out a theory of fairness based on completely different assumptions. Nozick argued that private property was a sacred right, and cannot possibly be taxed with some reference to the greater social good because there is no such thing as society.[93] For Nozick, pursuing equality of outcomes, or any other distribution undertaken with an end result in mind, was wrongheaded. Rather, Nozick defended inequality as long as property ownership resulted from "just" transactions. If initial property acquisition was conducted justly, and subsequent trades were also just, then property was off limits to any interference by the state, including taxation (which by this logic became theft). If the most important data points about property ownership are the original distribution of property and its historical transfer, then knowledge of the way in which property was originally acquired over time is important. Nozick paid no attention to that question, completely ignoring (for example) the theft of land from Native Americans by European settlers.[94]

The debate over distributive justice that began in earnest in the 1970s has continued, although in some sense both sides talk past each other. Libertarians and conservatives both tend to define economic "freedom" only in a negative sense—as the freedom from government restrictions on the deployment of their own property. Liberals, in contrast, point out that there is no substance to freedom if one lacks the resources to actually complete any life goals. In the words of the French novelist Anatole France, "The law, in its majestic equality, forbids the rich as well as the poor to sleep under bridges, to beg in the streets, and to steal bread."[95]

ROLE OF WOMEN

Just as the enfranchisement of white working men in the 1820s and black men in 1870 failed to provide economic equality, so women's enfranchisement in 1920 did not bring women economic justice. In 1963, the Kennedy administration created a Commission on the Status of Women, but while the commission revealed many state laws that kept women less prosperous and less well-educated than men, it recommended against an Equal Rights Amendment. The Civil Rights Act of 1964 had barred discrimination on the basis of sex, and an Equal Employment Opportunity Commission was created to police employment practices.

Within states, women lobbied for equal property rights for married women and to eliminate "protective" legislation. States had passed laws ostensibly to safeguard the health and reproductive capacities of women, but these also, handily, prevented women from earning overtime or participating in high-paid jobs.[96] A federal equal rights amendment was introduced, but it languished after being ratified by thirty-four states. Under pressure from conservative groups, including women lobbyists led by Phyllis Schlafly, several states rescinded their ratification. The amendment never became law despite its supporters being granted an extension of time for its ratification.

Large numbers of women, including, for the first time, mothers of young children, were moving into the workforce. This movement helped to disguise growing economic inequality, as women's wages offset the stagnating wages of their husbands. As they had been during the advent of the first textile factories in the nineteenth century, women were increasingly attractive to employers in the 1970s because firms were facing global competition, and women could be paid less than men. Some women achieved managerial positions, although they tended to be at the bottom of management hierarchies in the least-well-paid jobs. Occupational segregation, although it had eased somewhat by the end of the century, still existed in many fields, and women earned less than men at every educational level, with full-time women workers earning 59 cents on the dollar compared to men in 1974 and 79 cents on the dollar by 2014. Over the course of their careers, women tended to lose ground compared to men.[97]

Whereas racially discriminatory legislation had to face the legal test of "strict scrutiny" (no such law could stand without a "compelling state interest"), efforts to achieve gender equality foundered after the failure of the Equal Rights Amendment. While the federal government removed some barriers to women's participation in the workforce, it did little directly to aid that participation. The possibilities of federal daycare had been illustrated during World War II, when the government facilitated the construction of 24-hour care so that women could work in war industries. After the war these daycare centers closed. Although by the 1970s welfare policy encouraged poor, single mothers to work, no plan for large-scale child care was ever arranged. Headstart, an educational program for the children of the disadvantaged, provided care for too few hours each day to enable women to pursue jobs or job training.[98]

As this chapter has shown, the United States experienced a period of significant compression of inequality between 1945 and the early 1970s. It was impelled in part by economic growth, including a growing population and available high-wage manufacturing jobs; in part by home construction, underwritten by FHA loans; in part by an expansion of the middle class, supported by GI Bill–funded education; and in part by top tax rates above 70 percent. In the midst of this prosperity, groups were left behind: the urban poor, the migrant worker, the resident of Appalachia. These outcomes were not accidents but rather the result of policies like redlining (the refusal by mortgage lenders to underwrite mortgages in minority neighborhoods); by union seniority and apprenticeship policies that failed to benefit African

Americans; and by the failure of the extractive industries to reinvest in the towns they stripped of natural resources like coal.

Policymakers experimented creatively with programs intended to help the poor. Some programs, like Medicare and Medicaid, not only persist but also have constituencies that are very resistant to seeing them change. Other experiments, like the community action programs associated with the Office of Economic Opportunity, the Family Assistance Plan, the Humphrey-Hawkins Act, and the Program for Better Jobs and Income, have been consigned to the recycle bin of history, where they are described as misguided attempts to force equal outcomes rather than facilitating equal opportunities.

Although influential philosophers argued that liberal society would be a failed project unless the poorest had a decent standard of living, by the end of the 1970s, conservatives were successfully changing the discourse. Historians increasingly portray conservative opposition to federal attempts to increase equality in the as the culmination of decades of work by well-off suburbanites, Christians, and business leaders to build an effective ideology and organizations.[99] Conservative writers shifted the discourse on poverty during the 1970s, arguing that while the United States was a land of equal opportunity, liberals had made a hard left turn in favor of equality of results. They claimed that some people were poor due to their own bad choices and deserved to bear the consequences of those choices. They also argued that welfare destroyed initiative and family—that redistributive programs made people dependent or caused family instability by enabling poor people to divorce or to remain unmarried. In the worst formulation, they described the poor as devious "welfare queens."[100] As the next chapter will show, Ronald Reagan, long an opponent of welfare programs, made those associations and claims central tenets of his administration. Under the pressure of neoliberalism, the Great Compression quickly began to unravel.

CHAPTER 7

The Triumph of Neoliberalism: 1979–1999

Stagflation and the oil shocks of the 1970s had brought economic malaise to the United States, setting the stage for widespread acceptance of a new, "neoliberal" theory of prosperity, divorced from both equality of condition and equality of opportunity. Over the course of the next decade, Ronald Reagan's severe tax cuts and George H. W. Bush's "trickle-down" economics promoted the idea that Americans should nurture and cultivate "job creators," the wealthiest Americans, who, it was assumed, would reinvest in the economy and cause growth that would benefit all. The shift of much of the country's industrial base to the southern tier of states, where unions had always been weak or nonexistent, led to the emergence of a united call for deregulation of the economy.[1] However, not only did "trickle-down" economics fail to trickle down, but also many industrial jobs disappeared entirely, replaced by low-paid service jobs that relegated high-school graduates to poverty.[2] Free trade continued to be an article of faith, and American manufacturers claimed that the only way to remain competitive in globalized markets was to move their manufacturing to countries like Mexico where labor commanded a lower wage.

These global economic shifts, with which the United States had no policy to deal, occurred at the same time that a new consensus emerged about help for the poor. Although direct subsidies to income composed only a very small percentage of the annual U.S. budget, welfare programs and the people who used them came under attack by both Reagan and George H. W. Bush. Ultimately, a Democratic president, Bill Clinton, pressed on by the Congress of the "Contract with America," carried out one of the most drastic welfare reforms in American history. An escalation of the "war on drugs" also resulted in the large-scale imprisonment of many African American men, injuring black families and further exacerbating the economic inequality along racial lines that had persisted since Reconstruction. All of these factors combined replaced the trend toward greater economic equality that characterized the post–World War II period, with an upward-sloping trend toward greater inequality.

REAGAN AND FREE-MARKET ECONOMICS

The Austrian free-market school of economics is based on the tenet that an economy is full of rational, independent individuals. In this way of looking at the world, inequalities of condition are the natural result of inequalities of talent. It is wrong for the state to try to interfere with these inequalities, since the only way to do so is either by taking from one person what he or she has earned as a result of this differential talent or else ignoring the low valuation that the market has placed on the skills of the less-talented person. According to this way of thinking, poverty is important; it gives people a reason to excel, and forces them to participate in the market if they otherwise choose to do something different with their time.[3] Critiques of the distribution of wealth can be dismissed because they are based on envy. The free-marketeers believe that eventually, untrammeled free markets make everyone better off, as the most talented develop new commodities and technologies that percolate down to even the poorest.[4]

Upon assuming the presidency in 1981, former B-movie actor and California governor Ronald Reagan made these beliefs the cornerstone of his economic policies. His ideas marked such a departure from postwar norms that they came to be called "Reaganomics," although Reagan preferred to call them "New Federalism." New Federalism had three main elements: tax cuts, cuts in government spending, and deregulation. Reagan and his team argued that cutting taxes would increase government revenue. They based these arguments on the untested notions of Arthur Laffer, professor of business economics at the University of Southern California, who theorized in the 1970s that high taxes dissuaded people from working, thus harming productivity and economic growth. Lower tax rates, Laffer claimed, would reduce tax avoidance.[5] Tax cuts would energize the wealthiest, who were the most likely to invest in an expansion of productive capacity, thus increasing private employment.[6] The notion that tax cuts for the wealthiest would hasten economic growth was called "supply side" or "trickle-down" economics. The 1981 Economic Recovery Tax Act slashed the top income tax rate from

70 percent to 50 percent. A second piece of Reagan-era legislation in 1987 capped the top rate at 28 percent.[7]

With the advocacy of groups like Grover Norquist's Americans for Tax Reform, cutting taxes, or at the very least never raising taxes, became an article of Republican Party faith. Republicans suggested that government bureaucracy was always inferior to private-sector activity—that there was no difference, essentially, between democratic government and dictatorship. Journalist E. J. Dionne characterized Norquist's position: "Better, in this view, to have no health care and no pensions than to have the government embark on this terrible path. Environmental regulations are seen not as preserving streams and forests for future generation; they are viewed as ways of interfering with the free use of private property."[8]

Reaganomics also emphasized deregulation. Proponents argued that government regulations required businesses to spend money on compliance that they might otherwise have spent on growing productive capacity.[9] Reagan attacked the minimum wage, which he argued was a cause of unemployment, and attempted to institute a subminimum wage for young people, which was blocked by a House Democratic majority. As the minimum wage lost ground against inflation, Democrats in the House and Senate were ultimately forced to accept a subminimum "training wage" for certain kinds of on-the-job training, in order for any increase in the regular minimum wage to occur.[10]

Finally, Reagan's programs included cutbacks in spending on social services, education, and welfare. Conservatives claimed that large government bureaucracies could only be inefficient. Since they had no market competitors, and since they had privileged access to legislators, it was impossible to ensure that bureaucracies provided services in the most efficient and cheapest way.[11] The attack on government bureaucracies particularly harmed black families, as black women lost one of the better-paying occupational niches that they had gained since the 1960s—government employment.[12] Cutbacks in social services also harmed people with mental illness, contributing to an epidemic of homelessness.

Reaganomics included a great concern with diminishing inflation, and strong controls on federal spending, except for federal spending on the military budget. Political scientist Donald Wells noted in 1982 that one ironic side effect of Reaganomics was a growth in the "statism" that the Reagan administration said it deplored. Government expenditure was directed at wealthy military contractors.[13] The Reagan administration advocated for a Strategic Defense Initiative (SDI) or "Star Wars defense," which was intended to be a final salvo in the Cold War.[14] If SDI functioned as planned, the United States and its allies would be able to detect missiles launched by the Soviet Union and shoot them down in real time, using lasers. The total projected cost for this was $26 billion, but rather than being a government initiative like the Manhattan Project, the billions in this case were to be directed to military contractors in Europe, Israel, and the United States.[15] The combination of tax cuts and massive military spending immediately led to a deficit, and the deficit in turn led to rising interest rates. The administration's response was to roll back tax cuts for businesses, but not those for individuals, which had become a point of pride. By the time Reagan left office in 1989, the federal debt had risen from $900 billion to $2.6 trillion, and from 33 percent to 51 percent of GDP.[16]

DEINDUSTRIALIZATION

By the mid-1970s, the high growth of the postwar era had slowed, for several reasons. The oil shocks of the 1970s caused a huge outflow of American capital, and the economy stagnated under inflation. Although average incomes rose, rising prices diminished purchasing power for middle-income Americans to 70 percent of what it had been at the beginning of the decade.[17] A longitudinal study of Americans' incomes between 1974 and 1991 showed that, despite the much vaunted American Dream, mobility was very limited. Those who did manage to move up the income scale generally moved only to the next higher quintile. As Figure 7.1 shows, those income differentials,

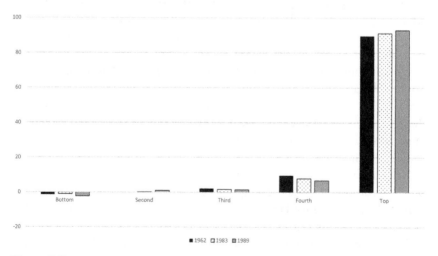

Figure 7.1
Percentage of Financial Net Wealth by Quintile. (Edward D. Wolff, "Trends in Household Wealth in the United States, 1962–1983 and 1983–1989," *Review of Income and Wealth Series* 40 no. 2 (June 1994): 143–174, at 153.)

and the ability of wealthier people to invest in a growing stock market, translated into a growing share of financial net wealth (net worth minus home equity) for the top quintile of wealth holders, and falling shares for other quintiles.

Part of the growth in inequality can be attributed to the decline in American manufacturing. In 1970, 26.4 percent of Americans were employed in manufacturing; by 1990, that share had decreased to 17.9 percent, and by 1998, to less than 16 percent. At the same time, employment in the service sector of the economy increased from 25.9 percent to 32.6 percent. The new jobs being created in the service sector were not primarily highly paid ones.[18] As wages for skilled workers increased, those for workers with less skill actually decreased, polarizing incomes. Computerized and automated processes displaced less-educated and less-experienced workers, who lacked trade unions to buffer them against losses. And unlike other countries that also experienced inequality growth, like the United Kingdom and Canada, the United States failed to offset the impact of inequality with redistributive taxation.[19]

The loss of highly paid manufacturing jobs may also have had the additional effect of promoting female-headed households, by sapping away some of the motivation for poorer couples to marry. As journalist Barbara Ehrenreich noted, the jobs available in the 1990s to the working poor paid so poorly that each woman would have had to marry 2.3 men in order for their combined incomes to carry them over the poverty line.[20]

STIGMATIZING THE POOR

At the same time that economic trends like deindustrialization, outsourcing, and offshoring were leaving workers behind, Republicans made poverty a moral issue. Between the nineteenth century and the 1980s, the notion of "dependency" was completely redefined. As has been noted in previous chapters, Americans thought economic independence so crucial for political participation that poor white men were prohibited from voting. When white men were enfranchised in the 1820s, the few black people and women with property who had once been able to vote were disenfranchised; now, dependency meant being a child or a female or a slave.

Wage workers were initially considered dependent, but as wage work became the norm, family members who did essential unpaid work in the home were classified as "dependent." Finally, in the twentieth century, the definition of dependency shifted yet again, to refer to those who neither worked nor received certain kinds of entitlements (Social Security recipients were not "dependent"—older people had successfully lobbied to ensure that their key program was seen as a matter of desert and of having "paid in").

By the 1970s, welfare recipients were doubly reviled. Out-of-wedlock births to black mothers increased from 25 percent to 57 percent, and the number of female-headed black families had doubled.[21] Since it was expected that all poor women, including mothers of young children, should work, welfare reformers affixed blame to the unemployed not only for their joblessness but also for their daring to have families at all. Reagan, who had long lobbied in favor of work requirements for welfare and limiting welfare eligibility, continued to stigmatize welfare recipients by referring to them as "welfare queens." This was a loaded term: "Black, female, a pauper, not a worker, a housewife and mother, yet practically a child herself—the new stereotype partakes of virtually every quality that has been coded historically as antithetical to independence," critical theorist Nancy Fraser and historian Linda Gordon noted. If welfare receipt is a social pathology, then any action that shrinks the welfare budget is a tough-love cure.[22] Critics of the antipoor discourse pointed out that the United States "devoted a smaller proportion of its gross national product to social programs than any other advanced industrialized nation," aside from Japan.[23]

Critics of welfare papered over the racial implications of their arguments. They claimed that they had the best interests of the poor in mind, and that welfare was harming recipients, miring them in a culture of dependency, and failing to inculcate the same "values and aspirations" shared by working Americans.[24] For example, libertarian political scientist Charles Murray claimed that welfare programs worsened poverty by giving the poor a disincentive either to work or to marry. This was bad because two-parent families were more likely to earn incomes above the poverty line. Murray argued that welfare recipients were clever calculators who took advantage of government largesse.[25] Historians Oscar and Lilian Handlin blamed the welfare state for everything from the decline of the middle-class family to the development of ethnic tribalism, inner-city violence, and white guilt. To them, it was wrong to favor "equality over efficiency" as a social goal, since to do so might result in "less for everyone." According to the Handlins, those seeking to survive amid the economic inequality of the modern economy should cultivate the "mainstream bonds" of family and mutual support.[26] Sociologist William Julius Wilson suggested that the government focus its energy on training and employing black men so that black women could escape poverty by marrying wage-earners.[27]

The moralistic rhetoric of Reagan's New Federalism was aimed at the white middle and lower-middle classes, and as sociologist Irving Horowitz pointed out, it encouraged middle-class whites to view recipients of federal aid as outsiders.[28] "To recognize that social stratification is an inevitable byproduct of economic and occupational differentiation is one thing; but it is quite another to accept as fiat differences between classes, ethnics, and races in the name of some higher principle of competitive society. The latter tendency seems to characterize the thrust of the New Federalism," Horowitz wrote, somewhat presciently.[29] While welfare cuts were on the table, any attempt to cut Social Security was met with a huge outcry, defining the limits of budget-cutting to the boundary at which cuts began to affect the white middle classes.[30] By targeting programs aimed largely at minorities and leaving intact those intended for white Americans, Reagan was able to attract large numbers of white working-class Democrats to vote for his re-election.[31]

Being able to stigmatize the poor as inferior—whether on the basis of race or of supposed shared cultural values—made it easier for white Americans at all income levels to hew to the notion of equal opportunity. Political scientist Jennifer Hochschild's 1981 study of Americans' beliefs about distributive justice showed that the white Americans who she interviewed supported egalitarianism in family and friend relationships and in terms of political and civil rights, but reflexively supported the economic status quo. "They define political freedom as strict equality, but economic freedom as an equal chance to become unequal—that is, as differentiation."[32] Hoschchild's study subjects believed that efficiency and productivity were crucial values, not just for the economic sphere, but also in the political domain. These beliefs, and 40 years of cold war with the Soviet Union, constrained the policy options that these study subjects were willing to endorse; job growth and job training were fine, but economic redistribution was not. Subjects readily differentiated between the deserving and the undeserving poor, with many stereotyping the poor as people with limited intelligence or limited drive.[33] Even those who did not believe that political liberalism depended on economic inequality accepted the status quo because the problems of the American economy and polity seemed too big to fix.[34]

The failure to support social spending fell disproportionately on black families, about 34 percent of whom lived in poverty in 1984 compared with 12 percent of white families. Among the items slashed were summer food programs for children, food stamps for many formerly eligible families, job training programs, federal aid to college students, and housing subsidies.[35] States assumed responsibility for the main welfare program, Aid to Families with Dependent Children (AFDC). By encouraging "subsidiarity," or the relegation of welfare responsibilities to the state and local levels, the Reagan administration conveniently ignored that poor states could not afford, and in the past had not afforded, to help their neediest residents. Instead states and localities competed for economic development by seeing which city or county could provide the greatest tax incentives for businesses to relocate. Many of these relocations ended up being temporary or providing fewer jobs than anticipated.[36]

What was the impact of Reaganomics? By 1986, inflation had fallen from 13.5 percent to 1.9 percent as the Federal Reserve reduced the money supply, but at the same time, unemployment grew from 7.2 percent in July 1981 to over 10 percent in 1982 before falling back into the range of 7 percent by 1985. While the anticipated productivity growth largely failed to appear, what did appear was a massive federal budget deficit. High interest rates resulting from the budget deficit produced much foreign investment in the United States, but the general tendency of those with money in the 1980s to spend lavishly rather than save produced a large trade imbalance.[37]

AFTER REAGAN

By the early 1990s, the free-trade, antitax, and antiwelfare rhetoric of the Reagan administration had become pervasive. Critics now assailed even pro-grams once considered somewhat sacred, like supplemental food for women, infants, and children (WIC). Dr. George Graham, a member of President Reagan's Task Force on Food Assistance, argued in *The Public Interest* that WIC "has failed because the evils that it tries to address stem from behavioral rather than nutritional causes. WIC is altogether unsuited to address the problems of disruptive behavior or failure in school, dropping out of school, delinquency, welfare dependency, substance abuse, promiscuity, illegitimacy, extreme prematurity, fetal alcohol syndrome, 'crack' babies, and infantile AIDS."[38]

Nor did the neoliberal turn solve the nation's economic problems. Between 1989, when Reagan's successor George H. W. Bush took office, and 1992, unemployment increased by 2 percentage points. Bush was a one-term president largely because when recession struck in 1990, as the United States attempted to unseat Saddam Hussein in the first Gulf War, Bush had to renege on his campaign promise not to raise taxes.[39] Bush's response to the recession and deficit was, among other things, to raise the marginal tax rate on the top tax bracket to 31 percent from 28 percent—still far below what it had been prior to Reagan. But only 16 percent of Americans surveyed professed to approve of the way in which he handled the economy.[40]

By 1992, neoliberalism had infected both political parties. Bill Clinton, although a Democrat, promised during his presidential campaign to "end welfare as we know it."[41] Clinton's plan, outlined in *Putting People First*, sought to craft a "third way." He triangulated between liberal welfarism of the kind pursued by Johnson and Roosevelt, and the hard line that Ronald Reagan had sought but was never able to obtain due to a Democratic House of Representatives through his eight-year administration. Clinton proposed reforming welfare by instituting time limits for welfare recipients but at the same time making jobs easier to get and retain. *Putting People First* advocated widespread subsidized daycare, job training, and federally supported jobs of last resort for those who were unable to find jobs in the private sector. Clinton also planned to expand Medicaid eligibility, thus removing the temptation for the poor to remain benefit recipients so that they could qualify for health insurance.[42]

When Republicans triumphed in the 1994 congressional midterm elections, held under the banner of Georgia Congressman Newt Gingrich's "Contract with America," they killed the more liberal aspects of Clinton's welfare reform. The Contract with America promised a balanced-budget amendment, a slashing of capital gains taxes, increased military spending, and term limits. Having obtained a congressional majority in the November midterms, the Republicans proceeded, in 1995, to shut down the government over the normally routine question of whether or not to raise the debt ceiling, indicating that compromise on the much more controversial question of welfare was going to be impossible.[43]

The bill that passed instead, the Personal Responsibility and Work Opportunity Reconciliation Act of 1996 (PRWORA), discarded AFDC and replaced it with a set of block grants to the states, called Temporary Assistance to Needy Families (TANF).[44] PRWORA set a time limit of five years for welfare eligibility and made work or job training compulsory for welfare recipients, despite the fact that the sort of work for which welfare recipients tended to qualify was often contingent and unlikely to lift anyone out of poverty. PRWORA also contained a preamble with paeans to marriage and the nuclear family.[45] Under the PRWORA, most state assistance to the poor came in the form of work-related supplementation, like child care assistance; but under the 1996 Child Care and Development Block Grant program, only 12 percent of eligible children could be served. On the plus side, when AFDC was eliminated, some states expanded the State Children's Health Insurance Program (SCHIP).[46]

What was the impact of the Clinton welfare reform? The picture is complicated, as PRWORA appears to have helped some welfare recipients and disadvantaged others. As political scientist Demetrios James Caraley wrote, when "welfare as we know it" ended, former recipients sorted themselves into three groups. A small number became fully employed; a second subset, especially single mothers, found low-paid work but were forced to have their children raised either by relatives or in substandard daycare situations; and a third group did not find or seek work and may have relied on other family members and on food stamps, perhaps benefiting from rises in income among those family members as the economy grew. Welfare reform also impacted long-term earnings. From 1996 to 1999, the total number of welfare recipients enrolled in higher education dropped from about 650,000 people to about 350,000, and four-year college enrollments did not rebound, unlike two-year college enrollments. This suggests a certain short-sightedness to PRWORA, since on average college graduates earn more than their peers without a college education.[47]

One of the stated goals of PRWORA was to encourage marriage for poor, unmarried mothers, on the theory that marriage should be a main route out of poverty. In fact, marriage rates among unmarried mothers after PRWORA did increase, but the partners that they chose were increasingly less educated, less likely to be employed, and more likely to have previous partners and existing children to whom they owed financial obligations. Such marriages provided no route out of poverty without some government policy commitment to available jobs at a living wage.[48]

After PRWORA, the welfare rolls fell 49 percent in five years, and politicians on both sides of the aisle celebrated the success of the Clinton welfare reforms. But they celebrated without taking into account whether or not other programs, like the expansion of the Earned Income Tax Credit and SCHIP, helped to offset welfare, or whether the Internet-related economic boom of the late 1990s (with real per capital GDP up 25 percent and 20 million new jobs) would have addressed unemployment through economic growth anyway. The new programs also offered insufficient support to people with mental illnesses and substance abuse problems that hampered their ability to get jobs.[49]

Clinton's administration had greater success in addressing inequality caused by low wages. Americans had been distinguishing between the unworthy poor and the worthy, working poor since the era of the Great Society. During the Clinton administration some questioned the existence of the category "the working poor." For example, the economist Bradley Schiller denied that people could work full time and still head poor families, showing little understanding that contingent workers are not in control of their schedules, yet often have to maintain open availability, and that one can work less than full time but still too many hours to have the sort of availability that permits a second job.[50] Clinton's administration combatted working poverty by expanding the Earned Income Tax Credit, acting on the premise that that no family with a fully employed household head should be living beneath the poverty line.[51] The administration also managed to increase the minimum wage, although only through a bargain with Republicans that resulted in tax cuts for small businesses.[52]

Health care costs, and the costs of untreated illnesses, were major sources of inequality. In contrast with citizens of many other developed countries, Americans in the 1990s still had differential access to health insurance and different levels of insurance coverage. People with pre-existing conditions either could not get health insurance at all or could only get policies through high-risk pools whose premiums were more than they could afford. Thus, an unexpected medical expense could bankrupt a family. While Clinton attempted to make health care expansion a centerpiece of his administration, the same discourse of the deserving and undeserving that inflected the welfare debate also shadowed health care reform. While in European countries health care was described as a human right, in the United States in the 1990s economists focused mainly on the high cost of health care. They even wrote about the "moral hazard" posed by people who used too much health care because their contribution, in the form of deductibles and copayments, was too small to deter use.

Responding to both of these issues, the Clinton plan sought to slow the growth of health-care expenses through the use of managed care plans (HMOs) and to expand the risk pool by compelling healthier people to become insured. President Clinton and his health-care collaborator, First Lady Hillary Clinton, intended to provide the employed with universal health care through regional health alliances or corporate alliances, while the unemployed would continue to receive Medicaid. Insurance plans would have been prohibited from excluding people for pre-existing conditions or failing to renew their insurance. The Clinton plan set caps on the acceptable growth of health-care premiums, directed employers to absorb 80 percent of health care premium costs, and subsidized premiums for those earning 150 percent of the poverty level.[53]

Unfortunately for the prospect of attacking this source of inequality, health insurance industry advocates killed the plan. The Health Insurance Association of America spent $6.5 million on a 1993 television campaign to convince the electorate that, were the Clinton plan to become law, people would lose all of their health care choices. In the commercials, average couple characters named "Harry" and "Louise" lamented their health care bills and lack of choice of doctors.[54] After a rancorous public debate, the failure of bipartisan attempts to craft a compromise, and much pushback against universal coverage by hard-liners within the Republican Party, the Clinton health care initiative died in the early fall of 1994.

As a so-called New Democrat, Clinton moved away from the Keynesianism that had characterized most postwar Democratic presidents. Although his *Putting People First* manifesto, inspired by the ideas of Secretary of Labor Robert Reich, had promised "massive investment in human capital, mainly education and training, and infrastructure programmes like transportation, communication, and technology to enhance America's global competitiveness," Clinton's actual policies did not match those promises.[55] Within his cabinet, Clinton was faced with two groups of conflicting advisors—one group in favor of deficit reduction, and the other in favor of public investment (this was similar to the inflation versus unemployment problem faced by Jimmy Carter). Ultimately, Clinton went along with the deficit hawks but realized that by doing so he was shifting away from the traditional priorities of the Democratic Party. "I hope you're all aware we're all Eisenhower Republicans," he noted.[56]

Clinton's impeachment and trial over his affair with intern Monica Lewinsky distracted Americans from the strong economic expansion of his administration, with an unemployment rate of only 4 percent and annual labor productivity growth of 2.7 percent per year.[57] He also successfully eliminated the federal deficit and replaced it with a surplus by "raising the top marginal tax rate to 39.6 percent, along with increased gasoline taxes, an uncapping of the payroll tax for Medicare, and increased taxation of Social Security benefits."[58]

INEQUALITY AND THE WAR ON DRUGS

As this chapter has shown, neoconservative doctrines about spending and welfare triumphed in the 1980s and 1990s, and welfare recipients were stigmatized, which divided Americans along both class and racial lines. The War on Drugs created by the Nixon administration accelerated during the Reagan era, worsening both inequality and racial divisiveness. In the 1980s, the moral panic surrounding the War on Drugs focused on crack cocaine, a rock-like distillation made by combining dissolved powder cocaine and baking soda in water and then heating. Smoking crack delivered a fast and cheap high and so was more popular in inner-city areas (whereas powder cocaine was a status symbol for wealthy whites). Crack use began in earnest around 1985, reached a peak in 1989, and then tapered off slightly, leaving social disruption, widespread violence, and incarceration in its wake.[59] But crack users were not the only victims of the drug wars; 80 percent of those arrested for drug offenses in the 1980s and 1990s were arrested for simple possession of marijuana, a drug that was subsequently considered harmless enough to be legalized for recreational use in some states.[60]

Successive Supreme Court decisions narrowed the Fourth Amendment right to be free from unreasonable searches, and the introduction of more discretion in policing meant that black people, particularly young black men, were much more likely than their white peers to be stopped and searched on a pretext and then arrested for drug possession. Law enforcement targeting of racially segregated inner city areas rather than (for example) college campuses led to more imprisonment of minority youth and to the widespread but false assumption that the inner cities were the site of most of the nation's drug use. In the suburbs, drug use was described as a public health issue that struck otherwise good children from "nice" families; in urban areas, it was portrayed as a crime wave.[61]

Law enforcement agencies came to have a material interest in stopping as many people as possible on suspicion of drug crimes once police departments were allowed to confiscate cars and houses. The final step in the direction of massive incarceration came when Clinton backed a three-strike rule for felons. Even when the racial impact of mandatory sentencing laws that weighted crack more heavily than powder cocaine became clear, Supreme Court decisions refused to question them unless legislators or judges in individual cases had admitted that they had sentenced individuals for racially discriminatory reasons.[62]

Ironically, the incarceration of over 30 percent of young black men by the end of the 1990s may have caused Americans to believe that inequality was waning. Racial disparities in wage inequalities are measured using the wages of people who are actually in the labor force. But as sociologists Bruce Western and Becky Pettit show, incarceration falls the most heavily on those who are either already unemployed or who are able to command very low wages. Since so many young black men were imprisoned, their low wage levels—the long tail of a bell curve—were excluded from statistical calculations of inequality. Not only did imprisonment hide the real racial disparities in economic equality, it also helped to perpetuate those disparities. Time in prison and out of the labor force translates into fewer skills, an even lower wage, and tremendous difficulties in actually getting hired.[63]

GLOBALIZATION AND FREE TRADE

While incarceration of young black men caused the statistical illusion that inequality was slowing in America in the 1990s, the jobs available were becoming more polarized into high-wage management jobs and low-wage service sector jobs with no hope of serving as a stepping stone to a middle-class career.[64] During the 1980s, improvements in communications technology and the expansion of "big box" stores like Walmart and Target provided greater markets in the United States for goods either produced or finished inexpensively overseas. Factories in Asia could quickly adapt to slight product changes.[65] Companies that could do so in the 1990s cut their costs by off-shoring portable jobs, maximizing profit through lower input costs (it is estimated that labor costs are "58 to 72 percent lower in China and 22 to 62 percent lower in Mexico"), but at the same time contributing to American unemployment.[66] Computers and telecommunication advances enabled companies to use smaller workforces to accomplish their goals, also helping to increase unemployment.[67]

Free trade became another vector of inequality during the Clinton administration, in the form of the North American Free Trade Agreement (NAFTA). NAFTA was designed to foster economic growth throughout the United States, Canada, and Mexico by lowering tariff barriers. After NAFTA, the value added to American manufacturing by Mexican assembly plants, or "maquiladoras," tripled.[68] "By 1999, tariff and non-tariff barriers had been removed on 65 percent of goods ... and the value of trade between the USA, Mexico, and Canada trebled between 1993 and 2007. Inward foreign direct investment increased fivefold over the same period."[69] This prosperity was not equally shared, however. NAFTA disadvantaged low-waged workers in the United States who were doing the sorts of assembly work that could be outsourced south of the border, and even Mexican workers employed by the new *maquiladoras* found that their wages fell. Even trucking was affected, as the Mexican transportation sector transported cheap Asian goods overland from Mexican ports to the United States.[70]

In order to secure enough Democratic votes to pass a bill that was designed mainly to benefit multinational corporations, the drafters of NAFTA included a labor side agreement, the North American Agreement on Labor Cooperation (NAALC). The agreement was intended to ensure enforcement of each country's own minimum wage, child labor, and occupational safety laws. In fact, between 1994 and 2011, only 39 cases were filed under the agreement, and none had generated sanctions against an offending firm, showing that the NAALC was basically a dead letter.[71]

INEQUALITY AND THE ENVIRONMENT

Finally, inequality during the 1980s and 1990s was manifested in the wage differentials for jobs available to different groups, and not only in the chance of incarceration caused by the War on Drugs but also in the purity of the environments in which they could afford to live. Beginning in the early 1980s, grassroots organizations began to challenge the location of landfills, toxic waste dumps, and other environmental harms in primarily low-income neighborhoods. They argued that although the economic benefits of such entities accrued to counties or states, the cost was borne by small pockets of disadvantaged people living in areas adjacent to the entities. On the Navajo reservation in New Mexico, the terrible environmental and health effects of mining uranium have been downplayed as mining companies tout economic development.[72] In Detroit, corporations counted on the inability of the poor to slow or stop the location of waste sites near their homes. In 1990, although they accounted for only a quarter of the U.S. population, minorities composed more than 40 percent of the population living within a mile of hazardous waste dumps.[73]

Corporations have claimed that their site location decisions, and subsequent decisions by poor people about where to live, are functions of value-neutral supply and demand, without acknowledging that it is possible, good, and sometimes necessary to mitigate the worst effects of capitalism in various ways.[74] As historian Alan Taylor noted, "Native Americans on reservations, African-Americans in cities and in the rural south, Appalachian mining families, and Mexican-American farmworkers in California have suffered disproportionately from our nation's environmental ills."[75] The 2016 crisis over the dangerous drinking water in Flint, Michigan—for years home to General Motors plants and other polluting industries—shows that the impact of environmental inequality persists in potentially devastating ways.[76]

As this chapter has shown, between 1979 and 1999 the Great Compression ended, and the United States reverted to the economic inequality characteristic of every other period since the nation's founding. Globalization gave multinational corporations the opportunity to cut labor costs by automating processes and by manufacturing or finishing their products overseas. As highly paid manufacturing jobs left the United States, there was no concerted effort either to replace them with other highly paid jobs or to redistribute the profits from labor cost savings to displaced workers.

The Reagan administration marked a turning point, as the rhetoric of free-market neoliberalism triumphed over Keynesianism. The best economy was the fastest growing, tax cuts to the wealthy would "trickle down" and mean prosperity for all, and the private sector was always more efficient and therefore better than government. Whereas New Deal and Great Society programs recognized the immorality of poverty amid wealth, during the Reagan administration, welfare recipients became "welfare queens," not just demoralized by a culture of dependency but also gaming the system. Even under

Bill Clinton, a Democrat, priorities like government stimulus for job creation were ignored in favor of deficit reduction. This 20-year period illustrated that one of the most durable pieces of capitalist folk wisdom was untrue: Not only did a rising tide not necessarily lift all boats, but it was even possible for seemingly unrelated policy measures, like the War on Drugs, to worsen economic inequality in ways that were very difficult to reverse.

CHAPTER 8

The New Inequality and the Lessons of the Past: 1999–Present

As the previous chapters have shown, socioeconomic inequality has always been a feature of American life, and although concern with it waxes and wanes, the political will to address the issue has been mostly nonexistent. The triumph of neoliberalism in the 1980s and 1990s made class easier to ignore. But in the first decades of the twenty-first century, interest in the issue spiked again. Journalists began to fret that something was systemically wrong, that the wealthy were no longer upholding their end of the social contract. Americans, who had long professed that anything was possible in the United States given enough hard work, were beginning to see inequalities of results that made that assertion problematic, and disparities between effort and compensation, or between the willingness to work full time and the ability to earn a living wage.[1]

The Great Recession that struck in 2007, with all of its similarities to the stock market crash of 1929 and the Great Depression, sparked anger and fueled a sense of futility about ever seeing change. The Tea Party movement to the right wing of the Republican Party, and the Occupy Wall Street movement to the left of the Democratic Party, both expressed inchoate unhappiness with the status quo. Dissatisfaction with inequality continues to be widespread, although the right and left wings of the American political spectrum have divergent prescriptions for the problem. Ideas about more equitable distribution, including proposals for a stakeholder society or a basic income guarantee, have not made much of an impact on popular consciousness.

The modern period has seen the widespread acceptance of Reaganite ideas, even by America's declining labor unions, and levels of inequality of wealth and income in the United States not seen since the first 25 years of the twentieth century. The Supreme Court's decision in *Citizens United* (2010) allowed unlimited funding to flow from corporations to political candidates, further decreasing the political impact of the middle and working classes. Even the privatization of the public schools further shrinks our sense of common purpose and collaborative effort.[2]

INEQUALITY IN THE TWENTY-FIRST CENTURY

During the administration of George W. Bush, poverty slipped off the national radar as a priority. Bush presided over massive tax cuts, and Congress reauthorized those tax cuts even after the economy worsened due to the terrorist attacks of September 11, 2001. As Reagan had, Bush claimed the best way to deal with an ailing economy was to put money back into the pockets of ordinary Americans.[3] Rhetoric aside, however, his $1.6 trillion in tax cuts and estate-tax reductions enriched the upper middle class and the wealthy. Unfortunately, those tax cuts were supported even by those Americans who, when interviewed, said they earned less than $50,000 a year, thought the rich should pay more in income tax, and hoped that the government would expand social programs. Part of this was due to voters' lack of information, but it also represented a deep-seated belief, even among working Americans, that people are entitled to do whatever they want with their private property, including giving unlimited inheritances to the people of their choice.[4]

Other Bush programs sought to uplift the poor through social engineering. While the notion of "Charitable Choice" had been included in Clinton's 1996 welfare reform, Bush created the White House Office of Faith-Based and Community Initiatives (OFBCI), intended to eliminate any regulations that prevented churches and other religious organizations from filling the gaps in the welfare system.[5] Religious organizations no longer had to separate out their social-service wings and keep them secular or nondenominational, and were allowed to discriminate in hiring on the basis of religious beliefs. But this change was not value-neutral; religious organizations tended to paint poverty as a moral failure rather than a result of structural economic problems. They depicted poor people as lacking social capital that only churches were able to provide.[6] The OFBCI also had a political purpose. Catholic bishops warmly supported the OFBCI because they saw it as affirming one of the key missions of the church; in response, the Bush administration hoped to pull Catholic voters from their traditional support of the Democratic Party.[7] Although the mission of the OFBCI was derailed by the September 11, 2001, attacks, tens of millions of dollars in federal aid was allocated to it through 2004.[8] Finally, the Bush administration focused on encouraging family formation and stigmatizing out-of-wedlock births through the Healthy Marriage Initiative, but since there were no effective federal programs to reduce the birth rate by (for example) distributing birth control, states were simply rewarded for happening to have birth-rate declines.

At the same time that welfare cash payments were largely cut back, the Earned Income Tax Credit (EITC) gained importance, providing nearly $36 billion in credits to 19.8 million families in 2002. EITC benefits are only available to working households, so it is not a substitute for welfare. The current welfare system cannot expand effectively to accommodate large numbers of unemployed during economic downturns, and welfare eligibility is capped at five years for a person's lifetime. Clinton's welfare changes were reauthorized by Congress in 2006, establishing as permanent the new norm that most recipients of welfare aid would not receive direct cash support.[9]

THE GREAT RECESSION AND INEQUALITY

In the years leading up to the Great Recession, the trend toward income and wealth inequality that dated from the Reagan era continued. As Figure 8.1 shows, the top quintile of income earners experienced steady growth in the percentage share of income received, while all other quintiles experienced a relative loss.

The wealth distribution pattern that had been established in the 1980s remained steady, but only because, up to 2006, house prices were generally rising, and most of the wealth of those in the bottom four quintiles of wealth holders was in the form of home equity. Rising home prices even offset the tendency of the middle three quintiles of wealth holders to draw on their home equity for lines of credit.[10] In a sense, most middle-class people had placed all of their wealth-earning eggs in the basket of home ownership.

In 1999, the repeal of the Glass-Steagall Act of 1933 removed federal oversight from large commercial banks that wished to branch out into speculative investments. During the Bush administration, mortgage lenders offered mortgages to many individuals who ordinarily would not have met income qualifications. Banks then packaged these "subprime" mortgages into instruments called collateralized debt obligations (CDOs), which were thought to be safe investments because generally, housing prices increased, and mortgage defaults were thought to be random. A housing crash in 2006, however, produced waves of mortgage defaults, showing that defaults were not random.[11] The collapse of

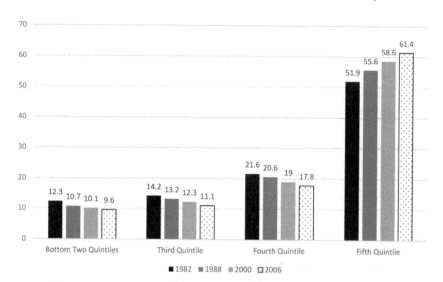

Figure 8.1
Percentage Share of Income by Quintile, 1982–2006. (Computed from Edward
Nathan Wolff, "Recent Trends in Household Wealth, 1983–2006: The Irresist-
ible Rise of Household Debt," *Review of Economics and Institutions* vol. 2 no. 1
(Winter 2001): 1–31, at 7.)

the housing market transformed CDOs into "toxic assets," precipitating the
failure of Lehman Brothers, one of the nation's largest banks. This propelled
the federal government to rescue other banks that were thought "too big to
fail." While the government had bailed out banks before, it was new and expensive for the government to rescue bank holding companies that had many assets
not insured by the FDIC.[12]

Economist Branko Milanovic argues that the economic crash of 2006 was
ultimately precipitated by inequality. Before the crash, the wealthiest Americans
needed places to invest vast sums, and this demand called into being a supply of
risky financial instruments. Middle- and low-income Americans had stagnant
real wages but could maintain or improve their quality of life with easy access
to credit, including subprime mortgages.

Debt as a share of income increased from 68.4 percent in 1983 to 118.7
percent in 2007 (see Figure 8.2). The net worth of minorities was much lower
than that of whites.[13]

When the economy collapsed, the media narrative emphasized the irre-
sponsibility of home-buyers in contracting such large levels of debt to begin
with. But as many economists have pointed out, existing levels of inequality
have made this level of borrowing not only necessary to maintain a reasonable

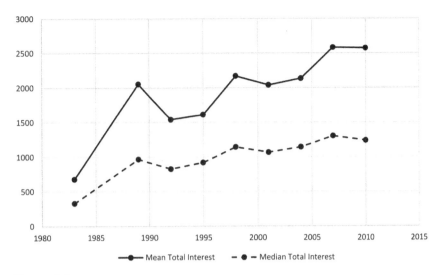

Figure 8.2
Mean and Median Household Consumption Debt Interest Payments, in 2011 Dollars, for Households with Debt. (Computed from Robert Scott and Steven Pressman, "Household Debt and Income Distribution," *Journal of Economic Issues* **vol. 47 no. 2 (June 2013): 323–331, at 328.)**

standard of living but also desirable from the perspective of wealthy people with money to lend. Although the Great Recession caused a contraction in the credit available to the bottom 95 percent of American income earners, shrinking the ratio of the debt they carried to their income, in the future the ratio of debt to income among poorer Americans is expected to increase.[14]

The Great Recession not only was caused by inequality but also had an unequal impact. Those at the bottom of the income distribution lost the most wealth in relative terms. The economy lost 3.5 percent of all jobs, the largest percentage loss of employment since 1945.[15] In 2011, the unemployment rate reached 9 percent, with 13.9 million people unemployed, not counting those who were underemployed or had left the labor force entirely out of despair. The first response of many firms was to cut the workforce and ask questions later, and as revenues shrank, public sector jobs at all levels were cut.[16]

Unemployment hurt some more than others; 15 percent of African Americans were unemployed, as contrasted with 8 percent of whites.[17] When discouraged workers who had left the labor force were included in the statistics for 2013, the 7.2 percent unemployment rate expanded to 13.6 percent. As the recession continued, the long-term unemployed had the most difficult time finding work, hampered by a stigma that unemployment meant unemployability. And those workers who managed to find jobs were relegated to contingent and part-time work, depriving them even of predictable work schedules.[18] The "reserve army of labor"—the underemployed or unemployed part of the labor force—has greatly grown, from about 5 million in the 1950s to around 30 million, making it always a buyers' market for employers.[19]

During the Great Depression, the government encouraged firms to avoid mass layoffs by reducing hours rather than jobs. During the Great Recession, the government exerted no such pressure. Although some economists called for an economic stimulus package on par with the New Deal, Republicans and most economists opposed the idea. They called for austerity instead, and President Barack Obama lacked the political capital to press the issue.[20] The Great Recession thus came and went with no significant steps taken to prevent inequality from causing another economic panic.

Many structural features of the modern American economy promote inequality. In his well-received book *Capital in the Twenty-First Century* (2013), economist Thomas Piketty argued that out-of-control executive compensation has caused much of the growth in inequality across Europe and in the United States. Executives are granted enormous salaries by boards of directors whom the CEOs themselves control, in a direct conflict of interest.[21] Executive compensation hides the real inequity in the share of compensation going to labor: "In 2002–2012 the bottom 90 percent of the population saw their average family income . . . drop by 11 percent, while those in the top .1 to .01 percent saw theirs rise by 30 percent." The top thousandth of workers saw their income rise by 76 percent.[22] Nor are there market norms that govern executive compensation. Political scientists Benjamin Page and Lawrence Jacobs conducted a number of public opinion surveys that bear this out. These show that while the average American is quite good at estimating how much people ranging from retail workers to surgeons earn, he or she underguesses executive compensation by a factor of almost 30. Americans polled guessed that the average corporate CEO earned $500,000 per year, when the actual average was around $14 million.[23]

Under the 2008 Troubled Assets Relief Program (TARP), federal dollars were used to bail out large firms and rescue banks that were "too big to fail." Despite this use of public money, financial institutions argued that no further regulations of Wall Street were necessary.[24] Large financial companies and automakers argued that to cut executives' cash pay to $500,000 a year—even though the vast majority of executive pay is not paid out in cash—would leave executives inappropriately cash-poor. Although the Dodd-Frank Act of 2010 gives shareholders an advisory "say on pay" for top salaries, this advice is not binding, nor are employees represented on boards of directors, as they are, for example, in Germany. As political scientist Sandra Suarez points out, CEOs of American companies are uniquely unembarrassed by compensation that far outstrips that of company heads in other countries. "During the period between 2000 and 2005, average worker pay stood at $36,136 compared to $9.2 million for the CEOs of the fifty largest publicly traded firms . . . in 2011, US CEOs in the largest 350 firms earned 209 times more than the typical worker."[25]

The wealthiest Americans insulate their assets from estate taxation through trusts and foundations whose records can be kept secret, thus evading the taxable moment in which it is easiest to calculate those assets. With the available records, economists have computed that the top 1 percent doubled its share of national income between the 1970s and the early 2000s, while the real income of lower- and middle-wage workers declined by 3 percent.[26] Political polarization in Congress favors keeping the status quo, which results in the protection of the assets and interests of the top 1 percent of earners, while measures that would lead to less inequality, like higher taxes or increases in the minimum wage, require the kind of bipartisan support that has been absent throughout the 2000s.[27] To the extent that anything has been gained from the top quintile by the other 80 percent of the population, it has been through home equity, but as the 2006 real estate crisis showed, this sort of paper wealth could be transitory.[28]

On the other end of the income spectrum, many workers today are paid at nor near a minimum wage that has lost 40 percent of its real value since the 1960s.[29] Had the minimum wage reflected the growth in the productivity of the American workforce, it would have been over $13 an hour by 2001.[30] Although polls show that most Americans favor an increase in the minimum wage, even if they believe that the market rather than government should set wage rates, the minimum wage has not been a legislative priority. Some of the largest and poorest-paying corporations—Walmart and fast food restaurants, for example—are subsidized by public programs that make up the difference for low-waged workers. Medicaid and the Supplemental Nutrition Assistance Program are two important examples.[31]

Poorly paid workers are in a double bind, since even these publicly funded programs are stigmatizing to those who qualify for them. Americans see work as a moral imperative and part of what makes them fit for citizenship, and many of the working poor take pride in differentiating themselves from those on public support (just as the poorest southern whites in the antebellum period took comfort in not being black). People whom sociologist Jennifer Sherman interviewed during the Great Recession preferred to live on Top Ramen, accept aid in kind from church food pantries, or borrow from relatives rather than accept transfer payments.[32]

DISSATISFACTION WITH THE STATUS QUO: OCCUPY WALL STREET

Although the government took few effective steps during the Great Recession to address American inequality and the resulting economic instability, the economic panic did produce dissent and discomfort with the status quo. On the left, disaffection with American inequality crystallized into the 2011 Occupy Wall Street movement, whose rhetoric pitted the top 1 percent of income-earners or wealth holders (the distinction seemed ambiguous) against the 99 percent with whom the movement's followers identified. Protesters occupied Zuccotti Park in Manhattan's Wall Street district and set up a campground and a "people's assembly." Later, Occupy movements sprouted up around the world.

Rhetorically, the Occupy movement had much in common with the egalitarian forebears described in previous chapters. As social critics had in the eighteenth century, Occupy protesters formulated a list of grievances, the "Declaration of the Occupation of New York City." Like their nineteenth-century progenitors, the protesters focused on the corporations: "corporations do not seek consent to extract wealth from the people and the Earth, and ... no true democracy is attainable when the process is determined by economic power."[33] They proposed an opposition between the rich and the poor:

> The Occupy Wall Street movement is not just demanding change. It is also transforming how we, the 99%, see ourselves. The same many of us felt when we couldn't find a job, pay down our debts, or keep our home is being replaced by a political awakening. Millions now recognize that we are not to blame for a weak economy, for a subprime mortgage meltdown, or for a tax system that favors the wealthy but bankrupts the government. The 99% are coming to see that we are collateral damage in an all-our effort by the super-rich to get even richer.[34]

Journalist Christopher Ketcham compared this rhetoric to that used by the Populists:

> There are ninety and nine who live and die
> In want, and hunger, and cold,
> That one may live in luxury
> And be wrapped in a silken fold.
> The ninety and nine in their hovel bare,
> The one in luxury with riches rare.[35]

Substantively, the Occupy movement pointed out that even though many Americans thought economic redistribution was un-American, tax policies since the 1970s had been redistributing money to the top 1 percent.[36]

Economist William K. Tabb noted that from 1973 to 2006, real wages grew by less than 1 percent, even while productivity increased by more than 80 percent.[37] Occupy protesters also resented changes in the banking system. Not only had banks grown so large that they were considered worthy of government bailouts, but also the suspension of the Glass-Steagall Act enabled banks to invest in ways that were in direct conflict with the interests of their depositors.[38]

The Occupy movement never gained much traction, for several reasons. First, it was impossible for Occupy protesters to pose a real alternative to capitalism without alienating the mainstream media and many Americans.[39] The impossibility, today, of really describing alternate economic arrangements without having them written off as "socialistic" testifies to the power of capital to silence other voices and to make change impossible by constricting the notion of alternatives.[40] Second, while the language and the tactics of the Occupy movement were promising, the movement was hindered by its lack of larger strategy. Some writers advocated for restructuring the banking system and reaffirming some of the limitations on banks that had been lifted in the 1980s in an attempt to return to community-centered banking. Others issued a vague call for tax restructuring, or job growth through the formation of local cooperative movements using environmentally sustainable practices.[41] English professor and Occupy participant Stephen Collis advocated expansion of public transit and free education and health care.[42] Some form of reviving collective bargaining, although perhaps not through a traditional union movement, was also suggested.[43] A slow movement overly focused on democratic process at the best of times, Occupy was open to being portrayed by the press as increasingly dirty, dangerous, unfocused, or even Marxist and laughable.[44] The Occupiers were so enamored of direct democracy that they celebrated divisions within the movement rather than making progress toward some common goal.[45] Nonetheless, the Occupy movement brought sustained public attention to the issue of inequality and the degree to which American politics had been captured by the wealthiest 1 percent. Awareness of the issue among young people arguably fueled Vermont Senator Bernie Sanders's popularity during the 2016 Democratic presidential primary.

DISSATISFACTION WITH THE STATUS QUO: THE TEA PARTY

A right-wing protest movement emerged a year before the Occupy movement. It was, in its own way, also a protest movement against inequality, but it defined the major issues differently. In 2009, Consumer News and Business Channel commentator Rick Santelli called for a "Tea Party" to resist the Obama administration's continuation of the Bush administration bank bailout. In the weeks that followed, Tea Party chapters were founded across the country, attracting mostly older, white, male participants who were generally nativist, authoritarian, and opposed to the policies of the nation's first African American president, particularly his talk of health care reform. By co-opting the name "Tea Party," the members of this movement linked themselves to an invented historical tradition, in which "real Americans" rejected statism to the greatest degree possible in favor of liberty from government intervention.[46] Tea Partiers called for small government (although not the elimination of programs like Medicare or Social Security that benefited many of them directly) and characterized recipients of government aid as undeserving.[47]

At first officially a grassroots movement, the Tea Party was quickly captured by large conservative funding organizations like Americans for Prosperity and FreedomWorks, and its focus shifted to the election of Republican candidates and away from symbolic protests. The 2010 midterm elections were disastrous for Democrats as a result.[48] After the 2010 midterm elections, the Tea Party remained significant as a Congressional caucus. By 2016, the Tea Party had moved the entire Republican Party to the right.[49] Republican presidential candidate Donald Trump addressed economic inequality through anti-immigrant stances, including the notion of a border wall to keep out migrant workers, and flirted with the idea of rejecting free trade. As previous chapters have shown, a political appeal to working people that exploits racial and ethnic divisions has been a tried-and-true American political strategy.

WHY INEQUALITY MATTERS

The Great Recession and the social unrest of the Occupy movement and the Tea Party show that inequality matters, but there are other reasons to pay attention to inequality as well. The first reason is permanence. Deindustrialization has removed good manufacturing jobs from the economy, leaving low-wage service jobs that notoriously pay poverty-level wages. Although repairing the nation's aging infrastructure might provide widespread employment at good wages, it has not been a priority, even in Great-Recession-linked stimulus packages.[50] Trade unions, which, despite their flaws (including sclerotic leadership and deep-seated racism and Cold War ideology) once provided a measure of job protection, pensions, and other benefits for their members, ebbed with deindustrialization and the rise of low-paid, insecure labor.[51] Trade globalization, it traditionally has been thought, lifts all boats, because even if well-paid manufacturing jobs are exported overseas, the price of goods and services becomes cheaper. This might have been true had the companies and individuals who benefited most from globalization been taxed, so that some of that gained wealth could have been redistributed to the net losers from globalization—but particularly in the United States, the political will for that kind of taxation just does not exist.[52]

Nobel Prize–winning economist Joseph Stieglitz argued that inequality harms the entire economy, decreasing demand, limiting growth, promoting a general sense of unfairness that makes workers unproductive, and sowing mistrust. But while individuals might see the theoretical virtues of a better distribution of income, no one wants to give up the perquisites of power that come with wealth. Moreover, in a capitalist system, while firms benefit from *other* firms paying their workers more, each individual firm has good prudential reasons to keep labor costs as low as possible.[53]

Inequality within a theoretically democratic republic not only has economic effects, it also has social and moral effects that undermine the commitment of both rich and poor to any version of the common weal. The percentage of Americans who believe that hard work makes the American dream accessible declined from 72 percent in 1997 to 62 percent in 2014. A majority of Americans of both parties say they believe that a few wealthy individuals have too much power.[54]

As Figure 8.3 shows, social mobility in the United States since the 1980s has been "sticky"—people who are born in the lowest economic quintile only have a 7.5 percent chance of reaching the highest quintile, but those born into the highest quintile have more than a 36 percent chance of remaining in the highest income quintile even as adults.

Upward mobility in the United States also compares unfavorably with other countries; the probability of rising from the lowest to the highest income quintile is 11.7 percent in Denmark and 13.3 percent in Canada.[55]

Tragically and dangerously, social and economic inequality have produced political inequality. Running for, and winning, political office today requires a personal fortune; more than 50 percent of members of Congress are millionaires.[56] Moreover, the equation of unlimited political spending with "free speech" has disadvantaged poor and middle-class Americans further. The *Citizens United* Supreme Court decision allows corporations or individuals to donate unlimited funds to political candidates through SuperPACs, political action committees that are not required to divulge their donors. *Citizens United* has been widely criticized, since the Supreme Court acted as

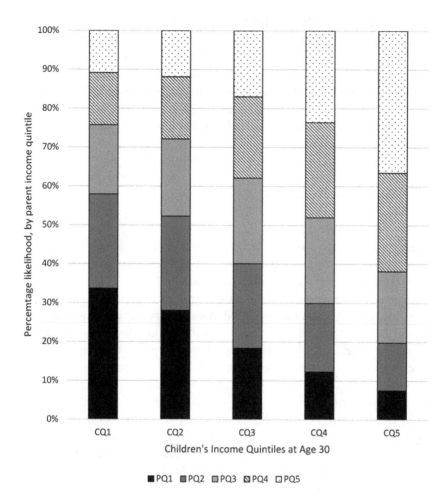

Figure 8.3
Quintile Transitions Over a Generation, 1980–2012. (Raj Chetty, Nathaniel
Hedren, Patrick Kline and Emmanuel Saez, "Where Is the Land of Opportunity:
The Geography of Intergenerational Mobility in the United States," *Quarterly
Journal of Economics* vol. 125 no. 4 (November 2014), 1577.)

though the interests of corporations were coextensive with those of the people who created them, despite the fact that gigantic, wealthy corporations
have much more power than do natural persons, and corporations generate
massive externalities (like pollution) that impact biological persons in unique
ways.[57] Predictably, given the possibility of unlimited individual donations, in
the 2016 election cycle, 400 individuals dominated campaign spending,
funneling money into anonymous SuperPACs.[58]

Voting is no substitute for being able to set the national agenda through donations. As professors of finance Donald J. Matthewson and Shelly Arsenault point out, not only does the United States have no labor party to advocate for the concerns of workers or the poor, Americans also see wealth as a proxy for hard work and moral success, so they are willing to choose candidates far removed from their own economic concerns. Voters are relegated to the position of spectators to this process, and the important act of voting is itself made more difficult with impediments like required picture identification at the polls, and voting on weekdays when many ordinary Americans need to be at work.[59]

As it has since the nation's founding, inequality has harsher impacts for minorities. Figure 8.4 shows trends in household income and wealth by race among non-Hispanic whites and non-Hispanic blacks. Mean incomes for whites and African Americans have risen faster than median incomes, showing that the top income earners outstrip the rest, but in all categories African American incomes continue to be lower.

Economic inequality along racial lines is supported by many white Americans' foundational belief that the "free market" is racially neutral. But as previous chapters have shown, this is just not the case. Even after the elimination of slavery, in places that had a high concentration of slaves in

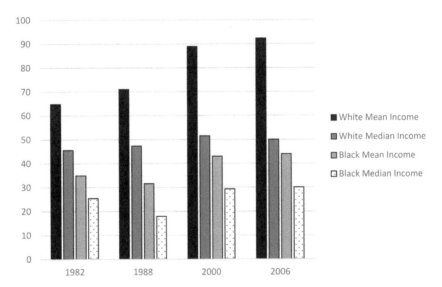

Figure 8.4
Incomes by Race, 1982–2006, in Thousands of Dollars. (Edward Nathan Wolff, "Recent Trends in Household Wealth, 1983–2009: The Irresistible Rise in Household Debt," *Review of Economics and Institutions* vol. 2 no. 1 (2011): 1–31, at 14.)

1860, place-based structural inequalities continued. African Americans in the formerly slaveholding South suffered from poor educational systems and from political marginalization that prevented them from achieving legislation for higher minimum wages and other economic reforms.[60] Slavery, share-cropping, housing segregation, white workers' job preferences for friends and relatives, the refusal of many banks to lend to black businesses, and denial of contractors' licenses to black artisans also complicated the "free market." Today, defenders of economic inequality claim that people who are unem-ployed or underemployed lack education or jobs skills or the motivation to show up to a job on a regular basis. Recognition that markets have never been race-neutral is crucial to support more systemic, redistributive changes.[61]

Economic inequality helps to perpetuate a criminal justice system that rele-gates hundreds of thousands of poor people, particularly young men of color, to second-class citizen status. Black unemployment rates are consistently higher than those of other groups. A 2012 study cited a 7.8 percent unemployment rate overall, and an official black unemployment rate of 14 percent, but this fig-ure rose to around 50 percent for young black men during the Great Reces-sion.[62] Cities and towns increase their revenues by fining the poor for petty offenses; in turn, those fines are collected by private companies that add their own transaction fees. When poor people cannot pay those fines, they are jailed for inability to pay, creating not only two-tiered justice system but even some-thing akin to the debtors' prisons of the eighteenth century.[63]

Those who have served time for felonies find insurmountable odds when they are released from prison. They do not qualify for public housing or other forms of federal aid, they cannot find a job in the private sector, and they may be unable to move around freely due to probation restrictions or lack of trans-portation or a driver's license. Many felons are reimprisoned because they cannot pay debts they owe for fines or for child support, or they end up back in the illegal sector of the economy due to the impossibility of finding work that pays well enough to discharge these fines.[64] Within a criminal justice sys-tem that discriminates against the poor, the lives of members of minority groups are at stake.[65] In 2015, the American public confronted case after case of differential justice. For example, Walter L. Scott was shot in the back while running away from a traffic stop in 2015. Scott was arrested 10 times during his life, mostly for drug charges and for contempt of court for not paying child support. He lost a good-paying job due to a 2003 imprisonment and then was never able to regain his footing, leading to more prison stays and thousands of additional dollars in unpaid child support.[66] While the police officer who shot Scott was charged with murder, such a charge was atypical, as other arrests or attempted arrests of black men and boys—Eric Garner,

Tamir Rice, Michael Brown, Freddie Gray—ended in death at the hands of the police. In none of the other cases was a murder charge levied. The confinement of African Americans in neighborhoods that have become increasingly segregated by both race and income helps people who do not live in those neighborhoods to blame the victims rather than to confront the fact that structural inequality is a contributing factor.

WHAT IS TO BE DONE? CHANGING THE DISCOURSE

Some historians and political philosophers, like Sean Wilentz and Michael Thompson, have tried to engage in public education on the topic of economic inequality. They have argued American history supports the idea that political equality requires some degree of economic and social independence. They call for bringing the notion of republicanism as it was viewed in the early republic back into the conversation.[67] That would not go far enough. As this book has shown, the history of the early republic was itself rife with inequality. Moreover, even leveling the playing field a little for political discourse would require a decision to override *Citizens' United* and to limit free speech to the speech of natural persons, rather than endowing owners and operators of corporations the right to speak twice. In contrast with the situation in the early republic, empowering women, younger voters, and people of color within the political system would, on average, force politicians to confront the problem of inequality, since empirical studies show that these groups are more likely to be egalitarian.

In addition to creating a more vibrant public political sphere, it is important to find new ways to talk about economic rights. It is difficult to claim a right against a multinational corporation. Rights claims are even more difficult to make when people do not see themselves as part of a collectivity. The twentieth century saw a successful campaign for rights-based economic justice by the elderly (during the 1930s), but other groups (such as welfare recipients) have been less successful. And in the long run, Americans are encouraged not to think of themselves as part of a collective that demands economic justice. As anthropologist Sally Engle Merry trenchantly puts it,

> The provision of adequate food, clothing, housing, and health care—core socioeconomic rights—is not simply the outcome of government efforts but requires a vast array of arrangements by states, corporations, and civil society. They depend on collective action and a consciousness that the well-being of a society means the well-being of all its members. This consciousness has been lost under

the sway of neoliberalism and ideas of responsibilization; rights frameworks do not bring it back.[68]

Steve Fraser argues that nineteenth-century revolts against industrial capitalism had their origins "in a realm before money and looked for gratification in a realm beyond money," suggesting that only by recognizing that "free market capitalism" harms politics, the family, and racial justice will we be able to push back against inequality.[69]

The nature of the public discourse until recently has also made it difficult to discuss inequality. Conservatives can endorse both equality of opportunity and capitalism without seeing conflict. Those who argue that equality of opportunity does not in fact exist have found less institutional support for their opinions and no alternate formulations of how things could be different. Polls show that supporters of the welfare state are less likely to express opinions about it in public opinion polls than are opponents of the welfare state. Although the impact of this bias is slight, it works in the same direction as other forms of political inequality, helping to marginalize the same voices.[70] Political scientists Stanley Feldman and John Zaller have found that opponents of government programs to promote equality find it easy to discuss big ideas like "individualism" and "opportunity." In contrast, proponents of social welfare spending refer to particular helpful or popular programs, or to the general notion that certain groups do not actually have equal opportunities.[71]

Because Americans do not know how to talk about inequality, social amenities widely available outside the United States, including guaranteed health care and parental leave, have not been secured. Over the past few decades, even investment in aspects of our common life once considered crucial for advancement of the economy—research universities, for example, and infrastructure—have been allowed to go begging. Fears about the slowing of the economy in general are met with calls for the education of the workforce, as though that, rather than increasing consumer demand, will guarantee that every individual somehow has a high-paying job. In fact, automation has caused the hollowing out of the wage structure; the highest-paid people continue to be highly paid, while middle- and low-skilled workers conduct a race to the bottom for lower-skilled jobs. Without some degree of redistribution and the provision of more public goods "such as food, housing, education and health care that are necessary for a modern life to go well," there is no guarantee that economic output will have any relationship to well-being.[72]

The path of the Patient Protection and Affordable Care Act (ACA, 2010) provides a good illustration of the problems caused by divergent partisan ideologies and powerful framing narratives. Like public education, public health programs are essential to our notion of equality of opportunity. It is often said that medical care in the United States is "the best in the world," but it is completely out of reach of those without medical insurance. In 2009, people living in the poorest counties in the United States had life expectancies that were, on average, six years less than those of their counterparts in the nation's wealthiest counties; life expectances in the former were similar to those in Mexico, while those in the latter were comparable with Japan.[73]

Instead of favoring a single-payer program like Britain's National Health Service or Medicare, President Barack Obama embraced a Republican-designed plan (one which Governor Mitt Romney had actually implemented in Massachusetts). Insurance exchanges would enable insurers to compete for participants in a national market, and participants (individuals without employer-provided insurance, and small businesses) would gain the advantages offered by a larger insurance market.[74] The basic plan for Obamacare had been mooted by the economist James Tobin as early as 1966:

> to make sure that adequate insurance coverage, either from government or from private insurers, is universally available for purchase; b) to require of everyone evidence of such coverage, or of equivalent financial protection for medical contingencies (just as automobile owners must prove financial responsibility) and c) to provide sufficient income to the indigent to enable them to pursue the required insurance coverage ...[75]

But what started as a Republican idea barely became law, passing the House and Senate without a single Republican vote. Due to the Democrats' loss of Massachusetts Senator Ted Kennedy's Senate seat, its sponsors sent the bill through a reconciliation process between the House and the Senate rather than take a chance that it would pass with significant changes. Then, as soon as the ACA became law, Republicans turned against it. Some states refused to create the competitive insurance exchanges, hoping instead that the Supreme Court would find Obamacare unconstitutional. States with Republican governments refused to expand Medicaid as the ACA intended, thus leaving some of their poorest residents with no health care. Many people who could have benefited from the availability of health insurance under Obamacare, or from subsidies based on income, made the economically irrational decision to reject it rather than to embrace a conflict with economic individualism. The rise of the Tea Party, with its polarizing rhetoric about federal overreach, transformed what should have been a popular policy initiative into a nonstarter. By January 2016, the House of Representatives had taken over 60 votes attempting to repeal the Affordable Care Act.[76]

Despite all this, it is possible that Obamacare, as feeble a step in the right direction as it may be, will contribute to an equalization of life chances in the United States that has been going on for more than 100 years. Widespread childhood vaccination programs, clean air and water, sewer systems, and other amenities common to developed countries have been acceptable projects for American municipalities because they serve everyone; infectious disease does not stop at the boundary line of segregated neighborhoods.

WHAT IS TO BE DONE? TANGIBLE SOLUTIONS

Historically, education has been held out as the great equalizer. When they were founded, American public schools were supposed to equip every child with the skills needed for employment and for citizenship. But the opportunity was fleeting. The *Brown* decision, which called for desegregation of schools, overlapped with housing segregation and the flight of better-off families from cities to suburbs. Prekindergarten programs demonstrably help poor children, but providing them is expensive.[77] Urban schools were left catering largely to underprepared students from challenging social environments, and court decisions preventing busing urban students to outlying suburbs, and vice versa, narrow the options.[78] In many urban areas, schools are more racially segregated now than they have ever been.[79]

President Obama suggested in 2015 that free community college tuition for all Americans might help address the inequality gap.[80] Higher education is touted as the surest road to a higher income than one's parents, but federal government studies now show that the greatest income benefits of a college education accrue to students who can afford to attend the highest tier of schools. At some state schools and at almost all for-profit schools, the average student fails to realize the supposed university income premium.[81] An expansion of educational opportunity therefore may not necessarily pay off in more equal incomes, as "the income advantages of inherited wealth, inter-vivos transfers, cultural capital and social connections, independent of education," help to estrange the richest and the poorest.[82] But even if it were the case that schools could fix inequality by producing a well-educated workforce, it is not clear that the postindustrial jobs that exist today—or that will exist in the future—will bear it out.

Another tangible possibility is for the federal government to resurrect the notion of becoming the employer of last resort, as Franklin Roosevelt had suggested in 1944, or as the Humphrey-Hawkins Bill of 1978 purported to do. As economist Helen Lachs Ginsburg has pointed out, our economy is shaped by human choices as much as it is by the "invisible hand." It would be possible, for example, for the government to prioritize full employment—not defined simply as some unemployment figure less than 5 percent but rather as the human right of each person to have work. It is difficult to move in that direction because people have been educated to believe that market efficiency ought to be the ultimate value of the economy, despite the fact that even perfectly efficient markets say nothing about distribution of incomes or about standards of living.[83]

The last few years have seen an active philosophical debate about the desirability of a basic income guarantee, a variation on the theme of the "negative income tax" attempted by Nixon in his Family Assistance Plan. There are several ways to frame a basic income guarantee, and one of those possible frames is that it enhances freedom.[84] Over the course of several generations, an ideally functioning free market will produce winners and losers, sometimes just due to moral bad luck. In those cases, people who are unable to meet their basic needs may end up accepting significant measures of personal coercion because they have no other choice. A universal basic income guarantee is a way to enable those people to opt out of coercive relationships without the stigma produced—or dependency supposedly produced—by other kinds of means-tested welfare.[85] A basic income guarantee could also reward activities like volunteering or caregiving that are not now rewarded by the market. A basic income guarantee is particularly crucial if the prediction that automation will produce mass unemployment in the future turns out to be correct.[86]

More modest than a basic income guarantee would be an expansion of the EITC, and equity in the payment of the tax credit to both custodial and non-custodial parents.[87] EITC expansion does not reach everyone, but it is politically practical; while the minimum wage has stagnated, the EITC has been expanded six times since 1975. As political scientist Larry Bartels explains, "tying the income subsidy to wages encourages work and sidesteps the association of traditional welfare programs with the 'undeserving poor' . . . this aspect of the program is reinforced by the designation of EITC as a 'tax credit,' despite the fact that most recipients have no income tax liability to offset."[88] Calling such transfers "earned income" credits makes them politically acceptable, in contrast to welfare.

Addressing American inequality also means addressing inequities in the legal system. Doing away with mandatory minimum sentencing might start to address incarceration rates and the long-term inequality that they bring for young male members of minority groups. Ron Haskins of the Brookings Institution also recommends a combination of programs to reduce teen birth rates, subsidize and facilitate marriage for poor minority couples, and help released prisoners find gainful employment.[89] Communication Studies professor Martin Carcasson suggests that the model for future beneficial change lies on the micro scale. For example, the living wage movement targets the minimum wage in individual cities, and "the devolution of welfare programs to the state level betters allows for grass-roots movements to make an impact and gives activists a critical sense of efficacy."[90] Borrowing from a vibrant tradition in Latin America, some communities in the United States are experimenting with programs like time banking, which enable participants simultaneously to build a sense of solidarity and to trade services with each other; community supported agriculture programs; or community producers' or consumers' cooperatives.[91]

Although it would do the most to reduce inequality, raising taxes on the nation's wealthiest seems the least likely tangible scenario. Studies show that even as Americans express discontentment with rising inequality, they are squeamish about the government expanding taxes—even taxes on the wealthy—or establishing admittedly redistributive government programs.[92] It is difficult to communicate to people that economic inequality undermines democracy itself, and that, at such a point, "reasonable envy" has to come into play to restore the political balance.[93] But Republicans' willingness to threaten government shutdown or even to countenance possible default over the debt ceiling shows that in general, negotiations about economic issues linked to equality—education, infrastructure, research and development, and health care—are off the table.[94]

Finally, the inequality problem might be partially addressed by regulating labor markets through higher minimum wages or even maximum wages. Few studies have measured voters' willingness to consider setting executive pay ceilings, but the studies that have been done show that Americans believe that government interference ruins markets. Even the current debate about whether it is just to raise the minimum wage to a "living wage" level betrays the fact that many Americans do not support an income floor. But again, framing appears to have powerful effects in determining how people perceive policies. Even though it constitutes market regulation, immigration restriction is seen as a positive step by many who would not otherwise countenance interference in labor markets.[95] Scholars and politicians who seek to confront economic inequality need to reframe their opponents' proposals as well as their own.

The preceding chapters have shown that almost without exception, the United States has advertised itself as a land of opportunity since its founding and then reneged on that promise. During the first 80 years of the nation's history, the nation depended on slavery in order to prosper. After the Civil War, as freed slaves graduated to the only marginally better status of sharecroppers, immigrant workers suffered the worst excesses of unregulated corporatism. The quiet critique of economic inequality that ran through the nineteenth century became louder in the twentieth, as the Progressives recognized that inequality threatened political participation; it became loudest during the Depression, forcing the government in the direction of the minimum wage, legal unionism, and Social Security.

World War II and the immediate postwar period saw some of the widest shared prosperity—not coincidentally, with the highest tax rates on the wealthiest Americans and plenty of government spending. But even during the 1950s and 1960s, hiring discrimination, truncated educational opportunities, residential redlining, and exploitation of resource-rich but poverty-stricken areas ensured that the United States still contained two nations, the rich and the poor.

As the United States entered a postindustrial era under the pressure of globalization, many of the high-paying jobs held by manual workers disappeared, only to be replaced by poorly paid and even worse-esteemed service jobs. And the ideological triumph of Reaganomics divided working people along political lines, along racial lines, and between those who managed to remain employed and those who could not find jobs. While we had our collective backs turned, distracted by the Internet bubble of the 1990s, the War on Terror, and the Great Recession, inequality has reached a dismal point not seen since the 1920s.

Americans need to learn how to think critically about the messages that reach them about the dangers of inequality. The notions that businessmen are heroes, and that the only worthwhile freedom is the freedom to make untrammeled fortunes, are very American myths that are hard to counter (particularly since alternative analyses of the economy were pushed aside by Cold War politics). The situation is worsened because Americans are largely credulous when it comes to political messaging, consistently falling for what historian Steven Fraser calls "populist plutocracy."[96] Opinion polls show that many people believe inequality makes America great; Americans surveyed about the best possible social organization consistently prefer inegalitarian to egalitarian distributions of income, although their preferred distributions are more equal than those that presently occur.[97] Occasionally the blinds are drawn up, as when presidential candidate Mitt Romney in the 2012 election referred to 47 percent of the electorate as social parasites. But for the most part, Americans are content to ignore class issues in pursuit of consumerism and individual choice. The notion that we should have a measure of economic solidarity, or enjoy some certain standard of living because we are Americans, does not resonate the way it does in some other countries. The concept that individuals get the outcomes they deserve remains strong.[98]

During the last great spike in American inequality, at the time of the "second industrial revolution," Theodore Roosevelt sketched out the ways in which government activity might counteract monopolies and reasonably regulate the economy. But although both Franklin Delano Roosevelt and Lyndon Johnson created programs that expanded the role of government, they did so almost apologetically, with an emphasis on as much local control as possible. As health care advocate Robert Kraig has pointed out, the doctrinaire refusal to consider any government solution as worthwhile deprives us of any way to move forward with common purpose.[99] Americans tend to forget that we are the government, and that antigovernment rhetoric hurts us.

In 1845, when Benjamin Disraeli lamented that Britain had become two nations, the rich and the poor, he had a solution in mind. Disraeli asked that the wealthy acknowledge that they had become rich by through the toil of their workers. In return, it was their responsibility of the rich to provide those workers with a reasonable standard of living. He tried to energize young people into a social movement: "We live in an age when to be young and to be indifferent can be no longer synonymous. We must prepare for the coming hour. The claims of the Future are represented by suffering millions; and the Youth of a Nation are the trustees of Posterity."[100] In the short run, Disraeli's critique produced little tangible change, but he drew attention to the problem, and over 150 years later, the safety net for which he advocated exists. While inequality has been a central feature of U.S. history since its founding, raising awareness of this long history will perhaps be a first step in creating change.

Notes

INTRODUCTION

1. Benjamin Disraeli, *Sybil: Or the Two Nations* (Aylesbury: Penguin Books, 1981), first published 1845, 96.

2. James L. Huston, *Securing the Fruits of Labor: The American Concept of Wealth Distribution, 1765–1900* (Baton Rouge: Louisiana State University Press, 1998), 383–384.

3. Robert Scott and Steven Pressman, "Household Debt and Income Distribution," *Journal of Economic Issues* vol. 47 no. 2 (June 2013): 323–331.

4. "Editorial Perspectives: On the Self-Interest of the Capitalist Ruling Class," *Science and Society* vol. 77 no. 1 (2013): 3–9.

5. Thomas Piketty and Emanuel Saez, "How Progressive Is the U.S. Federal Tax System? A Historical and International Perspective," *Journal of Economic Perspectives* vol. 21 no. 1 (Winter 2007): 3–24; Bret N. Bogenschneider, "Income Inequality and Regressive Taxation in the United States," *Interdisciplinary Journal of Economics and Business Law* vol. 4 no. 3 (2015): 8–28, at 12.

6. Jennifer Hoschchild, *What's Fair? American Beliefs about Distributive Justice* (Cambridge, MA: Harvard University Press, 1981), 4–5, 13.

7. Scott and Pressman, "Household Debt and Income Distribution," 325.

8. Zachary Roth, "Tea Party Congressman Suggests that Only Property Owners Should Vote," MSNBC, May 21, 2014, at http://www.msnbc.com/msnbc/tea-party-congressman-ted-yoho-voting-suggestion, accessed October 1, 2014; Steve Benen, "Political Animal," *Washington Monthly*, November 30, 2010, at http://www.washingtonmonthly.com/archives/individual/2010_11/026860.php, accessed October 1, 2014.

9. Janny Scott and David Leonhardt, "Shadowy Lines that Still Divide," *New York Times*, May 15, 2005, at http://www.nytimes.com/2005/05/15/us/class/shadowy-lines-that-still-divide.html, accessed August 31, 2015.

10. See, for example, Michael J. Thompson, *The Politics of Inequality* (New York: Columbia University Press, 2007).

11. Thomas Piketty, *Capital in the Twenty-First Century* (Cambridge, MA: Harvard University Press, 2014); Laura Bear, "Capital and Time: Uncertainty and Qualitative Measures of Inequality," *British Journal of Sociology* vol. 65 no. 4 (2014): 639–649; Steve Fraser, *The Age of Acquiescence: The Life and Death of American Resistance to Organized Wealth and Power* (New York: Little, Brown and Co., 2015).

12. Jim Tankersley, "The Thing Bernie Sanders Says about Inequality that No Other Candidate Will Touch," *Washington Post*, July 13, 2015, available online at http://www.washingtonpost.com/blogs/wonkblog/wp/2015/07/13/what-bernie-sanders-is-willing-to-sacrifice-for-a-more-equal-society/, accessed July 17, 2015.

13. Leslie McCall, *The Undeserving Rich: American Beliefs about Inequality, Opportunity and Redistribution* (Cambridge, MA: Cambridge University Press, 2013), 48.

14. Huston, *Securing the Fruits of Labor*, xi–xxiv, 383.

15. Jason Long and Joseph Ferrie, "Intergenerational Occupational Mobility in Great Britain and the United States since 1850," *American Economic Review* vol. 103 no. 4 (2013): 1109–1137.

16. Branko Milanovic, *The Haves and Have-Nots: A Brief and Idiosyncratic History of Global Inequality* (New York: Basic Books, 2010), 30.

17. Carole Shammas, "A New Look at Long-Term Trends in Wealth Inequality in the United States," *American Historical Review* vol. 98 no. 2 (April 1993): 412–431. To be fair, Williamson and Lindert did acknowledge that if slaves were added to the group of wealth-holders while being kept as part of the property of their owners, measurable inequality would have been even worse in the antebellum period than economic historians' studies suggest. See Jeffrey Williamson and Peter Lindert, "Three Centuries of American Inequality" (Madison: Wisconsin University Institute on Research on Poverty, 1976), 80.

18. Erik Sherman, "America Is the Richest, and Most Unequal, Country," *Fortune*, September 30, 2015, available online at http://fortune.com/2015/09/30/america-wealth-inequality/, accessed April 2, 2016.

19. Shammas, "A New Look," 420.

20. Williamson and Lindert, "Three Centuries of American Inequality," 11, 15, 20.

21. Mark W. Frank, "Inequality and Growth in the United States: Evidence from a New State-Level Panel of Income Inequality Measures," *Economic Inquiry* vol. 47 no. 1 (2009): 55–68.

22. Simon Kuznets, "Economic Growth and Income Inequality," *American Economic Review* vol. 45 no. 1 (1955): 1–30.

23. Milanovic, *Haves and Have-Nots*, 91.

24. Williamson and Lindert, "Three Centuries of American Inequality," 56, 59; Jeffrey Williamson and Peter H. Lindert, *American Inequality: A Macroeconomic History* (New York: Academic Press, 1980), 258.

25. Williamson and Lindert, *American Inequality,* 8.

CHAPTER 1

1. On the classical civilizations and ideas of equality, see Thompson, *The Politics of Inequality,* 30–40.

2. The historiography of the revolutionary period, and the extent to which historians have gravitated away from a Beardian socioeconomic analysis of the revolution toward an ideological analysis, are ably chronicled in Alfred Young, "Introduction," in Alfred F. Young, ed., *Beyond the American Revolution* (DeKalb: Northern Indiana University Press, 1993), 3–24.

3. Gordon Wood, *The Radicalism of the American Revolution* (New York: Vintage Books, 1991), 7.

4. Young, "Afterword," in *Beyond the American Revolution,* 317–367.

5. Stanley N. Katz, "The Strange Birth and Unlikely History of Constitutional Equality," *Journal of American History* vol. 75 no. 3 (1988): 747–762.

6. Alan Kulikoff, "Inequality in Boston," *William and Mary Quarterly* vol. 28 no. 3 (July 1971): 375–412, at 409.

7. G. B. Warden, "Inequality and Instability in Eighteenth-Century Boston: A Reappraisal," *Journal of Interdisciplinary History* vol. 6 no. 4 (1976): 585–620.

8. Wood, *Radicalism of the American Revolution,* 21.

9. Huston, *Securing the Fruits of Labor,* 78.

10. Sean Wilentz, "America's Lost Egalitarian Tradition," *Daedalus* vol. 131 no. 1 (2002): 66–80.

11. Ronald Schultz, "A Class Society? The Nature of Inequality in Early America," in Carla Gardina Pestana and Sharon V. Salinger, eds. *Inequality in Early America* (Hanover: University Press of New England, 1999): 203–221, at 213.

12. John Murrin, "In the Land of the Free and the Home of the Slave, Maybe There was Room Even for Deference," *Journal of American History* vol. 85 no. 1 (1998): 86–91; Richard Bushman, *The Refinement of America: Persons, Houses, Cities* (New York: Vintage Books, 1993).

13. Guido Pezzarozzi, "Camouflaging Consumption and Colonial Mimicry: The Materiality of an Eighteenth- and Nineteenth-Century Nipmuc Household," *International Journal of Historical Archaeology* vol. 18 (2014): 146–174.

14. Andrew Shankman, *Crucible of American Democracy: The Struggle to Fuse Egalitarianism and Capitalism in Jeffersonian Pennsylvania* (Lawrence: University Press of Kansas, 2004), 16.

15. Wood, *Radicalism of the American Revolution,* 27, 75.

16. J. R. Pole, *The Pursuit of Equality in American Society* (Berkeley: University of California Press, 1978), 29.

17. Peter H. Wood, "Liberty Is Sweet: African-American Freedom Struggles in the Years before Independence," in Young, ed., *Beyond the American Revolution*, 149–184.

18. Alex Gourevitch, "William Manning and the Political Theory of the Dependent Classes," *Modern Intellectual History* vol. 9 no. 2 (2012): 331–360; Edmund Morgan, "Slavery and Freedom: The American Paradox," *Journal of American History* vol. 59 no. 1 (1972): 5–29.

19. Peter H. Wood, "Liberty Is Sweet," 169; Billy G. Smith, "Black Women Who Stole Themselves in Eighteenth-Century America," in Pestana and Salinger, eds., *Inequality in Early America*, 134–159.

20. Maya Jasanoff, *Liberty's Exiles: American Loyalists in the Revolutionary World* (New York: Alfred A. Knopf, 2012), 48–50.

21. Philip D. Morgan, "Rethinking Early American Slavery," in Pestana and Salinger, eds., *Inequality in Early America*, 239–291 at 248.

22. Trevor Burnard, "Slavery and the American Revolution," in Andrew Shankman, ed., *The World of the Revolutionary American Republic: Land, Labor and the Conflict for a Continent* (New York: Routledge Press, 2014), 54–76. See also Peter Onuf, "The Empire of Liberty: Land of the Free and Home of the Slave," in Shankman, ed., *Revolutionary American Republic*, 195–217, at 201.

23. David Brion Davis, "American Equality and Foreign Revolutions," *Journal of American History* vol. 76 no. 3 (December 1989): 730–752.

24. Morgan, "Rethinking Early American Slavery," 239–291.

25. Pole, *Pursuit of Equality*, 32.

26. Morgan, "Rethinking Early American Slavery," 253; Stanley L. Engelmann, "Some Considerations Relating to Property Rights in Man," *Journal of Economic History* vol. 33 no. 1 (1973): 43–65.

27. Williamson and Lindert, *American Inequality*, 37.

28. Morgan, "Rethinking Early American Slavery," 257.

29. Huston, *Securing the Fruits of Labor*, 65.

30. Alan Kulikoff, "Such Things Ought Not to Be: The American Revolution and the First Great National Depression," in Shankman, ed., *The World of the Revolutionary American Republic*, 134–164, 149.

31. Sean Wilentz and Michael Merrill, *The Key of Liberty: The Life and Democratic Writings of William Manning* (Cambridge: Harvard University Press, 1993), 22.

32. Monroe Stearns, *Shays' Rebellion* (New York: Franklin Watts, 1968), 24; Thomas Slaughter, *The Whiskey Rebellion: Frontier Epilogue to the American Revolution* (New York: Oxford University Press, 1986), 48.

33. Stearns, *Shays' Rebellion*, 58.

34. Ibid., 30.

35. Kulikoff, "Inequality in Boston," 411; Allan Kulikoff, "The Revolution, Capitalism, and the Formation of Yeoman Classes," in Young, ed., *Beyond the American Revolution*, 80–119.

36. James M. Greene, "Ethan Allan and Daniel Shays: Contrasting Models of Political Representation in the Early Republic," *Early American Literature* vol. 48 no. 1 (2013): 125–151.

37. Shankman, *Crucible of American Democracy*, 6–7.

38. William Marina, "Revolution and Social Change: The American Revolution as a People's War," *Literature of Liberty: A Review of Contemporary Liberal Thought* vol. 1 no. 2 (April/June 1978): 5–39.

39. Francis D. Cogliano, *Revolutionary America, 1763–1815: A Political History* (New York: Routledge, 2000), 128.

40. Melancton Smith, "An Address to the People of the State of New York Showing the Necessity of Making Amendments to the Constitution Proposed for the United States, previous to Its Adoption," in Paul Leicester Ford, ed., *Pamphlets on the Constitution of the United States* (New York: NP, 1888), 110.

41. Smith, "An Address to the People," 94.

42. Richard Henry Lee, "Observation Leading to a Fair Examination of the System of Government Proposed by the Late Convention," in Ford, ed., *Pamphlets on the Constitution of the United States*, 318, 321.

43. Noah Webster, "An Examination into the Leading Principles of the Federal Constitution," in Ford, ed., *Pamphlets on the Constitution of the United States*, 59.

44. Webster, "An Examination," 44.

45. Shankman, *Crucible of American Democracy*, 28; Wilentz and Merrill, *Key of Liberty*, 38.

46. Gourevitch, "William Manning," 341.

47. Wilentz and Merrill, *Key of Liberty*, 131.

48. Ibid., 139.

49. Gourevitch, "William Manning," 355, 360.

50. Wilentz and Merrill, *Key of Liberty*, 32.

51. Ibid., 83.

52. Cogliano, *Revolutionary America*, 141.

53. Shankman, *Crucible of American Democracy*, 42, 50.

54. Paul Gilje, *The Road to Mobocracy: Popular Disorder in New York City, 1763–1834* (Chapel Hill: University of North Carolina Press, 1987), 100.

55. Katz, "History of Constitutional Equality," 751; Young, "Afterword," 328; "Declaration of the Rights of Man," August 26, 1789, available online at http://avalon.law.yale.edu/18th_century/rightsof.asp, accessed May 24, 2016.

56. Shankman, *Crucible of American Democracy*, 55.

57. Slaughter, *The Whiskey Rebellion*, 64, 67.

58. Ibid., 212.

59. Alan Taylor, "Agrarian Independence: Northern Land Rioters after the Revolution," in Young, ed., *Beyond the American Revolution*, 221–245.

60. Richard J. Ellis, "Rival Visions of Equality in American Political Culture," *Review of Politics* (2001): 253–280.

61. On the general notion of a "stakeholder society," see Anne Alstott and Bruce Ackerman, *The Stakeholder Society* (New Haven, CT: Yale University Press, 2000).

62. See Karl Widerquist, *Independence, Propertylessness, and Basic Income* (New York: Palgrave Macmillan, 2013), 123.

63. Thomas Paine, *Agrarian Justice*, available online at http://xroads.virginia .edu/~hyper/Paine/agrarian.html, accessed May 24, 2016.

64. Gregory Claeys, "Paine's *Agrarian Justice* and the Secularization of Natural Jurisprudence," *Bulletin of the Society for the Study of Labour History* vol. 52 no. 3 (November 1987): 21–31.

65. Paine, *Agrarian Justice*.

66. Paine, *Agrarian Justice*.

67. George Henry Evans, "Man's Inalienable Right to Land," *Radical, in Continuation of the Working Man's Advocate*, April 1841, p. 1. On Paine's later career, see "Biographical Notice of Paine," *New-England Galaxy and United States Literary Advertiser*, September 16, 1825.

68. Thomas Jefferson, *Notes on the State of Virginia*, Query XIX, available online at http://xroads.virginia.edu/~hyper/hns/yoeman/qxix.html, accessed May 24, 2016.

69. Peter Onuf, "Empire of Liberty," 205.

70. Kulikoff, "The Revolution, Capitalism, and the Formation of Yeoman Classes," 105.

71. Jefferson, quoted in John F. Manley, "American Liberalism and the Democratic Dream: Transcending the American Dream," *Policy Studies Review* vol. 10 no. 1 (1990): 89–102.

72. Quoted in Peter H. Wood, "Liberty Is Sweet," 162.

73. Peter Onuf, "Empire of Liberty," 207.

74. J. M. Opal, "Natural Rights and National Greatness: Economic Ideology and Social Policy in the American States, 1780s–1820," in Shankman, ed., *The World of the Revolutionary American Republic*, 295–323, at 304.

75. Peter Onuf, "Empire of Liberty," 203.

76. Christina Snyder, "Native Nations in the Age of Revolution," in Shankman, ed., *The World of the Revolutionary American Republic*, 77–94; Kathleen DuVal, "Independence for Whom? South and Southwest," in Shankman, *World of the Revolutionary American Republic*, 97–116.

77. Huston, *Securing the Fruits of Labor*, 53.

78. Max Edling, "Consolidating a Revolutionary Republic," in Shankman, ed., *The World of the Revolutionary American Republic*, 165–194, at 179.

79. Alan Taylor, "The War of 1812 and the Struggle for a Continent," in Shankman, ed., *The World of the Revolutionary American Republic*, 246–267.

80. Lee Soltow, "Inequality amidst Abundance: Land Ownership in Early Nineteenth-Century Ohio," *Ohio History* vol. 88 no. 2 (1979): 133–151.

81. Reeve Huston, "Land Conflict and Policy, 1780–1841," in Shankman, ed., *The World of the Revolutionary American Republic*, 324–345.

82. Opal, "Natural Rights and National Greatness," 309.

83. Ibid., 316.

84. Christopher Clark, *The Roots of Rural Capitalism: Western Massachusetts, 1780–1860* (Ithaca: Cornell University Press, 1990), 26.

85. Ibid., 16.

86. William J. Rorabaugh, "I Thought I Should Liberate Myself from the Thraldom," in Young, ed., *Beyond the American Revolution*, 185–217.

87. Thomas Ingersoll, " 'Riches and Honors Were Rejected by Them as Fearsome Vomit,': The Fear of Leveling in New England," in Pestana and Salinger, eds., *Inequality in Early America*, 46–66.

CHAPTER 2

1. Edward Pessen, "The Beleaguered Myth of Antebellum Egalitarianism: Cliometrics and Surmise to the Rescue," *Social Science History* vol. 6 no. 1 (1982): 111–128.

2. Edward Baptist, *The Half Has Never Been Told: Slavery and the Making of American Capitalism* (New York: Basic Books, 2014), 324.

3. Ibid., 20, 94–147.

4. James L. Huston, *Securing the Fruits of Labor: The American Concept of Wealth Distribution, 1765–1900* (Baton Rouge: Louisiana State University Press, 1998), 107, 124.

5. Charles Sellers, *The Market Revolution: Jacksonian America, 1815–1846* (New York: Oxford University Press, 1994).

6. Michael R. Haines, "Growing Incomes, Shrinking People—Can Economic Development Be Hazardous to Your Health?" *Social Science History* vol. 28 no. 2 (2004): 249–270.

7. Richard Carwardine, "The Whig Interpretation of History: A Review Essay," *Journal of Southern History* vol. 7 no. 4 (2008): 927–940.

8. Haines, "Growing Incomes, Shrinking People," 256.

9. Baptist, *The Half Has Never Been Told*, 114.

10. Huston, *Securing the Fruits of Labor*, 213, 217.

11. Haines, "Growing Incomes, Shrinking People," 250.

12. Alexis De Tocqueville, *Democracy in America*, first published 1835, available online at http://xroads.virginia.edu/~hyper/detoc/toc_indx.html, accessed February 6, 2016.

13. Edward Pessen, "On a Recent Cliometric Attempt to Resurrect the Myth of Antebellum Egalitarianism," *Social Science History* vol. 3 no. 2 (1979): 208–227.

14. Jeffrey Williamson and Peter Lindert, *American Inequality: A Macroeconomic History* (New York: Academic Press, 1980), 143; although see Scott D. Grosse, "On the Alleged Antebellum Surge in Wage Differentials: A Critique of Williamson and Lindert," *Journal of Economic History* vol. 42 no. 2 (June 1982): 413–418, who accuses Williamson and Lindert of misinterpreting the wages series, which Grosse claims show no significant wage differentials.

15. Seth Rockman, *Scraping By: Wage Labor, Slavery, and Survival in Early Baltimore* (Baltimore, MD: Johns Hopkins University Press, 2009), 77; Peter Way,

Common Labor: Workers and the Digging of North American Canals, 1780–1860 (Baltimore, MD: Johns Hopkins University Press, 1993), 6.

16. Williamson and Lindert, *American Inequality*, 102.

17. Theodore Hershberg, "Free Blacks in Antebellum Philadelphia: A Study of Ex-Slaves, Freeborn, and Socioeconomic Decline," *Journal of Social History* vol. 5 no. 2 (1971): 183–209; Rockman, *Scraping By*, 41.

18. Michael B. Katz, *The Underclass Debate* (Princeton, CT: Princeton University Press, 1993), 7.

19. Katz, "History of Constitutional Equality," 752.

20. Huston, *Securing the Fruits of Labor*, 46, 228, 233.

21. Baptist, *Half Has Never Been Told*, 250, 256.

22. Huston, *Securing the Fruits of Labor*, 247, 251.

23. Paul Gilje, *Road to Mobocracy: Popular Disorder in New York City, 1763–1834* (Chapel Hill: University of North Carolina Press, 1987), 178, 189.

24. Ibid., 267.

25. Roger Streitmatter, "Origins of the American Labor Press," *Journalism History* vol. 25 no. 3 (1999): 99–106, at 101.

26. Ibid., 104.

27. Sean Wilentz, *Chants Democratic* (New York: Oxford University Press, 1984) 172–216; C. K. McFarland and Robert L. Thistlethwaite, "20 Years of a Successful Labor Paper: *The Working Man's Advocate*, 1829–49," *Journalism Quarterly* vol. 60 no. 1 (Spring 1983): 35–40.

28. Alfred Young, *The Shoemaker and the Tea Party: Memory and the American Revolution* (New York: Beacon Press, 2000), 147.

29. Joshua Greenberg, " 'Powerful—Very Powerful Is the Parental Feeling': Fatherhood, Domestic Politics, and the New York City Working Men's Party," *Early American Studies, An Interdisciplinary Journal* vol. 2 no. 1 (2004): 192–227.

30. Gilje, *Road to Mobocracy*, 141–2; David Grimsted, *American Mobbing, 1828–1861: Toward Civil War* (New York: Oxford University Press, 1998), 199–217.

31. Gilje, *Road to Mobocracy*, 147–170.

32. Amos Gilbert, "A Sketch of the Life of Thomas Skidmore," *The Free Enquirer*, April 6, 1834, p. 24.

33. On Skidmore, see also Huston, *Securing the Fruits of Labor*, 290–292; J. R. Pole, *The Pursuit of Equality in American History* (Berkeley: University of California Press, 1978), 127.

34. Thomas Skidmore, *The Rights of Man to Property!* (New York: Author, 1829), 29.

35. Ibid., 60.

36. Skidmore, *Rights of Man to Property!* 378. Christopher L. Tomlins, *Law, Labor and Ideology in the Early American Republic* (New York: Cambridge University Press, 1993), 308–312; Rockman, *Scraping By*, 242.

37. Skidmore, *Rights of Man to Property!*, 77–78.

38. Thomas Hobbes, *Leviathan* (1651), chapter 14 paragraph 8, available online at http://www.bartleby.com/34/5/14.html, accessed July 29, 2015.

39. Skidmore, *Rights of Man to Property!*, 42.

40. John Locke, *Second Treatise on Government*, chapter 5 section 27, available online at http://www.constitution.org/jl/2ndtr05.htm, accessed July 29, 2015.

41. Skidmore, *Rights of Man to Property!*, 237.

42. Ibid., 33.

43. Ibid., 44.

44. Ibid., 141.

45. Ibid., 139.

46. Ibid., 140.

47. Here Skidmore anticipates Karl Widerquist's contention that government provision of cash is superior to provision of resources because it is more easily convertible into the many different goods and services that individuals would choose. Karl Widerquist,*Independence, Propertylessness, and Basic Income: Freedom as the Power to Say No* (New York: Palgrave Macmillan, 2013), 99.

48. Skidmore, *Rights of Man to Property!*, 142.

49. Ibid., 115.

50. Michael Levy, "Liberal Equality and Inherited Wealth," *Political Theory* vol. 11 no. 4 (November 1983): 545–564.

51. Skidmore, *Rights of Man to Property!*, 105, 157.

52. Skidmore, *Rights of Man to Property!*, 259. Skidmore was prescient; modern philosophers consider families to be a source of inequality. See Veronique Munoz-Darde, "Is the Family to Be Abolished Then?" *Proceedings of the Aristotelian Society* 99 (1999): 37–56.

53. Greenberg, "The Parental Feeling," 205.

54. Skidmore, *Rights of Man to Property!*, 264.

55. Ibid., 59.

56. Ibid., 160.

57. Ibid., 17.

58. For Thompson's assessment of Skidmore's nonstatism, see Michael Thompson, *The Politics of Inequality: A Political History of the Idea of Economic Inequality in America* (New York: Columbia University Press, 2007), 96.

59. Margaret Malamud, *Ancient Rome and Modern America* (London: Wiley Blackwell, 2009), 48–60.

60. A., "A most unjust attack was made this morning in the Courier & Enquirer upon our Mechanics," *New-York Morning Herald*, February 9, 1830; "A New Proposal," *New York Sentinel and Working Man's Advocate*, July 14, 1830, 43; Alexander Ming and Thomas Skidmore to Robert Dale Owen in *Free Enquirer*, January 23, 1830, 31; "The Friend of Equal Rights," *Workingman's Advocate*, April 24, 1830, 26; "Equalization of Property," *Workingman's Advocate*, January 16, 1830, 12.

61. Huston, *Securing the Fruits of Labor*, 265.

62. Thompson, *Politics of Inequality*, 96.

63. Gilje, *Road to Mobocracy*, 221.

64. Wilentz, *Chants Democratic*, 189.

65. Pole, *Pursuit of Equality*, 129.

66. Greenberg, "The Parental Feeling," 204.

67. On the National Reform movement for free homesteads, see Jamie L. Bron-stein, *Land Reform and Working-Class Experience in Britain and the United States, 1800–1862* (Stanford, CA: Stanford University Press, 1999); Sean Wilentz, *Chants Democratic*, 335–343.

68. Huston, *Securing the Fruits of Labor*, 173.

69. Reeve Huston, "Land Conflict and Land Policy in the United States, 1785–1841," in Andrew Shankman, ed., *World of the Revolutionary American Republic* (New York: Routledge, 2014), 323–344, at 340.

70. Roger W. Hecht, "'Rouse, Ye Anti-Renters': Poetry and Politics in the Anti-Rent Press," *Hudson River Valley Review* vol. 28 no. 2 (Spring 2012): 1–22.

71. Reeve Huston, "The Parties and 'The People': The New York Anti-Rent Wars and the Contours of Jacksonian Politics," *Journal of the Early Republic* vol. 20 no. 2 (2000): 241–271.

72. Thomas Goebel, "The Political Economy of American Populism: From Jack-son to the New Deal," *Studies in American Political Development* vol. 11 no. 1 (1997): 109–148, at 115.

73. Pole, *Pursuit of Equality in American History*, 138.

74. Orestes Brownson, *The Labouring Classes: An Article from the Boston Quar-terly Review* (Boston: Benjamin Greene, 1840), 9, 12.

75. Ibid., 14, 21.

76. Ibid., 11.

77. Ibid., 22.

78. Ibid., 3.

79. Patrick Carey, "Christian Socialism in the Early Brownson," *Records of the American Catholic Historical Society of Pennsylvania* vol. 99 no. 1 (1988): 17–38.

80. Paul Johnson, *A Shopkeeper's Millennium: Society and Revivals in Rochester, New York, 1815–1837* (New York: Hill and Wang, 2004); Randall Ballmer, "An End to Unjust Inequality in the World," *Church History and Religious Culture* vol. 94 no. 4 (2014): 505–530.

81. Kirsten E. Wood, "Broken Reeds and Competent Farmers: Slaveholding Wid-ows in the Southeastern United States, 1783–1861," *Journal of Women's History* vol. 13 no. 2 (2001): 34–57, at 47.

82. Jeanne Boydston, *Home and Work: Housework, Wage and the Ideology of Labor in the Early Republic* (New York: Oxford University Press, 1990); Christine Stansell, *City of Women: Sex and Class in New York, 1789–1860* (New York: Alfred A. Knopf, 1986); Rockman, *Scraping By*, 185–193.

83. Rockman, *Scraping By*, 140, 156.

84. Wood, "Broken Reeds," at 48.

85. Dianne Avery, "The Daughters of Job: Property Rights and Women's Lives in Mid-Nineteenth-Century Massachusetts," *Law and History Review* vol. 10 no. 2 (1992): 323–357.

86. Norma Basch, "Equity vs. Equality: Emerging Concepts of Women's Political Status in the Age of Jackson," *Journal of the Early Republic* vol. 3 no. 3 (1983): 297–318.

87. Rowland Berthoff, "Conventional Mentality: Free Blacks, Women, and Business Corporations as Unequal Persons, 1820–1870," *Journal of American History* vol. 76 no. 3 (1989): 753–784.

88. Thomas Dublin, *Women at Work* (New York: Columbia University Press, 1979), 128–130.

89. Berthoff, "Conventional Mentality," 763, 773, 777.

90. Baptist, *Half Has Never Been Told*, 179.

91. Damian Alan Pargas, " 'Various Means of Providing for Their Own Tables': Comparing the Slave Family Economies in the Antebellum South," *American Nineteenth-Century History* vol. 7 no. 3 (September 2006): 361–387.

92. Baptist, *Half Has Never Been Told*, 113, 130, 410.

93. Pessen, "On a Recent Cliometric Attempt," 218.

94. Pargas, "Their Own Tables," 364, 379.

95. Peter A. Coclanis and Stanley Engerman, "Would Slavery Have Survived without the Civil War? Economic Factors in the American South during the Antebellum and Postbellum Eras," *Southern Cultures* vol. 19 no. 2 (Summer 2013): 66–90.

96. Chad Morgan, "Progressive Slaveholders: Planters, Intellectuals, and Georgia's Antebellum Economic Development," *Georgia Historical Quarterly* vol. 86 no. 3 (2002): 398–422.

97. Steven Hahn, "The 'Unmaking' of the Southern Yeomanry: The Transformation of the Georgia Upcountry, 1860–1890," in Hahn and Jonathan Prude, eds., *The Countryside in the Age of Capitalist Transformation* (Chapel Hill, NC: University of North Carolina Press, 1985), 179–204.

98. Patrick Wolfe, "Race and Citizenship," *OAH Magazine of History* vol. 18 no. 5 (October 2004): 66–71.

99. Thomas R. Dew, "Review of the Debate in the Virginia Legislature," in Eric L. McKittrick, ed., *Slavery Defended: The Views of the Old South* (Englewood Cliffs, NJ: Prentice-Hall, 1963), 31.

100. John Calhoun, "Disquisition on Government," in McKittrick, ed., *Slavery Defended*, 10–11.

101. John C. Calhoun, "Speech on the Importance of Domestic Slavery," in McKittrick, ed., *Slavery Defended*, 19.

102. George Fitzhugh, *Sociology for the South*, reprinted in McKittrick, ed., *Slavery Defended*, 37–8, 45; Jeremy J. Tewell, "A Difference of Complexion: George Fitzhugh and the Birth of the Republican Party," *Historian* vol. 73 no. 2 (2011): 235–254.

103. Robert Loewenberg, "John Locke and the Antebellum Defense of Slavery," *Political Theory* vol. 13 no. 2 (1985): 266–291; George Fitzhugh, *Cannibals All!* (Cambridge, MA: Harvard University Press, 1960), first published 1857, 235–236.

104. Jeremy J. Tewell, "A Difference of Complexion: George Fitzhugh and the Birth of the Republican Party," *Historian* vol. 73 no. 2 (2011): 223, 253–254.

105. Peter Kolchin, "In Defense of Servitude: American Proslavery and Russian Pro-Serfdom Arguments, 1760–1860," *American Historical Review* vol. 85 no. 4 (1980): 809–827.

106. Baptist, *Half Has Never Been Told*, 329, 346.

107. Wilentz, "America's Lost Egalitarian Tradition," 75; Huston, *Securing the Fruits of Labor*, 327.

108. Although as Tyler Anbinder notes, poorer draftees had additional options, including failing to report and risking arrest, or claiming medical exemptions. See "Which Poor Man's Fight? Immigrants and the Federal Conscription of 1863," *Civil War History* vol. 52 no. 4 (2006): 344–372.

109. Iver Bernstein, *The New York City Draft Riots* (New York: Oxford University Press, 1990).

110. Peter Carlson, "Abraham Lincoln Meets Frederick Douglass," *American History* vol. 45 no. 6 (2011): 28–29.

CHAPTER 3

1. Huston, *Securing the Fruits of Labor*, 328; Pole, *Pursuit of Equality*, 201; Roger Ransom, "Reconstructing Reconstruction: Options and Limitations to Federal Policies on Land Distribution in 1866–67," *Civil War History* vol. 51 no. 4 (2005): 364–377, at 368.

2. Paul Cimbala, "The Freedmen's Bureau, The Freedmen, and Sherman's Grant in Reconstruction Georgia, 1865–1867," *Journal of Southern History* vol. 55 no. 4 (1989): 597–632.

3. Ransom, "Reconstructing Reconstruction," 372.

4. William Toll, "Free Men, Freedmen, and Race: Black Social Theory in the Gilded Age," *Journal of Southern History* vol. 44 no. 4 (1978): 571–596.

5. Melinda C. Miller, "Land and Racial Wealth Inequality," *American Economic Review, Papers and Proceedings* vol. 101 no. 3 (2011): 371–376.

6. Huston, *Securing the Fruits of Labor*, 331, 336.

7. Stanley N. Katz, "The Strange Birth and Unlikely History of Constitutional Equality," *Journal of American History* vol. 75 no. 3 (Dec. 1988): 747–764, at 756.

8. Jonathan Lurie, "One Hundred and Twenty-Five Years after *Slaughterhouse*: Where's the Beef?" *Journal of Supreme Court History* vol. 24 no. 3 (2011): 269–281.

9. *Santa Clara County v. Southern Pacific Railroad Company* 118 US 394, decided May 10, 1886, available online at https://supreme.justia.com/cases/federal/us/118/394/case.html, accessed April 7, 2016.

10. Ciara Torres-Spelliscy, "The History of Corporate Personhood," *Brennan Center for Justice*, April 7, 2014, available online at https://www.brennancenter.org/blog/hobby-lobby-argument, accessed April 7, 2016.

11. Jacqueline Jones, "Southern Diaspora: Roots of the Northern 'Underclass,' " in Michael B. Katz, ed., *The Underclass Debate* (Princeton, NJ: Princeton University Press, 1993), 29.

12. James L. Huston, "An Alternative to the Tragic Era: Applying the Virtues of Bureaucracy to the Reconstruction Dilemma," *Civil War History* vol. 51 no. 4 (2005): 403–415, at 406.

13. Huston, "An Alternative to the Tragic Era," 408, 413.

14. W. F. Brundage, ed., *Up from Slavery: A Brief History with Documents* (New York: Bedford Books, 2002), 9.

15. Eric Rauschway, *Blessed among Nations* (New York: Hill and Wang, 2006), 58–59, 68.

16. Steve Fraser, *The Age of Acquiescence: The Life and Death of American Resistance to Organized Wealth and Power* (New York: Little, Brown and Co., 2015), 57.

17. Ibid., 63.

18. Rauschway, *Blessed among Nations*, 99.

19. Katz, *The Underclass Debate*, 10; Fraser, *Age of Acquiescence*, 57.

20. Scott Reynolds Nelson, "A Storm of Cheap Goods: New American Commodities and the Panic of 1873," *Journal of the Gilded Age and Progressive Era* vol. 10 no. 4 (2011) 447–453.

21. Scott Reynolds Nelson, "A Financial Crisis in Prints and Cartoons," *Journal of the Gilded Age and Progressive Era* vol. 10 no. 4 (2011): 425–433; Nicolas Barreyre, "The Politics of Economic Crises: The Panic of 1873, the End of Reconstruction, and the Realignment of American Politics," *Journal of the Gilded Age and Progressive Era* vol. 10 no. 4 (2011): 403–423.

22. Toby Higbie, "Crossing Class Boundaries: Tramp Ethnographers and Narratives of Class," *Social Science History* vol. 21 no. 4 (Winter 1997): 559–592, at 573.

23. Fraser, *Age of Acquiescence*, 117–124.

24. Mark Aldrich, *Death Rode the Rails: American Railroad Accidents and Safety, 1828–1965* (Baltimore, MD: Johns Hopkins University Press, 2007), 103.

25. Jessica Piper, "The Great Railroad Strike of 1877: A Catalyst for the American Labor Movement," *The History Teacher* vol. 47 no. 1 (2013): 93–110; Gerald G. Eggert, "Gunfire and Brickbats: The Great Railway Strike of 1877," *American History Illustrated* vol. 16 no. 2 (1981): 16–25; Brian Luskey, "Riot and Respectability: The Shifting Terrain of Class Language and Status in Baltimore during the Great Strike of 1877," *American Nineteenth-Century History* vol. 4 no. 3 (2003): 61–96.

26. Richard White, *Railroaded: The Transcontinentals and the Making of Modern America* (New York: W.W. Norton and Co., 2011), 334.

27. Thomas Goebel, "The Political Economy of American Populism from Jackson to the New Deal," *Studies in American Political* Development vol. 11 no. 1 (1997), 109–148, at 132.

28. White, *Railroaded*, 289; Richard Oestreicher, "A Note on Knights of Labor Membership Statistics," *Labor History* vol. 25 no. 1 (1984): 102–108.

29. Kenneth Kann, "The Knights of Labor and the Southern Black Worker," *Labor History* vol. 18 no 1 (1977): 49–70.

30. Pole, *Pursuit of Equality*, 207; White, *Railroaded*, 301.

31. Robert E. Weir, "A Fragile Alliance: Henry George and the Knights of Labor," *American Journal of Economics and Sociology* vol. 56 no. 4 (October 1997): 421–439, at 430.

32. White, *Railroaded*, 342, 343; Oestreicher, "A Note on Knights of Labor Membership Statistics," 106.

33. Helga Kristin Hallgrimsdottir and Cecelia Benoit, "From Wage Slaves to Wage Workers: Cultural Opportunity Structures and the Evolution of the Wage Demands of the Knights of Labor and the American Federation of Labor, 1880–1900," *Social Forces* vol. 85 no. 3 (March 2007): 1393–1411.

34. Julie Greene, *Pure and Simple Politics: The American Federation of Labor and Political Activism, 1881–1917* (Cambridge, UK: Cambridge University Press, 1999), 21–27.

35. See Jefferson Cowie and Nick Salvatore, "The Long Exception: Rethinking the Place of the New Deal in American History," *International Labor and Working-Class History* No. 74 (Fall 2008): 3–32, at 6–7.

36. Rauschway, *Blessed among Nations*, 90.

37. White, *Railroaded*, 16, 24, 35, 87, 96.

38. Ibid., 160.

39. Rauschway, *Blessed among Nations*, 52, 77.

40. Goebel, "Political Economy of American Populism," 129.

41. Robert C. McMath Jr., "Sandy Land and Hogs in Timber: (Agri)Cultural Origins of the Farmers' Alliance in Texas," in Steven Hahn and Jonathan Prude, eds. *The Countryside in the Age of Capitalist Transformation* (Chapel Hill: University of North Carolina Press, 1985): 205–229; Matthew Hild, "The Knights of Labor and the Third-Party Movement in Texas 1886–1896," *Southwestern Historical Quarterly* vol. 119 no. 1 (2015): 24–43.

42. Goebel, "Political Economy of American Populism," 124.

43. Irvin D. W. Winsboro and Moses Musoke, "Lead Us Not into Temptation: Race, Rhetoric and Reality in Southern Populism," *Historian* vol. 65 no. 6 (2003): 1354–1374, at 1355; Fraser, *Age of Acquiescence*, 93.

44. "Omaha Platform," *The World Almanac, 1893* (New York: 1893), 83–85. Reprinted in George Brown Tindall, ed., *A Populist Reader, Selections from the Works of American Populist Leaders* (New York: Harper & Row, 1966), 90–96.

45. Worth Robert Miller, ed., "The Populist Vision: A Roundtable Discussion," *Kansas History: A Journal of the Central Plains* vol. 32 (Spring 2008): 18–45, at 21; J. A. Thompson, "The Age of 'Reform' in America," *Historical Journal* vol. 19 no. 1 (1976): 257–274, at 268.

46. Lawrence Goodwyn, *The Populist Moment: A Short History of the Agrarian Revolt in America* (New York: Oxford University Press, 1978).

47. Richard J. Ellis, "Rival Visions of Equality in American Political Culture," *Review of Politics* vol. 54 no. 2 (1992): 253–280, at 268.

48. Fraser, *Age of Acquiescence*, 105; Miller, "The Populist Vision," 23.

49. Gene Clanton, "Populism, Progressivism, and Equality: The Kansas Paradigm," *Agricultural History* vol. 51 no. 3 (1977): 559–581.

50. Edward Caudill, "E. L. Godkin and the Science of Society," *Journalism Quarterly* vol. 66 (1989): 57–64; Pole, *Pursuit of Equality*, 206.

51. Thomas C. Leonard, "Mistaking Eugenics for Social Darwinism: Why Eugenics Is Missing from the History of American Economics," *History of Political Economy* vol. 1 (2005): 201–233.

52. Steve J. Shone, "Cultural Relativism and the Savage: The Alleged Inconsistency of William Graham Sumner," *American Journal of Economics and Sociology* vol. 63 no. 3 (July 2004): 697–715; Jeff Sklansky, "Pauperism and Poverty: Henry George, William Graham Sumner, and the Ideological Origins of Modern American Social Science," *Journal of the History of the Behavioral Sciences* vol. 35 no. 2 (Spring 1999): 111–138.

53. Christopher R. Versen, "What's Wrong with a Little Social Darwinism (in Our Historiography)?" *History Teacher* vol. 42 no. 4 (August 2009): 403–423; Andrew Carnegie, "Wealth," in *North American Review* vol. 391 (1889), available online at https://www.swarthmore.edu/SocSci/rbannis1/AIH19th/Carnegie.html, accessed October 21, 2015.

54. Carnegie, "Wealth."

55. Andrew Vincent, "Becoming Green," *Victorian Studies* vol. 48 no. 3 (Spring 2006): 487–504.

56. Wendy J. Deichmann, "The Social Gospel as Grassroots Movement," *Church History* vol. 84 no. 1 (March 2015): 203–206; Bradley W. Bateman, "Clearing the Ground: The Demise of the Social Gospel Movement and the Rise of Neoclassicism in American Economics," *History of Political Economy* vol. 30 (1998): 29–52.

57. Henry Demarest Lloyd, *Wealth Against Commonwealth* (Englewood Cliffs, NJ: Prentice-Hall, 1963), 90.

58. Ibid., 157.

59. Thompson, *Politics of Inequality*, 113.

60. Lloyd, *Wealth Against Commonwealth*, 160.

61. Ibid., 182.

62. White, *Railroaded*, 232.

63. Ibid., 356.

64. Ibid., 384, 420.

65. Huston, *Securing the Fruits of Labor*, 348.

66. Charles Barzillai Spahr, *An Essay on the Present Distribution of Wealth in the United States* (New York: Johnson Reprint Corporation, 1970, first published 1896), 69.

67. Ibid., 128.

68. Ibid., 158.

69. Charles Barzillai Spahr, *America's Working People* (London: Longmans Green, 1900), 45.

70. Spahr, *America's Working People*, 51, 110.

71. Ibid., 135.

72. Ibid., 166.

73. David Montgomery. "George, Henry," *American National Biography Online* February 2000, available online at http://www.anb.org/articles/15/15-00261.html, accessed October 14, 2015.

74. Weir, "A Fragile Alliance," 428, 432.

75. Pole, *Pursuit of Equality*, 209; Henry George, *Progress and Poverty* (New York: Robert Schalkenbach Foundation, 1990), 286.

76. George, *Progress and Poverty*, 339; James M. Dawsey, "Henry George and the Economic Fruits of a Good Society," *American Journal of Economics and Sociology* vol. 74, no. 1 (January 2015): 63–92.

77. George, *Progress and Poverty*, 245, 277, 285.

78. Ibid., 299–327, 404.

79. Ibid., 420.

80. Ibid., 427.

81. Charles R. McCann Jr., "Apprehending the Social Philosophy of Henry George," *American Journal of Economics and Sociology* vol. 67 no. 1 (January 2008): 67–88; Ian Inkster, "Henry George, Protectionism and the Welfare of the Working Class," *American Journal of Economics and Sociology* vol. 49 no. 3 (1990): 375–384.

82. George, *Progress and Poverty*, 456.

83. Ibid., 468.

84. Ibid., 538.

85. Toll, "Free Men, Freedmen, and Race," 585.

86. Edward Gordon Clark, "Henry George's Land Tax," *The North American Review*, vol. 144 no. 362 (January 1887): 107–110; Isaac L. Rice, "Has Land a Value?" *The North American Review*, vol. 134 no. 307 (June 1882): 617–630.

87. Weir, "A Fragile Alliance," 424.

88. "Looking Backward," available online at http://www.digitalhistory.uh.edu/disp_textbook.cfm?smtID=2&psid=3123, accessed April 7, 2016.

89. Hoschchild, *What's Fair?*, 61.

90. Edward Bellamy, *Looking Backward* (New York: Penguin Classics, 1982), first published 1888, at 65.

91. Ibid., 66.

92. Ibid., 69.

93. Matthew Hartman, "Utopian Evolution: The Sentimental Critique of Social Darwinism in Bellamy and Peirce," *Utopian Studies* vol. 10 no. 1 (1999): 26–41.

94. Bellamy, *Looking Backward*, 72; Nicholas P. Gilman, " 'Nationalism' in the United States," *Quarterly Journal of Economics* vol. 4 (October 1889): 50–76.

95. Bellamy, *Looking Backward*, 83.

96. Gilman, " 'Nationalism,' " 58. The same "membership in a nation" reasoning is used by Anne Alstott and Bruce Ackerman in their book *The Stakeholder Society* (New Haven, CT: Yale University Press, 2000).

97. Bellamy, *Looking Backward*, 88.

98. Ibid., 90.

99. Ibid., 70. For the difference between mandatory-participation and voluntary-participation economies, see Karl Widerquist, *Independence, Propertylessness, and Basic Income* (New York: Palgrave Macmillan, 2013), 116.

100. John Hope Franklin, "Edward Bellamy and the Nationalist Movement," *New England Quarterly* vol. 11 no. 4 (December 1938): 739–772; Gilman, " 'Nationalism,' " 56.

101. Pole, *Pursuit of Equality*, 213.

102. Louise Knight, *Citizen: Jane Addams and the Struggle for Democracy* (Chicago, IL: University of Chicago Press, 2005), 154.

103. Knight, *Citizen*, 169; Rima Lunin Schultz, "Jane Addams, Apotheosis of Social Christianity," *Church History* vol. 84 no. 1 (March 2015): 207–219.

104. Knight, *Citizen*, 199, 205, 266.

105. Deichmann, "The Social Gospel," 204.

106. Eric H. Monkkonen, "Nineteenth-Century 'Institutions: Dealing with the Urban 'Underclass,' " in Michael B. Katz, ed., *The Underclass Debate* (Princeton, NJ: Princeton University Press, 1993), 334–365.

107. Knight, *Citizen*, 282.

108. Herman C. Voeltz, "Coxey's Army in Oregon, 1894," *Oregon Historical Quarterly* vol. 65 no. 3 (1964): 263–295.

109. Homer E. Socolofsky, "Jacob Coxey: Ohio's Fairly Respectable Populist," *Kansas Quarterly* vol. 1 no. 4 (1969): 62–75.

110. Quoted in Voeltz, "Coxey's Army in Oregon," 268.

111. Ibid., 273.

112. Carlos A. Schwantes, "Coxey's Montana Navy: A Protest against Unemployment on the Wageworkers' Frontier," *Pacific Northwest Quarterly* vol. 73 no. 3 (1982): 98–107.

113. Voeltz, "Coxey's Army in Oregon," 293.

114. Socolofsky, "Jacob Coxey," 70.

115. Knight, *Citizen*, 315.

116. Fraser, *Age of Acquiescence*, 138.

117. Sean Wilentz, "America's Lost Egalitarian Tradition," *Daedalus* vol. 131 no. 1 (Winter 2002): 66–80, at 77.

118. Huston, *Securing the Fruits of Labor*, 366.

CHAPTER 4

1. Gene Smiley, "A Note on New Estimates of the Distribution of Income in the 1920s," *Journal of Economic History* vol. 60 no. 4 (2000): 1120–1128.

2. Daniel T. Rodgers, "Capitalism and Politics in the Progressive Era and in Ours," *Journal of the Gilded Age and Progressive Era* vol. 13 no. 3 (June 2014): 379–386.

3. Phillip Deen, "John Atkinson Hobson and the Roots of John Dewey's Economic Thought," *European Journal of the History of Economic Thought* vol. 20 no. 4 (2013): 646–665, at 648.

4. David Huyssen. *Progressive Inequality: Rich and Poor in New York, 1890–1920* (Cambridge, MA: Harvard University Press, 2014), 4, 16; Paul Starr, *Freedom's Power: The True Force of Liberalism* (New York: Basic Books, 2007), 8; Daniel Bender, "Perils of Degeneration: Reform, the Savage Immigrant, and the Survival of the Unfit," *Journal of Social History* vol. 42 no. 1 (2008): 5–29.

5. J. R. Pole, *The Pursuit of Equality in American History* (Berkeley: University of California Press, 1979), 215.

6. Rodgers, "Capitalism and Politics," 384.

7. Glen Gendzel, "What the Progressives Had in Common," *Journal of the Gilded Age and Progressive Era* vol. 10 (2011): 331–339.

8. Eric Rauschway, *Blessed among Nations* (New York: Hill and Wang, 2006), 14.

9. Maureen A. Flanagan, *America Reformed: Progressives and Progressivisms, 1890s–1920s* (New York: Oxford University Press, 2007), 259.

10. Jeffrey Williamson and Peter Lindert, *American Inequality: A Macroeconomic History* (New York: Academic Press, 1980), 105, 120.

11. Huyssen, *Progressive Inequality*, 52.

12. Flanagan, *America Reformed*, 26.

13. Robin D. G. Kelley, "The Politics of Opposition," in Michael B. Katz, ed., *The Underclass Debate* (Princeton, NJ: Princeton University Press, 1993), 293–333, at 302.

14. Mark Stern. "Poverty and Family Composition," in Katz, ed., *The Underclass Debate*, 220–253, at 222.

15. Katheryn M. Neckerman, "Underclass Family Patterns," in Katz, ed., *The Underclass Debate*, 194–219, at 210.

16. Robert Miraldi, "Charles Edward Russell, Chief of the Muckrakers," *Journalism & Mass Communication Monographs* 150 (1995): 1–27.

17. Toby Higbie, "Crossing Class Boundaries: Tramp Ethnographers and Narratives of Class in Progressive-Era America," *Social Science History* vol. 21 no. 1 (1997): 557–592, at 584.

18. Susan Estabrook Kennedy, "Poverty, Respectability, and Ability to Work," *International Journal of Women's Studies* vol. 2 no. 5 (1979): 401–418.

19. Rodgers, "Capitalism and Politics," 385.

20. Thomas Goebel, "The Political Economy of American Populism from Jackson to the New Deal," *Studies in American Political Development* vol. 11 no. 1 (1997): 109–148, at 134.

21. David A. Gamson, "District Progressivism: Rethinking Reform in Urban School Systems, 1900–1928," *Paedagogica Historica* vol. 3 no. 4 (2003): 417–434, at 428.

22. Glen Gendzel, "What the Progressives Had in Common," *Journal of the Gilded Age and Progressive Era* vol. 10 no. 3 (2011): 331–339, at 338.

23. Melvin I. Urofsky, "State Courts and Protective Legislation during the Progressive Era: A Reevaluation," *Journal of American History* vol. 72 no. 1 (1985): 63–91, at 64.

24. Robert Alexander Kraig, "The 1912 Election and the Rhetorical Foundations of the Liberal State," *Rhetoric and Public Affairs* vol. 3 no. 3 (2000): 363–393, at 377; Theodore Roosevelt, "The New Nationalism," *Theodore Roosevelt Association Journal* vol. 33 no. 1–3 (2012): 54–64.

25. Roosevelt, "The New Nationalism," 58.

26. Ibid., 60.

27. Eric Rauschway, "The High Cost of Living in the Progressives' Economy," *Journal of American History* vol. 88 no. 3 (December 2001): 898–924.

28. Patrick Porter, "Source Material for Economic History: Records of the Bureau of Corporations," *Prologue* vol. 2 no. 1 (1970): 31–33.

29. G. Edward White, "Constitutional Change and the New Deal: The Internalist/Externalist Debate," *American Historical Review* vol. 110 no. 4 (2005): 1095–1115; Flanagan, *America Reformed*, 106; Rauschway, *Blessed Among Nations*, 115.

30. *Lochner v. People of the State of New York*, 198 US 45 (1905), available online at http://caselaw.findlaw.com/us-supreme-court/198/45.html, accessed January 3, 2016.

31. Richard G. Frederick, *William H. Taft* (New York: Nova Science Publishers, 2010), 101–121.

32. Frederick, *Taft*, 142–144; Justin Crowe, "The Forging of Judicial Autonomy: Political Entrepreneurship and the Reforms of William Howard Taft," *Journal of Politics* vol. 69 no. 1 (2007): 73–87, at 78; James C. German Jr., "The Taft Administration and the Sherman Antitrust Act," *Mid-America* vol. 54 no. 3 (1972): 172–186.

33. Robert Alexander Kraig, "The 1912 Election and the Rhetorical Foundations of the Liberal State," *Rhetoric and Public Affairs* vol. 3 no. 3 (2000): 363–395.

34. Flanagan, *America Reformed*, 154–156.

35. Priscilla Murolo and A. B. Chitty, *From the Folks Who Brought You the Weekend* (New York: New Press, 2001), 148.

36. Huyssen, *Progressive Inequality*, 157.

37. Higbie, "Crossing Class Boundaries," 574.

38. Steve Fraser, *The Age of Acquiescence: The Life and Death of American Resistance to Organized Wealth and Power* (New York: Little, Brown and Co., 2015), 186.

39. Murolo and Chitty, *Folks Who Brought You the Weekend*, 128.

40. John P. Enyeart, "Revolution or Evolution: The Socialist Party, Western Worker, and Law in the Progressive Era," *Journal of the Gilded Age and Progressive Era* vol. 2 no. 4 (2003): 377–402, at 384.

41. Murolo and Chitty, *Folks Who Brought You the Weekend*, 159.

42. Flanagan, *America Reformed*, 50.

43. Murolo and Chitty, *Folks Who Brought You the Weekend*, 156.

44. Diane Kirkby, " 'The Wage-Earning Woman and the State': The National Women's Trade Union League and Protective Labor Legislation, 1903–1923," *Labor History* vol. 28 no. 1 (1987): 54–74.

45. Flanagan, *America Reformed*, 69.

46. Enyeart, "Revolution or Evolution," 382.

47. Ibid., 392, 399.

48. Allison L. Hurst, "Languages of Class in US Party Platforms, 1880–1936," *Journal of Historical Sociology* vol. 23 no. 4 (2010): 542–569; Flanagan, *America Reformed*, 128.

49. Shigeo Hirano and James M. Snyder Jr., "The Decline of Third-Party Voting in the United States," *Journal of Politics* vol. 69 no. 1 (2007): 1–16.

50. Flanagan, *America Reformed*, 63; Sybil Lipschultz, "Hours and Wages: The Gendering of Labor Standards in America," *Journal of Women's History* vol. 8 no. 1 (1996): 114–136.

51. Alice Kessler-Harris, *In Pursuit of Equity: Women, Men and the Quest for Economic Citizenship in 20th-Century America* (Oxford, UK: Oxford University Press, 2001); 4, 32.

52. Lipschultz, "Hours and Wages," 127.

53. Melvin I. Urofsky, "State Courts and Protective Legislation during the Progressive Era: A Reevaluation," *Journal of American History* vol. 72 no. 1 (1985): 6–91, at 69.

54. *Hammer v. Dagenhart* 247 US 251 (1918), available online at https://www.law.cornell.edu/supremecourt/text/247/251, accessed December 18, 2015.

55. Flanagan, *America Reformed*, 128; Alana Semuels, "How Common Is Child Labor in the U.S.?" *The Atlantic*, December 15, 2014, available online at http://www.theatlantic.com/business/archive/2014/12/how-common-is-chid-labor-in-the-us/383687, accessed December 18, 2015.

56. Huyssen, *Progressive Inequality*, 65, 77, 98, 113.

57. Joyce E. Williams and Vicky M. Maclean, "In Search of the Kingdom: The Social Gospel, Settlement Sociology, and the Science of Reform in America's Progressive Era," *Journal of the History of the Behavioral Sciences* vol. 48 no. 4 (2012): 339–362.

58. Kennedy, "Poverty, Respectability, and Ability to Work," 406–407.

59. Flanagan, *America Reformed*, 34.

60. Louise Knight, *Citizen: Jane Addams and the Struggle for Democracy* (Chicago, IL: University of Chicago Press, 2005), 404.

61. Huyssen, *Progressive Inequality*, 139.

62. Cooper, quoted in Derrick P. Alridge, "Of Victorianism, Civilizationism, and Progressivism: The Educational Ideas of Anna Julia Cooper and W. E. B. Du Bois, 1892–1940," *History of Education Quarterly* vol. 47 no. 4 (Winter 2007): 416–446, at 443.

63. Huyssen, *Progressive Inequality*, 146.

64. Flanagan, *America Reformed*, 47.

65. Eric Monkkonen, "Nineteenth-Century Institutions: Dealing with the Urban Underclass," in Katz, ed., *The Underclass Debate*, 334–365, at 355.

66. Mark H. Left, "Consensus for Reform: The Mothers' Pension Movement in the Progressive Era," *Social Service Review* vol. 47 no. 3 (1973): 397–417.

67. Bender, "Perils of Degeneration," 15, 21.

68. Melissa J. Wilde and Sabrina Danielsen, "Fewer and Better Children: Race, Class, Religion and Birth Control Reform in America," *American Journal of Sociology* vol. 119 no. 6 (2014): 1710–1960, at 1733.

69. Ben Harris, "Arnold Gesell's Progressive Vision: Child Hygiene, Socialism and Eugenics," *History of Psychology* vol. 14 no. 3 (2011): 311–334; Kennedy, "Poverty, Respectability, and Ability to Work," 410.

70. Kevin Mattson, "Doing Democracy: An Exploration of Progressive-Era Reform and Its Legacy for American Politics," *National Civic Review* vol. 87 no. 4 (1998): 337–346.

71. Ely, quoted in Gendzel, "What the Progressives Had in Common," 334.

72. Wilfred M. McClay, "Croly's Progressive America," *Public Interest* September 1, 1999, 56.

73. Herbert Croly, *Promise of American Life* (New York: Capricorn, 1964), first published 1911, 23.

74. Ibid., 45, 59.

75. Ibid., 117.

76. Ibid., 169.

77. Thompson, *Politics of Inequality*, 130.

78. Croly, *Promise of American Life*, 203–204, 383.

79. Ibid., 387.

80. Claudio J. Katz, "Syndicalist Liberalism: The Normative Economics of Herbert Croly," *History of Political Thought* vol. 22 no. 4 (2001): 669–702.

81. Croly, *Promise of American Life*, 407.

82. Ibid., 414.

83. Jim Garrison, "Individuality, Equality, and Creative Democracy—the Task Before Us," *American Journal of Education* vol. 118 (May 2012): 369–379.

84. Walter Weyl, *The New Democracy* (New York: Harper and Row, 1964), first published 1912, 21.

85. Ibid., 87, 90–91.

86. Ibid., 131.

87. Ibid., 133.

88. Ibid., 166–167.

89. Flanagan, *America Reformed*, 54.

90. Ibid., 110.

91. William Toll, "Free Men, Freedmen, and Race: Black Social Theory in the Gilded Age," *Journal of Southern History* vol. 44 no. 4 (November 1978): 571–596, at 595.

92. Alridge, "Of Victorianism, Civilizationism, and Progressivism," 416–446.

93. W. Fitzhugh Brundage, ed., *Up from Slavery, with Related Documents* (New York: Bedford Books, 2003), 143.

94. Ibid., 143.

95. Brundage, ed., *Up from Slavery*, 18–19; Ramon G. Vela, "The Washington–DuBois Controversy and African-American Protest: Ideological Conflict and Its Consequences," *Studies in American Political Development* vol. 16 no. 1 (2002): 88–109.

96. Mark Bauerlein, "Washington, DuBois, and the Black Future," *The Wilson Quarterly* vol. 28 no. 4 (Autumn 2004): 74–86.

97. Ashraf H. A. Rushdy, *American Lynching* (New Haven, CT: Yale University Press, 2012); Jacqueline Jones Royster, ed., *Southern Horrors and Other Writings: The Anti-Lynching Campaign of Ida B. Wells, 1892–1900* (New York: Bedford/St. Martins, 1997).

98. David Levering Lewis, "*The Souls of Black Folk* a Century Hence," *Crisis* (March–April 2003): 17–21.

99. Mary Stovall, "The *Chicago Defender* in the Progressive Era," *Illinois Historical Journal* vol. 83 no. 3 (1990): 159–172.

100. Jacqueline Jones, "Southern Diaspora: Origins of the Northern 'Underclass,'" in Stephanie Coontz, ed., *American Families: A Multicultural Reader* (New York, Routledge, 1999), 153–179; J. W. Trotter, "Blacks in the Urban North," in Katz, *The Underclass Debate*, 55–81, at 59.

101. William J. Collins and Marianne H. Wanamajer, "Selection and Economic Gains in the Great Migration of African Americans: New Evidence from Linked Census Data," *National Bureau of Economic Research Papers* No. 19124 (June 2013), available online at http://www.nber.org/papers/w19124, accessed April 29, 2016.

102. Trotter, "Blacks in the Urban North," 73; John Tipple, *Crisis of the American Dream: A History of American Social Thought, 1920–1940* (New York: Pegasus Books, 1968), 43.

103. Trotter, "Blacks in the Urban North," 81.

104. Alridge, "Of Victorianism, Civilizationism, and Progressivism," 444.

105. Flanagan, *America Reformed*, 269; Tipple, *Crisis of the American Dream*, 75–80.

106. Williamson and Lindert, *American Inequality*, 81; Smiley, "A Note on New Estimates," 1124.

107. "Socialist Party Platform," in New York State Legislature, ed., *Revolutionary Radicalism: Report of the Joint Legislative Committee to Investigate Seditious Activities* (Albany, NY: JB Lyon, 1920), 1801.

108. Tipple, *Crisis of the American Dream*, 58.

109. Ibid., 129.

110. Ibid., 107.

111. Ibid., 182–183.

112. Lizabeth Cohen, *Making a New Deal: Industrial Workers in Chicago, 1919–1939* (New York: Cambridge University Press, 1990), 171.

113. Kessler-Harris, *In Pursuit of Equity*, 47.

114. Richard J. Jensen, "The Causes and Cures of Unemployment in the Great Depression," *Journal of Interdisciplinary History* vol. 19 no. 4 (1989): 553–583, at 562.

115. H. M. Gitelman, "Welfare Capitalism Reconsidered," *Labor History* vol. 33 no. 1 (1992): 5–31; Cohen, *Making a New Deal*, 208.

116. Tipple, *Crisis of the American Dream*, 138.

117. Ibid., 147.

118. E. J. Dionne Jr., "A New Progressive Era," *National Civic Review* vol. 87 no. 1 (1998): 5–36, at 25.

CHAPTER 5

1. See Jefferson Cowie and Nick Salvatore, "The Long Exception: Rethinking the Place of the New Deal in American History," *International Labor and Working-Class History* no. 74 (Fall 2008): 3–32, at 5.

2. Jeffrey Williamson and Peter Lindert, *American Inequality: A Macroeconomic History* (New York: Academic Press, 1980), 84, 188.

3. Williamson and Lindert, *American Inequality*, 212; Mae Ngai, *Impossible Subjects: Illegal Aliens and the Making of Modern America* (Princeton, NJ: Princeton University Press, 2004), 72.

4. John Tipple, *Crisis of the American Dream: A History of American Social Thought, 1920–1940* (New York: Bobbs-Merrill, 1968), 173.

5. Barry Eichengreen, "Did International Economic Forces Cause the Great Depression?" *Contemporary Policy Issues* vol. 6 no. 2 (April 1988): 90–114.

6. Tipple, *Crisis of the American Dream*, 31, 164.

7. Gene Smith, *The Shattered Dream: Herbert Hoover and the Great Depression* (New York: William and Morrow, 1970), 16.

8. Anastassios D. Karayiannis and Ray Petridis, "Keynes and the Constraints on Policy," *History of Economic Ideas* vol. 9 no. 1 (2001): 103–120.

9. Steve Boisson, "When America Sent Her Own Packing," *American History* vol. 41 no. 4 (2006): 20–27.

10. Smith, *The Shattered Dream*, 60, 100, 153, 156, 165.

11. Jonathan Alter, *The Defining Moment FDR's Hundred Days and the Triumph of Hope* (New York: Simon and Schuster, 2006), 2, 75.

12. Lizabeth Cohen, *Making a New Deal: Industrial Workers in Chicago, 1919–1939* (New York: Cambridge University Press, 1990), 222.

13. Michael Kumhof, Romain Ranciere, and Pablo Winant, "Inequality, Leverage, and Crises," *American Economic Review* vol. 105 no. 3 (2015): 1217–1245, at 1225.

14. Studs Terkel, *Hard Times: An Oral History of the Great Depression* (New York: New Press, 1986), 86, 93, 243.

15. Alter, *The Defining Moment*, 134.

16. Ibid., 216, 271, 277.

17. Ibid., 150.

18. Ibid., 230, 305.

19. Sandra L. Suarez, "Symbolic Politics and the Regulation of Executive Compensation: A Comparison of the Great Depression and the Great Recession," *Politics and Society* vol. 42 no. 1 (2014): 73–105.

20. Jason Taylor, "Cartel Code Attributes and Cartel Performance: An Industry-Level Analysis of the National Industrial Recovery Act," *Journal of Law and Economy* vol. 50 (2007): 597–622; Alter, *The Defining Moment*, 302.

21. Larry Gerber, "The National Industrial Recovery Act in Comparative Perspective: Organized Labor's Role in American and British Efforts at Industrial Planning, 1929–1933," *Journal of Policy History* vol. 6 no. 4 (1994): 403–438.

22. Sora H. Friedman, "Planned Communities of the New Deal," *Communal Studies* vol. 26 no. 2 (2006): 99–120.

23. Alter, *The Defining Moment*, 299.

24. Jason Scott Smith, "New Deal Public Works at War: The WPA and Japanese American Internment," *Pacific Historical Review* vol. 72 no. 1 (2003): 63–92, at 63, 68.

25. Ibid., 69.

26. Richard J. Jensen, "The Causes and Cures of Unemployment in the Great Depression," *Journal of Interdisciplinary History* vol. 19 no. 4 (Spring 1999): 553–583, at 580. Jensen asserts, without any evidence, that widespread training and education would have eased the Depression and been preferable to New Deal programs.

27. Neil M. Maher, " 'Work for Others but None for Us': The Economic and Environmental Inequalities of New Deal Relief," *Social History* vol. 40 no. 3 (2015): 312–334.

28. Alter, *The Defining Moment*, 295, 297.

29. James Branscombe, "The TVA: It Ain't What It Used to Be," *American Heritage* vol. 28 no. 2 (1977): 69–78.

30. Carl Kitchens, "The Role of Publicly Provided Electricity in Economic Development: The Experience of the Tennessee Valley Authority, 1929–1955," *Journal of Economic History* vol. 74 no. 2 (June 2014): 389–419; Karen M. O'Neill, "Why the TVA Remains Unique: Interest Groups and the Defeat of New Deal River Planning," *Rural Sociology* vol. 67 no. 2 (2002): 163–182.

31. Alter, *The Defining Moment*, 288.

32. Alter, *The Defining Moment*, 273; Steve Valocchi, "The Racial Basis of Capitalism and the State, and the Impact of the New Deal on African Americans," *Social Problems* vol. 41 no. 3 (1994): 347–362.

33. Cohen, *Making a New Deal*, 280.

34. Briggs Depew, Price V. Fishback, and Paul W. Rhode, "New Deal or No Deal in the Cotton South: The Effect of the AAA on the Agricultural Labor Structure," *Explorations in Economic History* vol. 50 (2013): 466–486.

35. Jerold S. Auerbach, "Southern Tenant Farmers: Socialist Critics of the New Deal," *Arkansas Historical Quarterly* vol. 27 no. 2 (1968): 3–18.

36. Taylor, "Cartel Code Attributes," 622; Raymond Wolters, "Section 7a and the Black Worker," *Labor History* vol. 10 no. 3 (1969): 459–474.

37. Jill Quadagno, *The Color of Welfare* (New York: Oxford University Press, 1994), 21; Alter, *The Defining Moment*, 315; Alice Kessler-Harris, *In Pursuit of Equity: Women, Men and the Quest for Economic Citizenship in 20th-Century America* (Oxford, UK: Oxford University Press, 2001), 132.

38. Henry P. Guzda, "Frances Perkins' Interest in the New Deal for Blacks," *Monthly Labor Review* vol. 103 no. 4 (April 1980): 31–35.

39. B. Joyce Ross, "Mary McLeod Bethune and the National Youth Administration: A Case Study of Power Relationships in the Black Cabinet of Franklin D. Roosevelt," *The Journal of Negro History* vol. 60, no. 1 (Jan., 1975): 1–28.

40. J. D. Gaydowski, "Eight Letters to the Editor: The Genesis of the Townsend National Recovery Plan," *Southern California Quarterly* vol. 52 no. 4 (1970): 365–382.

41. Phillip Deen, "John Atkinson Hobson and the Roots of John Dewey's Economic Thought," *European Journal of the History of Economic Ideas* vol. 20 no. 4 (2013): 646–665, at 657–658.

42. George R. Rising, "An EPIC Endeavor: Upton Sinclair's 1934 California Gubernatorial Campaign," *Southern California Quarterly* vol. 79 no. 1 (Spring 1997): 101–124.

43. Ray Argyle, "The Last Utopians," *Beaver* vol. 87 no. 5 (Oct/Nov2007): 42–46.

44. Daniel J. B. Mitchell, "The Lessons of Ham and Eggs: California's 1938 and 1939 Pension Ballot Propositions," *Southern California Quarterly* vol. 82 no. 2 (2000): 193–218.

45. Gaydowski, "Eight Letters to the Editor," 375.

46. Daniel J. B. Mitchell, "Townsend and Roosevelt: Lessons from the Struggle for Elderly Income Support," *Labor History* vol. 42 no. 3 (2001) 255–276.

47. Upton Sinclair, *I, Governor of California, and How I Ended Poverty: A True Story of the Future* (Los Angeles, CA: Poverty League, 1933), 15; see also Rising, "Sinclair's 1934 Gubernatorial Campaign," 105.

48. Sinclair, *I, Governor of California*, 37.

49. Ibid., 43.

50. Ibid., 52.

51. Fay M. Blake, "Upton Sinclair's EPIC Campaign," *California History* vol. 63 no. 4 (1984): 305–312; Rising, "Sinclair's 1934 Gubernatorial Campaign," 116.

52. Daniel Hanne, " 'Ham and Eggs' Left and Right: The California Scrip Pension Initiatives of 1938 and 1939," *Southern California Quarterly* vol. 80 no. 2 (1998): 183–230.

53. Hanne, "Ham and Eggs," 199; Mitchell, "Lessons of Ham and Eggs," 199.

54. Tom Zimmerman, "Ham and Eggs, Everybody!" *Southern California Quarterly* vol. 62 no. 1 (1980): 77–96.

55. Mitchell, "Lessons of Ham and Eggs," 214.

56. Jerry P. Sanson, " 'What He Did and What He Promised to Do ...' Huey Long and the Horizons of Louisiana Politics," *Louisiana History* vol. 47 no. 3 (2006): 261–276; but also see Glen Jeansonne, "The Apotheosis of Huey Long," *Biography* vol. 12 no. 4 (1989): 283–301.

57. William Leuchtenberg, "FDR and the Kingfish," *American Heritage* vol. 36 no. 6 (1985): 56–63.

58. Glen Jeansonne, "Gerald L. K. Smith and the 'Share Our Wealth' Movement," *Red River Valley Historical Review* vol. 3 no. 3 (1978): 52–65.

59. Alan Brinkley, "Huey Long, the Share-Our-Wealth Movement, and the Limits of Depression Dissidence," *Louisiana History* vol. 22 no. 2 (1981): 117–134.

60. Leuchtenberg, "FDR and the Kingfish," 62.

61. Edwin Amenta, Kathleen Dunleavy, and Mary Bernstein, "Stolen Thunder? Huey Long's 'Share Our Wealth,' Political Mediation, and the Second New Deal," *American Sociological Review* vol. 59 no. 5 (Oct. 1994): 678–702.

62. Ibid., at 688.

63. Mitchell, "Lessons of Ham and Eggs," 198.

64. Amenta, Dunleavy, and Bernstein, "Stolen Thunder?" 686, 698.

65. James P. Shenton, "The Coughlin Movement and the New Deal," *Political Science Quarterly* vol. 73 no. 3 (September 1958): 352–373.

66. David A. Horowitz, "Senator Borah's Crusade to Save Small Business from the New Deal," *Historian* vol. 55 no. 4 (1993): 693–708.

67. William E. Leuchtenberg, "Comment on Laura Kalman's Article," *American Historical Review* vol. 110 no. 4 (2005): 1081–1092; Alan Brinkley, "The Debate over the Constitutional Revolution of 1937," *American Historical Review* vol. 110 no. 4 (2005): 1046–1051.

68. Frederic Krome, "From Liberal Philosophy to Conservative Ideology? Walter Lippman's Opposition to the New Deal," *Journal of American Culture* vol. 10 no. 1 (1987): 57–64.

69. Laura Kalman, "The Constitution, The Supreme Court, and the New Deal," *American Historical Review* vol. 110 no. 4 (2005): 1052–1080; G. Edward White, "Constitutional Change and the New Deal: The Internalist/Externalist Debate," *American Historical Review* vol. 110 no. 4 (2005): 1094–1115; William Leuchtenberg, "The Nine Justices Respond to the 1937 Crisis," *Journal of Supreme Court History* vol. 1 (1997): 55–75.

70. Joseph Postell, "The Anti-New Deal Progressive: Roscoe Pound's Alternative Administrative State," *Review of Politics* vol. 74 (2012), 53–85.

71. Larry M. Bartels, "Federal Government Activism and the Political Response: Political Effects of the Great Recession," *Annals of the American Academy of Political and Social Sciences* vol. 650 no. 47 (2013): 47–75, at 68.

72. Alan Derickson, " 'Take Health from the List of Luxuries': Labor and the Right to Health Care, 1915–1949," *Labor History* vol. 41 no. 2 (2000): 171–187; Jaap Kooijman, "'Licked by a Group of Doctors': The Exclusion of a National Health Insurance Program from the Social Security Act of 1935," in *Social and Secure? The Politics and Culture of the Welfare State* (Amsterdam: VU University Press, 1996), 129–145.

73. Michael Thompson, *The Politics of Inequality: A History of the Political Idea of Economic Inequality in America* (New York: Columbia University Press, 2007), 137; Cohen, *Making a New Deal*, 302.

74. Kessler-Harris, *In Pursuit of Equity*, 108.

75. Lisa Gayle Hazirjian, "Combating NEED: Urban Conflict and the Transformations of the War on Poverty and the African American Freedom Struggle in Rocky Mount, North Carolina," *Journal of Urban History* vol. 34 no. 4 (May 2008): 639–664, at 642.

76. Daniel P. Gitterman, "Making the New Deal Stick: The Minimum Wage and American Political History," *Journal of the Historical Society* vol. 12 no. 1 (March 2012): 47–78.

77. David Plotke. "The Endurance of New Deal Liberalism," *Studies in American Political Development* vol. 10 no. 2 (1996): 415–420.

78. Margaret Weir, "States, Race, and the Decline of New Deal Liberalism," *Studies in American Political Development* vol. 19 (2005): 157–172.

79. J. R. Vernon, "World War II Fiscal Policies and the End of the Great Depression," *Journal of Economic History* vol. 54 no. 4 (Dec. 1994): 850–868.

80. Robert Higgs, "Wartime Prosperity? A Reassessment of the U.S. Economy in the 1940s," *Journal of Economic History* vol. 52 no. 1 (Mar. 1992): 41–60; Paul Evans, "The Effects of General Price Controls in the United States during World War II," *Journal of Political Economy* vol. 90 no. 5 (1982): 944–966.

81. Higgs, "Wartime Prosperity," 58.

82. Thomas Sugrue, *The Origins of the Urban Crisis: Race and Inequality in Postwar Detroit* (Princeton, NJ: Princeton University Press, 1996), 19.

83. Claudia Goldin and Claudia Olivetti, "Shocking Labor Supply: A Reassessment of the Role of World War II on Women's Labor Supply," *American Economic Review: Papers and Proceedings* vol. 103 no. 3 (2013): 257–262.

84. Evans, "General Price Controls," 954.

85. Sugrue, *Origins of the Urban Crisis*, 28; Robert Margo, "Explaining Black–White Wage Convergence, 1940–1950," *Industrial and Labor Relations Review* vol. 48 no. 4 (1995): 470–481, at 471; William L. Collins, "Race, Roosevelt and Wartime Production: Fair Employment in World War II Labor Markets," *American Economic Review* vol. 91 no. 1 (2001): 272–286.

86. Aimee Dechter and Glen H. Elder Jr., "World War II Mobilization in Men's Work Lives: Continuity or Disruption for the Middle Class?" *American Journal of Sociology* vol. 110 no. 3 (September 2004): 761–793.

87. Smith, "New Deal Public Works," 71.

88. Robert Shaffer, "Opposition to Internment: Defending Japanese American Rights during World War II," *Historian* vol. 61 no. 3 (1999): 597–620.

89. Aimee Chin, "Long Term Labor-Market Effects of Japanese American Internment during World War II on Working-Age Male Internees," *Journal of Labor Economics* vol. 23 no. 3 (2005): 491–525.

90. Lilian and Oscar Handlin, "America and Its Discontents: A Great Society Legacy," *American Scholar* 64 (1995): 15–37; Don Yalung-Matthews, "Business Perspectives on the Full Employment Bill of 1945 and Passage of the Employment Act of 1946," *Essays in Economic and Business History* vol. 8 (1990): 331–342.

91. Franklin Delano Roosevelt, "State of the Union Address, January 11, 1944," available online at http://www.fdrlibrary.marist.edu/archives/address_text.html, accessed January 5, 2016.

92. Helen Lachs Ginsburg, "Historical Amnesia: The Humphrey-Hawkins Act, Full Employment and Employment as a Right," *Review of Black Political Economy* 39 (2012): 121–136, at 125.

93. Ginsburg, "Historical Amnesia," 126.

94. Kessler-Harris, *In Pursuit of Equity*, 62.

95. J. R. Pole, *The Pursuit of Equality in American History* (Berkeley: University of California Press, 1993), 255.

96. Cowie and Salvatore, "Rethinking the Place of the New Deal," 9; Cohen, *Making a New Deal*, 287.

CHAPTER 6

1. Jefferson Cowie and Nick Salvatore, "The Long Exception: Rethinking the Place of the New Deal in American History," International Labor and Working-Class History, 74 (2008): 1-32, 14.

2. Claudia Goldin and Robert A. Margo, "The Great Compression: The Wage Structure in the United States at Mid-Century," *Quarterly Journal of Economics* vol. 107 no. 1 (February 1992): 1–34; Jeffrey G. Williamson and Peter Lindert, *American Inequality: A Macroeconomic History* (New York: Academic Press, 1980), 94.

3. Dale W. Jorgenson, "Productivity and Postwar U.S. Economic Growth," *Journal of Economic Perspectives* vol. 2 no. 4 (Fall 1988): 23–41, at 24.

4. Theodore Rosenof, "Freedom, Planning, and Totalitarianism: The Reception of F.A. Hayek's 'The Road to Serfdom,'" *Canadian Review of American Studies* vol. 5 no. 2 (1974): 149–165.

5. Michael K. Brown, "Bargaining for Social Rights: Unions and the Reemergence of Welfare Capitalism, 1945–1952," *Political Science Quarterly* vol. 112 no. 4 (1997): 645–672.

6. Leslie Lenkowsky, "Welfare Reform and the Liberals," *Commentary* vol. 67 no. 3 (1979): 56–61, at 58.

7. "Layoff Cut Seen in Auto Industry," *New York Times,* April 5, 1975, p. 37; Agis Salpukas, "22 of Ford Plants to Shut for Week; Closings Will Affect 55% of the Company's Hourly Work Force in U.S.," *New York Times,* January 11, 1975, L1; "Down and Out in America," *New York Times,* February 9, 1975, 221.

8. Murray Weidenbaum, "The Employment Act of 1946: A Half Century of Presidential Policymaking," *Presidential Studies Quarterly* vol. 26 no. 3 (1996): 880–885.

9. Bertram Gross, "Job Rights under Capitalism," *Social Policy* vol. 5 no. 6 (1975): 20–33.

10. Yalung-Matthews, "Business Perspectives on the Full Employment Bill of 1945," 336–337.

11. Ronald V. Dellums, "Welfare State vs. Warfare State: The Legislative Struggle for Full Employment," *Urban League Review* vol. 10 no. 1 (1986): 49–60.

12. Fred Magdoff and John Bellamy Foster, "The Plight of the U.S. Working Class," *Monthly Review* vol. 65 no. 8 (January 2014): 1–22, at 3.

13. Brown, "Bargaining for Social Rights," 653.

14. Jacqueline Jones, "Southern Diaspora: Origins of the Northern 'Underclass,'" in Michael Katz, ed., *The Underclass Debate: Views from History* (Princeton, NJ: Princeton University Press, 1993), 27–55, at 49, 52.

15. Michael Harrington, *The Other America: Poverty in the United States* (New York: Macmillan, 1963), 72.

16. Mark Stern, "Poverty and Family Composition," in Katz, ed., *The Underclass Debate,* 220–253, at 236.

17. Thomas Sugrue, *The Origins of the Urban Crisis: Race and Inequality in Postwar Detroit* (Princeton, NJ: Princeton University Press, 1996), 94.

18. Ibid., 149.

19. Sugrue, *Origins of the Urban Crisis*, 220; Ira Katznelson, "New Deal, Raw Deal," *Souls* vol. 8 no. 1 (2006): 8–11.

20. Sugrue, *Origins of the Urban Crisis*, 38, 48, 87.

21. Stanley N. Katz, "The Strange Birth and Unlikely History of Constitutional Equality," *Journal of American History* vol. 75 no. 3 (1988): 747–762, at 759.

22. Sugrue, *Origins of the Urban Crisis*, 176.

23. Richard J. Schaefer, "Reconsidering *Harvest of Shame*: The Limitations of a Broadcast Journalism Landmark," *Journalism History* vol. 19 no. 4 (1994): 121–133; Edward R. Murrow, *Harvest of Shame*, CBS Reports, November 1960, available online at https://www.youtube.com/watch?v=yJTVF_dya7E, accessed January 7, 2016.

24. Murrow, *Harvest of Shame*, at 19:30.

25. Murrow, *Harvest of Shame*, at 27:20.

26. Gabriel Kolko, *Wealth and Power in America: An Analysis of Social Class and Income Distribution* (New York: Praeger, 1962), 90–91, 98–99.

27. Ibid., 104.

28. Ibid., 119.

29. Harry Caudill, *Night Comes to the Cumberlands* (Boston: Little, Brown and Co., 1963), xi; Margaret Ripley Wolfe, "Lifting Up His Eyes unto the Hills: Harry M. Caudill and His Appalachia," *Filson History Quarterly* vol. 76 no. 1 (2002): 1–32.

30. Caudill, *Night Comes to the Cumberlands*, 13, 96.

31. Caudill, *Night Comes to the Cumberlands*, 114, 132; Edward R. Schmitt, "The Appalachian Thread in the Antipoverty Politics of Robert F. Kennedy," *Register of the Kentucky Historical Society* vol. 107 no. 3 (Summer 2009): 371–400, at 389.

32. Harrington, *The Other America*, 15.

33. Ibid., 71.

34. Katz, ed., *The Underclass Debate*, 13; Daniel Patrick Moynihan, *The Negro Family: The Case for National Action* (U.S. Department of Labor Office of Policy Planning and Research, 1965), available online at http://www.dol.gov/oasam/programs/history/webid-meynihan.htm, accessed February 17, 2016; Daryl Michael Scott, "The Politics of Pathology: The Ideological Origins of the Moynihan Controversy," *Journal of Policy History* vol. 8 no. 1 (1996): 81–105.

35. Daniel P. Gitterman, " 'Making the New Deal Stick': The Minimum Wage and American Political History," *Journal of the Historical Society* vol. 12 no. 1 (March 2012): 47–78, at 66.

36. Schmitt, "Antipoverty Politics of Robert F. Kennedy," 371–400.

37. Martha J. Bailey and Nicolas J. Duquette, "How Johnson Fought the War on Poverty: The Economics and Politics of Funding at the Office of Economic Opportunity," *Journal of Economic History* vol. 74 no. 2 (June 2014): 351–388; Cowie and Salvatore, "Rethinking the New Deal," 16.

38. J. R. Pole, *The Pursuit of Equality in American History* (Berkeley: University of California Press, 1993), 264.

39. Lyndon B. Johnson, "State of the Union Address," January 8, 1964, available online at http://www.pbs.org/wgbh/americanexperience/features/primary-resources/lbj-union64/, accessed January 7, 2016.

40. Carl M. Brauer, "Kennedy, Johnson and the War on Poverty," *Journal of American History* vol. 69 no. 1 (June 1982): 98–119, at 108.

41. David Torstensson, "Beyond the City: Lyndon Johnson's War on Poverty in Rural America," *Journal of Policy History* vol. 25 no. 4 (2013): 587–613, at 593.

42. Ibid., 603.

43. Bailey and Duquette, "War on Poverty," 360.

44. Quadagno, *Color of Welfare*, 57–58.

45. Lisa Gayle Hazirjian, "Combating NEED: Urban Conflict and the Transformations of the War on Poverty and the African American Freedom Struggle in Rocky Mount, North Carolina," *Journal of Urban History* vol. 34 no. 4 (2008): 639–664, at 658.

46. Bailey and Duquette, "War on Poverty," 367.

47. Bailey and Duquette, "War on Poverty," 351; Robert Dallek, "Medicare's Complicated Birth," *American Heritage* vol. 60 no. 2 (2010): 28.

48. Gitterman, "Minimum Wage," 68.

49. Bailey and Duquette, "War on Poverty," 381.

50. Lester C. Thurow, "The Political Economy of Income Redistribution Policies," *Annals of the American Academy of Political and Social Science* vol. 408 (1973): 146–155, at 151.

51. Kolko, *Wealth and Power in America*," ix.

52. Cowie and Salvatore, "Rethinking the New Deal," 18.

53. Quadagno, *Color of Welfare*, 65.

54. Torstensson, "Beyond the City," 587–61; Sugrue, *Origins of the Urban Crisis*, 259.

55. Sean Wilentz, "America's Lost Egalitarian Tradition," *Daedalus* vol. 131 no. 1 (2002): 66–80, at 78–79.

56. Lilian Handlin and Oscar Handlin, "America and Its Discontents: A Great Society Legacy," *The American Scholar* vol. 65 no. 1 (1995): 15–37, at 23.

57. Ibid., 21.

58. Kevin Boyle, "Why Is There No Social Democracy in America?" *International Labor and Working-Class History* no. 74 (Fall 2008): 33–37, at 35; Suzanne Model, "The Ethnic Niche and the Structure of Opportunity: Immigrants and Minorities in New York City," in Michael Katz, ed., *The Underclass Debate*, 161–193; Quadagno, *Color of Welfare*, 195.

59. John Cheves and Bill Estep, "Fifty Years of Night," *Lexington Herald-Leader*, December 21, 2012, at www.kentucky.com/2012/12/21/2451229/chapter-4-disillusioned-harry.html, accessed February 27, 2015.

60. Charles A. Murray, "The Two Wars against Poverty: Economic Growth and the Great Society," *Public Interest* vol. 69 no. 3 (1982): 3–16, at 6.

61. Bailey and Duquette, "War on Poverty," 383.

62. Schmitt, "Antipoverty Politics of Robert F. Kennedy," 394.

63. Thurow, "Income Redistribution Policies," 152.

64. William Crafton, "The Incremental Revolution: Ronald Reagan and Welfare Reform in the 1970s," *Journal of Policy Studies* vol. 26 no. 1 (2014): 27–47; Thurow, "Income Redistribution Policies," 153.

65. Robert F. McNown, "The Story of the Family Assistance Plan," *Current History* vol. 65 no. 384 (1973): 57–86.

66. James Tobin, "The Case for an Income Guarantee," *The Public Interest* vol. 4 (1966): 31–41, at 33.

67. Ibid., 36.

68. Robert Asen, "Nixon's Welfare Reform: Enacting Historical Contradictions of Poverty Discourses," *Rhetoric and Public Affairs* vol. 4 no. 2 (Summer 2001): 261–279, at 266.

69. Ibid., 273.

70. Steve Evera, "The Family Assistance Plan: 40 Acres and a Mule?" *New South* (Fall 1971): 70–74.

71. Jill Quadagno, "Race, Class and Gender in the U.S. Welfare State: Nixon's Family Assistance Plan," *American Sociological Review* vol. 55 no. 1 (Feb. 1990): 11–28, at 20; Quadagno, *Color of Welfare*, 130.

72. Crafton, "The Incremental Revolution," 30.

73. Quadagno, "Race, Class and Gender," 21.

74. Nancy Fraser and Linda Gordon, "A Genealogy of Dependency: Tracing a Keyword of the U.S. Welfare State," *Signs* vol. 19 no. 2 (1994): 309–336, at 329.

75. Crafton, "Incremental Revolution," 33; Asen, "Nixon's Welfare Reform," 265; McNown, "Family Assistance Plan," 59.

76. Crafton, "Incremental Revolution," 38.

77. Otto A. Davis, "The Senate Defeat of the Family Assistance Plan," *Public Policy* vol. 22 no. 3 (1974): 245–273; Quadagno, "Race, Class and Gender," 24.

78. Quadagno, *Color of Welfare*, 152.

79. " 'Welfare Queen' Becomes Issue in Reagan Campaign," *New York Times*, February 15, 1976, p. 51; " 'Welfare Queen' Loses Cadillac Limousine," *New York Times*, February 29, 1976, p. 42.

80. Jeff Bloodworth, " 'The Program for Better Jobs and Income': Welfare Reform, Liberalism, and the Failed Presidency of Jimmy Carter," *International Social Science Review* vol. 82 no. 3–4 (2006): 135–150; Lenkowsky, "Welfare Reform and the Liberals," 59.

81. Lenkowsky, "Welfare Reform and the Liberals," 58.

82. Bloodworth, "Program for Better Jobs and Income," 146.

83. Gross, "Job Rights under Capitalism," 25.

84. Bernard Anderson, "Robert Browne and Full Employment," *Review of Black Political Economy* vol. 35 (2008): 91–101, at 96.

85. Michael Harrington, "How to Reshape America's Economy," *Dissent* vol. 23 no. 2 (1976): 119–123.

86. Helen Lachs Ginsburg, "Historical Amnesia: The Humphrey-Hawkins Act, Full Employment and Employment as a Right," *Review of Black Political Economy* vol. 39 (2012): 121–136, at 132.

87. Iwan Morgan, "Jimmy Carter, Bill Clinton, and the New Democratic Economies," *Historical Journal* vol. 47 no. 4 (December 2004): 1015–1039, at 1020.

88. John Rawls, *A Theory of Justice* (Cambridge, MA: Harvard University Press, 1971), passim.

89. R. George Wright, "The High Cost of Rawls's Inegalitarianism," *Western Political Quarterly* vol. 3 no. 1 (1977): 73–79.

90. Philip A. Michaelbach, John T. Scott, Richard E. Matland, and Brian H. Bornstein, "Doing Rawls Justice: An Experimental Study of Income Distribution Norms," *American Journal of Political Science* vol. 47 no. 3 (July 2003): 523–539.

91. Jeffrey Edward Green, "Rawls and the Forgotten Figure of the Most Advantaged: In Defense of Reasonable Envy toward the Superrich," *American Political Science Review* vol. 107 no. 1 (February 2013): 123–138, at 125.

92. Charles Frankel, "The New Egalitarianism and the Old," *Commentary* vol. 56 no. 3 (1973): 34–61, at 58.

93. Robert Nozick, *Anarchy, State, and Utopia* (New York: Basic Books, 1974); Mark Walker, *Free Money for All* (New York: Palgrave, 2015), 72.

94. On Rawls, see Pole, *Pursuit of Equality*, 349. On the impact of land acquisition on Native Americans, see Steve Fraser, *Age of Acquiescence: The Life and Death of American Resistance to Organized Wealth and Power* (New York: Little, Brown and Co., 2015), 42.

95. George Brandes, *Anatole France* (London: William Heinemann, 1908), 6.

96. Pole, *Pursuit of Equality*, 314, 316, 321.

97. Michael B. Katz, Mark J. Stern, and Jamie J. Fader, "Women and the Paradox of Economic Inequality in the Twentieth Century," *Journal of Social History* vol. 39 no. 1 (Fall 2005): 65–88.

98. Quadagno, *Color of Welfare*, 137, 142.

99. Kim Phillips-Fein, "Conservatism: A State of the Field," *Journal of American History* vol. 98 no. 3 (December 2011): 723–742.

100. Lenkowsky, "Welfare Reform and the Liberals," 59.

CHAPTER 7

1. Michael Thompson, *The Politics of Inequality: A Political History of the Idea of Economic Inequality in America* (New York: Columbia University Press, 2007), 143.

2. Harvey Kantor and Brenda Brenzel, "Urban Education and the 'Truly Disadvantaged': The Historical Roots of the Contemporary Crisis, 1945–1980," *Teachers College Record* vol. 94 no. 2 (1992): 278–314.

3. Donald J. Matthewson and Shelly Arsenault, "Conservatives, Federalism, and the Defense of Inequality," *National Review of Political Science* vol. 11 (2007): 335–351, at 339.

4. Thompson, *Politics of Inequality*, 157, 161.

5. Richard McGahey, "The Political Economy of Austerity in the United States," *Social Research* vol. 80 no. 3 (Fall 2013): 717–748, at 729; Monica Prasad, "The Popular Origins of Neoliberalism in the Reagan Tax Cut of 1981," *Journal of Policy History* vol. 14 no. 3 (2012): 351–383, at 354; Jude Wanniski, "Taxes, Revenues and the Laffer Curve," *The Public Interest* vol. 50 (1978): 3–16.

6. Chris J. Dolan, "In His Shadow: The Impact of the Reagan Economic Regime and Institutional Structure on the Bush Administrations," *White House Studies* vol. 7 no. 3 (2007): 235–250.

7. Jill Quadagno, *The Color of Welfare: How Racism Undermined the War on Poverty* (Oxford, UK: Oxford University Press, 1996), 167.

8. E. J. Dionne Jr., "A New Progressive Era," *National Civic Review* vol. 87 no. 1 (1998): 5–26, at 20.

9. Michael Comiskey, "The Promise and Performance of Reaganomics," *Polity* vol. 20 no. 2 (1987): 316–331.

10. Daniel P. Gitterman, "Making the New Deal Stick? The Minimum Wage and American Political History," *Journal of the Historical Society* vol. 12 no. 1 (March 2012): 47–78, at 73.

11. Matthewson and Arsenault, "Conservatives, Federalism and the Defense of Inequality," 341.

12. Michael B. Katz, Mark J. Stern, and Jamie J. Fader, "Women and the Paradox of Economic Inequality in the Twentieth Century," *Journal of Social History* vol. 39 no. 1 (2005): 65–88, at 76.

13. Donald T. Wells, "Reaganomics: Micro-Perspectives and Macro-Effects," *Studies in the Social Sciences* vol. 21 (1982): 53–71.

14. Doug Rossinow, "The Legend of Reagan the Peacemaker," *Raritan* vol. 32 no. 3 (2013): 56–76.

15. Peter J. Westwick, "The International History of the Strategic Defense Initiative: American Influence and Economic Competition in the Late Cold War," *Centaurus* vol. 52 (2010): 338–351, at 342.

16. McGahey, "Political Economy of Austerity," 730; Prasad, "Popular Origins of Neoliberalism," 351.

17. Irving Horowitz, "From the New Deal to the New Federalism: Presidential Ideology in the U.S. from 1932 to 1987," *American Journal of Economics and Sociology* vol. 42 no. 2 (April 1983): 129–148, at 141

18. Albert Chevan and Randall Stokes, "Growth in Family Income Inequality, 1970–1990: Industrial Restructuring and Demographic Change," *Demography* vol. 37 no. 3 (August 2000): 365–380.

19. Peter Gottschalk, "Inequality, Income Growth, and Mobility: The Basic Facts," *Journal of Economic Perspectives* vol. 11 no. 2 (1997): 21–40.

20. Barbara Ehrenreich, "American Style Welfare Reform: Inequality in the Clinton Era," in Edward Broadbent, ed. *Democratic Equality: What Went Wrong?* (Toronto: University of Toronto Press, 2001), 148–161, at 150.

21. Joe William Trotter Jr., "Blacks in the Urban North: The 'Underclass Question' in Historical Perspective," in Katz, ed., *The Underclass Debate*, 57.

22. Nancy Fraser and Linda Gordon, "A Genealogy of Dependency: Tracing a Keyword of the U.S. Welfare State," *Signs* vol. 19 no. 2 (1994): 309–336, at 327; Tracey R. Carpenter, "Construction of the Crack Mother Icon," *Western Journal of Black Studies* vol. 36 no. 4 (2012): 264–275.

23. Sar A. Levitan, "How the Welfare System Promotes Economic Security," *Political Science Quarterly* vol. 100 no. 3 (Autumn 1985): 447–459.

24. Ibid., 456.

25. Charles A. Murray, "The Two Wars against Poverty: Economic Growth and the Great Society," *Public Interest* vol. 69 (1982): 3–16; Charles A. Murray, *Losing Ground: American Social Policy, 1950–1980* (New York: Basic Books, 1981).

26. Oscar Handlin and Lilian Handlin, "America and Its Discontents: A Great Society Legacy," *American Scholar* (Winter 1995): 15–37, at 34.

27. Katz, *The Underclass Debate*, 16–18.

28. Quadagno, *The Color of Welfare*, 178.

29. Horowitz, "New Deal to New Federalism," 145.

30. Quadagno, *The Color of Welfare*, 162–163.

31. Michelle Alexander, *The New Jim Crow: Mass Incarceration in the Age of Colorblindness* (New York: New Press, 2010), 48.

32. Jennifer Hoschchild, *What's Fair? American Beliefs about Distributive Justice* (Cambridge, MA: Harvard University Press, 1986), 278.

33. Ibid., 175, 253.

34. Ibid., 190, 255.

35. Maurice A. St. Pierre, "Reaganomics and Its Implications for African-American Family Life," *Journal of Black Studies* vol. 21 no. 3 (Mar., 1991): 325–340.

36. Levitan, "How the Welfare System Promotes Economic Security," 458.

37. Michael Comiskey, "The Promise and Performance of Reaganomics," *Polity* vol. 20 no. 2 (1987): 316–331.

38. George G. Graham, "WIC: A Food Program that Fails," *The Public Interest* vol. 103 (1991): 66–75, at 71.

39. Prasad, "The Reagan Tax Cut of 1981," at 374.

40. Dolan, "In His Shadow," 242.

41. Martin Carcasson, " 'Ending Welfare as We Know It': President Clinton and the Rhetorical Transformation of Welfare Culture,"*Rhetoric and Public Affairs* vol. 9 no. 4 (2006): 655–692.

42. Brendan O'Connor, "Policies, Principles, and Polls: Bill Clinton's Third Way Welfare Policies, 1992–1996," *Australian Journal of Politics and History* vol. 48 no. 13 (2002): 396–411, at 406.

43. James Fallows, "Washington and the Contract with America," *The Atlantic* (1994), available online at http://www.theatlantic.com/past/docs/unbound/jfnpr/jfreview.htm, accessed November 2, 2015.

44. Crafton, "The Incremental Revolution: Ronald Reagan and Welfare Reform in the 1970s," *Journal of Policy History* vol. 26 no. 1 (January 2014): 27–47, at 41.

45. Melinda Cooper, "Workfare, Familyfare, Godfare: Transforming Contingency into Necessity," *The South Atlantic Quarterly* vol. 111 no. 4 (2012) 643–661;

Matthewson and Arsenault, "Conservatives, Federalism and the Defense of Inequality," 344.

46. Demetrios James Caraley, "Ending Welfare as We Know It: A Reform Still in Progress," *Political Science Quarterly* vol. 116 no. 4 (2001–2002): 525–559.

47. Jounghee Kim, "Welfare Reform and College Enrollment among Single Mothers," *Social Science Review* vol. 86 no. 1 (March 2012): 69–91, at 70.

48. Deborah Roempke Graefe and Daniel T. Lichter, "Marriage Patterns among Unwed Mothers: Before and After PRWORA," *Journal of Policy Analysis and Management* vol. 27 no. 3 (2008): 479–497.

49. Douglas J. Besharov and Peter Germanis, "Welfare Reform: Four Years Later," *Public Interest* vol. 140 (2000): 17–38; Scott W. Allard, "The Changing Face of Welfare under the Bush Administration," *Publius: The Journal of Federalism* vol. 37 no. 3 (2007): 304–332; Sunshine Role and Jill Quadagno, "Depression and Alcohol Dependence among Poor Women: Before and After Welfare Reform," *Social Science Review* vol. 85 no. 2 (June 2011): 230–245.

50. Bradley Schiller, "Who Are the Working Poor?" *The Public Interest* vol. 115 (Spring 1994): 61–71.

51. O'Connor, "Policies, Principles, and Polls," 409.

52. Gitterman, "Minimum Wage," 75.

53. David M. Cutler, "A Guide to Health Care Reform," *Journal of Economic Perspectives* vol. 8 no. 3 (1994): 13–29.

54. Stuart Elliott, "The Media Business; Advertising; Health Care Commercials Bring a Scolding from the White House, as Well as a Lot of Attention," *New York Times*, November 8, 1993, available online at http://www.nytimes.com/1993/11/08/business/media-business-advertising-health-care-commercials-bring-scolding-white-house.html, accessed November 1, 2015.

55. Iwan Morgan, "Jimmy Carter, Bill Clinton, and the New Democratic Economics," *Historical Journal* vol. 47 no. 4 (December 2004): 1015–1039.

56. Ibid., 1032.

57. Ibid., 1035.

58. McGahey, "Political Economy of Austerity," 732.

59. Ronald G. Fryer Jr., Paul S. Heaton, Steven D. Levitt, and Kevin M. Murphy, "Measuring Crack Cocaine and Its Impact," *Economic Inquiry* vol. 51 no. 3 (January 2013): 1651–1681, at 1656.

60. Philippe Bourgeois, "Crack and the Political Economy of Suffering," *Addiction Research and Theory* vol. 11 no. 1 (2003): 31–37, at 36.

61. Matthew D. Lassiter, "Impossible Criminals: The Suburban Imperatives of the War on Drugs," *Journal of American History* vol. 102 no. 1 (June 2015): 126–140.

62. Alexander, *New Jim Crow*, 56, 101, 111, 130, 180; Ron Haskins, "Moynihan Was Right: Now What?" *Annals of the American Academy of Political Science* vol. 621 no. 1 (January 2009): 281–314, at 290.

63. Bruce Western and Becky Pettit, "Black–White Wage Inequality, Employment Rates, and Incarceration," *American Journal of Sociology* vol. 111 no. 2 (2005): 553–578.

64. Ted Mouw and Arne L. Kalleberg, "Occupations and the Structure of Wage Inequality in the United States, 1980 to 2000s," *American Sociological Review* vol. 75 no. 3 (2010): 402–431.

65. Robert C. Feenstra, "Integration of Trade and Disintegration of Production in the Global Economy," *Journal of Economic Perspectives* vol. 12 no. 4 (1988): 31–50.

66. Susan Houseman, Christopher Kurz, Paul Lengerman, and Benjamin Mandel, "Offshoring Bias in U.S. Manufacturing," *Journal of Economic Perspectives* vol. 25 no. 1 (Spring 2011): 111–132.

67. Stephen Bates, "Levelling Leviathans," *Wilson Quarterly* vol. 37 no. 3 (Summer 2013): 10–12.

68. Paul R. Bergin, Robert C. Feenstra, and Gordon H. Hanson, "Offshoring and Volatility: Evidence from Mexico's Maquiladora Industry," *American Economic Review* vol. 99 no. 4 (2008): 1664–1671.

69. Daniel Ozarow, "Pitching for Each Other's Teams: The North American Free Trade Agreement and Labor Transnationalism," *Labor History* vol. 54 no. 5 (2013): 512–526, at 516.

70. Richard D. Vogel, "The NAFTA Corridors: Offshoring US Transportation Jobs to Mexico," *Monthly Review* vol. 57 no. 9 (February 2006): 16–29; Dionne, "A New Progressive Era," 31.

71. Feenstra, "Integration of Trade," 46; Ozarow, "Pitching for Each Other's Teams," 513.

72. Christy Roye, "Unleashing Leetso: A Labor History of Navajo Uranium," M.A. Thesis, Department of History, New Mexico State University, 2010.

73. Liam Downey, "The Unintended Significance of Race: Environmental Racial Inequality in Detroit," *Social Forces* vol. 83 no. 3 (2005): 971–1008; Paul Mohai and Robin Saha, "Racial Inequality in the Distribution of Hazardous Waste: A National Level Reassessment," *Social Problems* vol. 54 no. 3 (2007): 343–370, at 361.

74. Robert W. Williams, "Environmental Injustice in America and Its Politics of Scale," *Political Geography* vol. 18 no. 1 (1999): 49–73.

75. Alan Taylor, "Unnatural Inequalities: Social and Environmental Histories," *Environmental History* vol. 1, no. 4 (Oct. 1996): 6–19, at 16.

76. Tim Carmody, "How the Flint River Got So Toxic," *The Verge*, February 26, 2016, available online at http://www.theverge.com/2016/2/26/11117022/flint-michigan-water-crisis-lead-pollution-history, accessed June 17, 2016.

CHAPTER 8

1. Leslie McCall, *The Undeserving Rich: American Beliefs about Inequality, Opportunity, and Redistribution* (Cambridge, UK: Cambridge University Press, 2013), 72, 161, 182.

2. Daniel Rodgers, "Capitalism and Politics in the Progressive Era and in Ours," *Journal of the Gilded Age and Progressive Era* vol. 13 no. 3 (June 2014): 379–386, at 386.

3. Christopher Dolan, "In His Shadow: The Impact of the Reagan Economic Regime and Institutional Structure on the Bush Administrations," *White House Studies* 7, no. 3 (2007): 235–250, at 244.

4. Richard McGahey, "The Political Economy of Austerity in the United States," *Social Research* vol. 80 no. 3 (Fall 2013): 717–749, at 720; Larry Bartels, "A Tale of Two Tax Cuts, a Wage Squeeze and a Tax Credit," *National Tax Journal* vol. 49 no. 3 (2006): 403–423; Nozar Hashemzadeh, "The Effects of Bush's Tax Cuts on Income Distribution and Economic Growth in the United States," *Perspectives and Problems in Management* vol. 3 (2004): 111–120.

5. Derek H. Davis, "President Bush's Office of Faith-Based and Community Initiatives: Boon or Boondoggle?" *Journal of Church and State* vol. 43 no. 3 (2001): 411–423.

6. Alexander Kenneth Nagel, "Charitable Choice: The Religious Component of the US Welfare Reform: Theoretical and Methodological Reflections on 'Faith Based Organizations' as Social Service Agencies," *Numen* vol. 53 (2006): 78–111.

7. Jo Renee Formicola and Mary Segers, "The Bush Faith-Based Initiative: The Catholic Response," *Journal of Church and State* vol. 44 no. 4 (Autumn 2002): 693–715.

8. Staley W. Carlson-Thies, "Implementing the Faith-Based Initiative," *Public Interest* vol. 155 (Spring 2004): 57–74, at 67.

9. Scott W. Allard, "The Changing Face of Welfare during the Bush Administration," *Publius: The Journal of Federalism* vol. 37 no. 3 (2007): 304–332, at 305, 309, 314, 318.

10. Edward Nathan Wolff, "Recent Trends in Household Wealth, 1983–2006: The Irresistible Rise of Household Debt," *Review of Economics and Institutions* vol. 2 no. 1 (Winter 2001): 1–31, at 12.

11. Peter Temin, "The Great Recession and the Great Depression," *Daedalus* vol. 4 no. 9 (2010): 115–130, at 118.

12. James R. Barth and Apanard Penny Prabha, "An Analysis of Resolving Too-Big-to-Fail Banks throughout the United States," *The Journal of Regional Analysis and Policy* vol. 44 no. 1 (2014): 1–19.

13. Fabian T. Pfeffer, Sheldon Danziger, and Robert F. Schoeni, "Wealth Disparities Before and After the Great Recession," *Annals of the American Academy of Political and Society Science* no. 650 (2013): 98–123.

14. Branko Milanovic, *Haves and Have-Nots: A Brief and Idiosyncratic History of Global Inequality* (New York: Basic Books, 2010). 196; Michael Tavel Clarke, "After the Welfare State: The New Marxism and Other Rough Beasts," *American Quarterly* vol. 61 no. 1 (2009): 173–184, at 182; Michael Kumhof, Romain Ranciere, and Pablo Winant, "Inequality, Leverage and Crises," *American Economic Review* vol. 105 no. 3 (2015): 1217–1245; Barry Z. Cynamon and Steven M. Fazzari, "Inequality, the Great Recession, and Slow Recovery," Institute for New Economic Thinking, Working Group on the Political Economy of Distribution, Working Paper No. 1 (October 2014): 1–41, at 4, available online at http://ineteconomics.org/uploads/papers/Cyn-Fazz-ConsInequ-141024-revised-Oct.pdf, accessed April 27, 2016.

15. Richard McGahey, "The Political Economy of Austerity in the United States," *Social Research* vol. 80 no. 3 (Fall 2013): 717–748, at 724.

16. Richard Freeman, "Failing the Test? The Flexible US Job Market in the Great Recession," *Annals of the American Academy of Political and Social Science* vol. 650 (2013): 78–97.

17. Helen Lachs Ginsburg, "Historical Amnesia: The Humphrey-Hawkins Act, Full Employment and Employment as a Right," *Review of Black Political Economy* 39 (2012): 121–136.

18. Fred Magdoff and John Bellamy Foster, "The Plight of the US Working Class," *Monthly Review* vol. 65 no. 8 (January 2014): 1–22.

19. Depankar Basu, "The Reserve Army of Labor in the Postwar U.S. Economy," *Science and Society* vol. 77 no. 2 (2013): 179–201.

20. Peter Temin, "The Great Recession and the Great Depression," *Daedalus* vol. 4 no. 9 (2010): 115–130, at 123.

21. Thomas Piketty, *Capital in the Twenty-First Century* (New York: Belknap Press, 2013), 224.

22. Magdoff and Foster, "Plight of the US Working Class," at 19.

23. Benjamin Page and Larry Jacobs, *Class War? What Americans Really Think about Economic Inequality* (Chicago: University of Chicago Press, 2009), 38.

24. Charles R. Geisst, "The Great Recession," *Financial History* vol. 104 (Fall 2012): 37–38.

25. Sandra L. Suárez, "Symbolic Politics and the Regulation of Executive Compensation: A Comparison of the Great Depression and the Great Recession," *Politics & Society* vol. 42, no. 1 (2014): 73–105, at 90.

26. Benjamin Page and Larry Jacobs, *Class War? What Americans Really Think about Economic Inequality* (Chicago: University of Chicago Press, 2009), 6.

27. Ray Kwon, "Does Radical Partisan Politics Affect National Income Distributions? Congressional Polarization and Income Inequality in the United States, 1913–2008," *Social Science Quarterly* vol. 96 no. 1 (2015): 49–64.

28. Carole Shammas, "A New Look at Long-Term Trends in Wealth Inequality in the United States," *American Historical Review* vol. 98 no. 2 (April 1993): 412–431, at 427.

29. Bartels, "Tale of Two Tax Cuts," at 416.

30. Donald J. Matthewson and Shelly Arsenault, "Conservatives, Federalism, and the Defense of Inequality," *National Review of Political Science* 11 (2007): 335–351, at 345; Kevin Mattson, "Doing Democracy: An Exploration of Progressive-Era Reform and Its Legacy for American Politics," *National Civic Review* vol. 87 no. 4 (1998): 337–346.

31. Magdoff and Foster, "Plight of the US Working Class," at 16.

32. Jennifer Sherman, "Surviving the Great Recession: Growing Need and the Stigmatized Safety Net," *Social Problems* vol. 60 no. 4 (2013): 409–432.

33. Sarah Van Gelder, *This Changes Everything: Occupy Wall Street and the 99% Movement* (San Francisco: Berrett-Koehler, 2011), 36.

34. Ibid., 2.

35. Christopher Ketcham, "The New Populists," *American Prospect*, December 12, 2011, 10–24.

36. Van Gelder, *This Changes Everything*, 3–4.

37. William K. Tabb, "The Crisis: A View from Occupied America," *Monthly Review* vol. 64 no. 4 (2012): 15–21.

38. Gary Dorrien, "The Case against Wall Street," *Christian Century*, November 15, 2011, pp. 22–29.

39. Stephen Collis, *Dispatches from the Occupation: A History of Change* (Vancouver, BC: Talonbooks, 2012), 127, 198.

40. Allison L. Hurst, "Languages of Class in US Party Platforms, 1880–1936," *Journal of Historical Sociology* vol. 23, no. 4 (2010): 542–569, at 567.

41. Van Gelder, *This Changes Everything*, 58, 62, 66.

42. Collis, *Dispatches from the Occupation*, 115.

43. Amy Dean, "Occupy Wall Street: A Protest against the Broken Economic Compact," *Harvard International Review* vol. 33 no. 4 (Spring 2012): 12–15.

44. Collis, *Dispatches from the Occupation*, 81; P. J. O'Rourke, "Are the Peasants Revolting? Occupy Wall Street Takes on the World," *World Affairs* (January–February 2012): 6–14.

45. Collis, *Dispatches from the Occupation*, 91.

46. Ritchie Savage, "From McCarthyism to the Tea Party: Interpreting Anti-Leftist Forms of US Populism in Comparative Perspective," *New Political Science* vol. 34 no. 4 (December 2012): 564–584.

47. Rory McVeigh, Kraig Beyerlein, Burrell Vann Jr., and Priyamvada Trivedi, "Educational Segregation, Tea Party Organizations, and Battles over Distributive Justice," *American Sociological Review* vol. 79 no. 4 (2014): 630–652.

48. Larry M. Bartels, "Federal Government Activism and the Political Response: Political Effects of the Great Recession," *Annals of the American Academy of Political and Social Science* vol. 650 no. 47 (2013): 47–75.

49. Andrew J. Perrin, Stephen Tepper, Neal Caren, and Sally Morris, "Political and Cultural Dimensions of Tea Party Support, 2009–2012," *Sociological Quarterly* vol. 55 (2014): 625–652; Paul J. Saunders, "The GOP's Identity Crisis," *National Interest* 130 (March/April 2014): 9–19.

50. Steve Fraser, *Age of Acquiescence: The Life and Death of American Resistance to Organized Wealth and* Power (New York: Little, Brown and Co., 2015), 225, 250.

51. Ibid., 352.

52. Binyamin Appelbaum, "Perils of Globalization when Factories Close and Towns Struggle," *New York Times*, May 17, 2015, available online at http://www.nytimes.com/2015/05/18/business/a-decade-later-loss-of-maytag-factory-still-resonates.html, accessed May 19, 2015.

53. Joseph Stiglitz, "The 1 Percent's Problem," *Vanity Fair*, June 2, 2012; "Editorial Perspectives: On the Self-Interest of the Capitalist Ruling Class," *Science and Society* vol. 77 no. 1 (2013): 3–7.

54. Paul J. Saunders, "The GOP's Identity Crisis," *National Interest* vol. 130 (March/April 2014): 9–19, at 19.

55. Raj Chetty, Nathaniel Hendren. Patrick Kline, and Emmanuel Saez, "Where Is the Land of Opportunity? The Geography of Intergenerational Mobility in the United States," *Quarterly Journal of Economics* vol. 129 no. 4 (November 2014): 1553–1623, at 1578.

56. Andrew Katz, "Congress Is Now Mostly a Millionaires Club," *Time*, January 9, 2014, at http://time.com/373/congress-is-now-mostly-a-millionaires-club/, accessed January 20, 2015.

57. Steven Gereneser, "The Corporate Person and Democratic Politics," *Political Research Quarterly* vol. 58 no. 4 (2005): 625–635.

58. Philip Michelbach, John T. Scott, Richard Matland, and Brian H. Bornstein, "Doing Rawls Justice: An Experimental Study of Income Distribution Norms," *American Journal of Political Science* vol. 47 no. 3 (July 2003): 523–539, at 535; Nicholas Confessore, Sarah Cohen, and Karen Yourish, "Small Pool of Donors Dominates Election Giving," *New York Times*, August 1, 2015, available online at http://www.nytimes.com/2015/08/02/us/small-pool-of-rich-donors-dominates-election-giving.html?_r=0, accessed June 18, 2016.

59. Matthewson and Arsenault, "Conservatives, Federalism and the Defense of Inequality," 346.

60. Heather A. O'Donnell, "The Impact of Slavery on Racial Inequality in Poverty in the Contemporary US South," *Social Forces* vol. 90 no. 3 (2012): 713–734.

61. Rhonda M. Williams and William E. Spriggs, "How Does It Feel to Be Free? Reflections on Black-White Economic Inequality in the Era of 'Color Blind' Law," *Review of Black Political Economy* vol. 27 no. 1 (Summer 1999): 9–22.

62. Rose M. Brewer, "21st-Century Capitalism, Austerity, and Black Economic Dispossession," *Souls: A Critical Journal of Black Politics, Culture and Society* vol. 14 no. 3–4 (2012): 227–239, at 233.

63. Jessica Pishko, "Locked Up for Being Poor," *The Atlantic*, February 25, 2015, available online at http://www.theatlantic.com/national/archive/2015/02/locked-up-for-being-poor/386069/, accessed August 10, 2015; Campbell Robertson, "A City Where Policing, Discrimination and Raising Revenue Went Hand in Hand," *New York Times*, March 4, 2015, available online at http://www.nytimes.com/2015/03/05/us/us-details-a-persistent-pattern-of-police-discrimination-in-a-small-missouri-city.html?_r=0, accessed August 10, 2015; "A Modern System of Debtor Prisons," *New York Times*, March 28, 2016, available online at http://www.nytimes.com/2016/03/28/opinion/a-modern-system-of-debtor-prisons.html, accessed June 18, 2016.

64. Michelle Alexander, *The New Jim Crow: Mass Incarceration in the Age of Color-blindness* (New York: New Press, 2010), 147–148, 192.

65. Jon Swaine, Oliver Laughland, and Jamiles Lartey, "Black People Killed by Police Twice as Likely to Be Unarmed as White People," *Guardian*, June 1, 2015, available online at http://www.theguardian.com/us-news/2015/jun/01/black-americans-killed-by-police-analysis, accessed June 2, 2015.

66. David Zucchino, "In Funeral Sermon for Walter Scott, Pastor Decries 'Act of Racism,' " *Los Angeles Times*, April 11, 2015, available online at http://www.latimes

.com/nation/la-na-walter-scott-funeral-20150411-story.html, accessed June 1, 2015.

67. Michael Thompson, *The Politics of Inequality* (New York: Columbia University Press, 2007), 196; Sean Wilentz., "America's Lost Egalitarian Tradition," *Daedalus* 131, no. 1 (2002): 66–80.

68. Sally Engle Merry, "Inequality and Rights: Commentary on Michael McCann's 'The Unbearable Lightness of Rights,' " *Law and Society Review* vol. 48 no. 2 (2014): 285–295.

69. Fraser, *Age of Acquiescence*, 420.

70. Adam J. Berinsky, "Silent Voices: Social Welfare Policy Opinions and Political Equality in America," *American Journal of Political Science* vol. 46 no. 2 (April 2002): 276–287.

71. Stanley Feldman and John Zaller, "The Political Culture of Ambivalence: Ideological Responses to the Welfare State," *American Journal of Political Science* vol. 36 no. 1 (Feb. 1992): 268–307.

72. Rebecca Blank, "What Drives American Competitiveness?" *Annals of the American Academy of Political and Social Science* vol. 663 (2016) 8–29; Joel Mokyr, Chris Vickers, and Nicholas L. Ziebarth, "The History of Technological Anxiety and the Future of Economic Growth: Is This Time Different?" *Journal of Economic Perspectives* vol. 29 np. 3 (Summer 2015): 31–50.

73. Sam Peltzman, "Mortality Inequality," *Journal of Economic Perspectives* vol. 23 no. 4 (Fall 2009): 175–190.

74. David K. Jones, Katharine W. V. Bradley, and Jonathan Oberlander, "Pascal's Wager: Health Insurance Exchanges, Obamacare, and the Republican Dilemma," *Journal of Health Politics, Policy and Law* vol. 39, no. 1 (2014): 97–137.

75. James Tobin, "The Case for an Income Guarantee." *The Public Interest* vol. 4 (1966): 31–41, at 40.

76. Jones, Bradley, and Oberlander, "Pascal's Wager," 127; Deirdre Walsh, "House Sends Obamacare Repeal Bill to White House," available online at http://www.cnn.com/2016/01/06/politics/house-obamacare-repeal-planned-parenthood/, accessed February 1, 2016.

77. Ron Haskins, "Moynihan Was Right: Now What?" *Annals of the American Academy of Political and Social Science* vol. 621 no. 1 (January 2009); 281–314, at 306.

78. Harvey Kantor and Barbara Brenzel, "Urban Education and the 'Truly Disadvantaged': The Historical Roots of the Contemporary Crisis, 1945–1990," in Katz, ed., *The Underclass Debate*, 366–402, at 378.u.

79. Nikole Hannah-Jones, "Choosing a School for My Daughter in a Segregated City," *New York Times*, June 9, 2016, available online at http://www.nytimes.com/2016/06/12/magazine/choosing-a-school-for-my-daughter-in-a-segregated-city.html, accessed June 18, 2016.

80. Ashley Smith, "Obama Steps up Push for Free," *Inside Higher Ed*, September 9, 2015, available online at https://www.insidehighered.com/news/2015/09/

09/obama-unveils-new-push-national-free-community-college, accessed February 1, 2016.

81. Kevin Carey, "Gaps in Earnings Stand Out in Release of College Data," *New York Times*, September 14, 2015, p. A3.

82. Deirdre Bloome and Bruce Western, "Cohort Change and Racial Differences in Educational and Income Mobility," *Social Forces* vol. 90 no. 2 (2011): 375–395.

83. Ginsburg, "Historical Amnesia," 134.

84. Mark Walker, *Free Money for All* (New York: Palgrave, 2015), 8, 64.

85. Frank Lovett, "Domination and Distributive Justice," *Journal of Politics* vol. 71 no. 3 (2009): 817–830.

86. Eduardo Porter, "Jobs Threatened by Machines: A Once 'Stupid' Concern Gains Respect," *New York Times*, June 8, 2016, available online at http://www.nytimes.com/2016/06/08/business/economy/threatened-by-machines-a-once-stupid-concern-gains-respect.html, accessed June 18, 2016.

87. Haskins, "Moynihan Was Right," 298.

88. Bartels, "Tale of Two Tax Cuts," at 419.

89. Haskins, "Moynihan Was Right," 309.

90. Martin Carcasson, "Ending Welfare as We Know It: President Clinton and the Rhetorical Transformation of the Anti-Welfare Culture," *Rhetoric and Public Affairs* vol. 9 no. 4 (2005): 655–692, at 677.

91. Ethan Miller, "Solidarity Economy: Key Concepts and Issues," in Emily Kawano, Thomas Neal Masterson, and Jonathan Teller-Ellsberg, eds., *"Solidarity Economy I: Building Alternatives for People and the Planet* (Amherst, MA: Center for Popular Economics, 2009), 25–42.

92. McCall, *The Undeserving Rich*, 204.

93. Jeffrey Edward Green, "Rawls and the Forgotten Figure of the Most Advantaged: In Defense of Reasonable Envy Toward the Superrich," *American Political Science Review* vol. 107 no. 1 (February 2013): 123–138. at 129; E. J. Dionne Jr., "A New Progressive Era," *National Civic Review* 87, no. 1 (1998): 5–36, at 32.

94. McGahey, "Political Economy of Austerity," at 737.

95. McCall, *The Undeserving Rich*, 212.

96. Fraser, *Age of Acquiescence,* 300.

97. David Miller, "Distributive Justice; What the People Think," *Ethics* vol. 102 no. 3 (1992): 555–593.

98. Fraser, *Age of Acquiescence,* 305; Miller, "Distributive Justice," 590; Frank Lovett, "Domination and Distributive Justice," *Journal of Politics* vol. 71 no. 3 (2009): 817–830, at 820.

99. Robert Alexander Kraig, "The 1912 Election and the Rhetorical Foundations of the Liberal State," *Rhetoric and Public Affairs* vol. 3 no. 3 (2000): 363–395.

100. Benjamin Disraeli, *Sybil: Or the Two Nations* (Aylesbury, UK: Penguin Books, 1981), first published 1845, 422.

Select Bibliography

Alexander, Michelle. *The New Jim Crow: Mass Incarceration in the Age of Colorblindness.* New York: New Press, 2010.

Alstott, Anne, and Bruce Ackerman. *The Stakeholder Society.* New Haven, CT: Yale University Press, 2000.

Alter, Jonathan. *The Defining Moment: FDR's Hundred Days and the Triumph of Hope.* New York: Simon and Schuster, 2006.

Bailey, Martha J., and Nicolas J. Duquette. "How Johnson Fought the War on Poverty: The Economics and Politics of Funding at the Office of Economic Opportunity." *Journal of Economic History* 74, no. 2 (June 2014): 351–388.

Baptist, Edward. *The Half Has Never Been Told: Slavery and the Making of American Capitalism.* New York: Basic Books, 2014.

Basch, Norma. "Equity vs. Equality: Emerging Concepts of Women's Political Status in the Age of Jackson." *Journal of the Early Republic* 3, no. 3 (1983): 297–318.

Bellamy, Edward. *Looking Backward.* New York: Penguin Classics, 1982.

Blake, Fay M. "Upton Sinclair's EPIC Campaign." *California History* 63, no. 4 (1984): 305–312.

Bloodworth, Jeff. " 'The Program for Better Jobs and Income': Welfare Reform, Liberalism, and the Failed Presidency of Jimmy Carter." *International Social Science Review* 82, nos. 3–4 (2006): 135–150.

Bogenschneider, Bret N. "Income Inequality and Regressive Taxation in the United States." *Interdisciplinary Journal of Economics and Business Law* 4, no. 3 (2015): 8–28.

Boyle, Kevin. "Why Is There No Social Democracy in America?" *International Labor and Working-Class History* no. 74 (Fall 2008): 33–37.

Brauer, Carl M. "Kennedy, Johnson and the War on Poverty." *Journal of American History* 69, no. 1 (June 1982): 98–119.

Brinkley, Alan. "Huey Long, the Share-Our-Wealth Movement, and the Limits of Depression Dissidence." *Louisiana History* 22, no. 2 (1981): 117–134.

Bronstein, Jamie L. *Land Reform and Working-Class Experience in Britain and the United States, 1800–1862.* Stanford, CA: Stanford University Press, 1999.

Brownson, Orestes. *The Labouring Classes: An Article from the Boston Quarterly Review.* Boston: Benjamin Greene, 1840.

Brundage, W. F., ed. *Up from Slavery: A Brief History with Documents.* New York: Bedford Books, 2002.

Caraley, Demetrios James. "Ending Welfare as We Know It: A Reform Still in Progress." *Political Science Quarterly* 116, no. 4 (2001–2): 525–559.

Carnegie, Andrew. "Wealth." *North American Review* 391 (1889), available online at https://www.swarthmore.edu/SocSci/rbannis1/AIH19th/Carnegie.html, accessed May 24, 2016.

Caudill, Harry. *Night Comes to the Cumberlands.* Boston: Little, Brown and Co., 1963.

Chetty, Raj, Nathaniel Hendren. Patrick Kline, and Emmanuel Saez. "Where Is the Land of Opportunity? The Geography of Intergenerational Mobility in the United States." *Quarterly Journal of Economics* 129, no. 4 (November 2014): 1553–1623.

Chevan, Albert, and Randall Stokes, "Growth in Family Income Inequality, 1970–1990: Industrial Restructuring and Demographic Change." *Demography* 37, no. 3 (August 2000): 365–380.

Cimbala, Paul. "The Freedmen's Bureau, The Freedmen, and Sherman's Grant in Reconstruction Georgia, 1865–1867." *Journal of Southern History* 55, no. 4 (1989): 597–632.

Claeys, Gregory. "Paine's *Agrarian Justice* and the Secularization of Natural Jurisprudence." *Bulletin of the Society for the Study of Labour History* 52, no. 3 (November 1987): 21–31.

Cohen, Lizabeth. *Making a New Deal: Industrial Workers in Chicago, 1919–1939.* New York: Cambridge University Press, 1990.

Collins, William J., and Marianne H. Wanamaker. "Selection and Economic Gains in the Great Migration of African Americans: New Evidence from Linked Census Data." *National Bureau of Economic Research Papers* no. 19124 (June 2013), available online at http://www.nber.org/papers/w19124, accessed May 24, 2016.

Collins, William L. "Race, Roosevelt and Wartime Production: Fair Employment in World War II Labor Markets." *American Economic Review* 91, no. 1 (2001): 272–286.

Collis, Stephen. *Dispatches from the Occupation: A History of Change.* Vancouver, BC: Talonbooks, 2012.

Comiskey, Michael. "The Promise and Performance of Reaganomics." *Polity* 20, no. 2 (1987): 316–331.

Cowie, Jefferson, and Nick Salvatore. "The Long Exception: Rethinking the Place of the New Deal in American History." *International Labor and Working-Class History* no. 74 (Fall 2008): 3–32.

Crafton, William. "The Incremental Revolution: Ronald Reagan and Welfare Reform in the 1970s." *Journal of Policy Studies* 26, no. 1 (2014): 27–47.

Croly, Herbert. *Promise of American Life.* New York: Capricorn, 1964.

Davis, Otto A. "The Senate Defeat of the Family Assistance Plan." *Public Policy* 22, no. 3 (1974): 245–273.

Dawsey, James M. "Henry George and the Economic Fruits of a Good Society." *American Journal of Economics and Sociology* 74, no. 1 (January 2015): 63–92.

Dean, Amy. "Occupy Wall Street: A Protest against the Broken Economic Compact." *Harvard International Review* 33, no. 4 (Spring 2012): 12–15.

Dechter, Aimee, and Glen H. Elder Jr. "World War II Mobilization in Men's Work Lives: Continuity or Disruption for the Middle Class?" *American Journal of Sociology* 110, no. 3 (September 2004): 761–793.

"Declaration of the Rights of Man." August 26, 1789, available online at http://avalon.law.yale.edu/18th_century/rightsof.asp, accessed May 24, 2016.

Dellums, Ronald V. "Welfare State vs. Warfare State: The Legislative Struggle for Full Employment." *Urban League Review* 10, no. 1 (1986): 49–60.

De Tocqueville, Alexis. *Democracy in America* (1835), available online at http://xroads.virginia.edu/~hyper/detoc/toc_indx.html, accessed May 24, 2016.

Dionne, E. J., Jr. "A New Progressive Era." *National Civic Review* 87, no. 1 (1998): 5–36.

Disraeli, Benjamin. *Sybil: Or the Two Nations.* Aylesbury: Penguin Books, 1981.

Dolan, Chris J. "In His Shadow: The Impact of the Reagan Economic Regime and Institutional Structure on the Bush Administrations." *White House Studies* 7, no. 3 (2007): 235–250.

Dorrien, Gary. "The Case against Wall Street." *Christian Century* (November 15, 2011): 22–29.

Eggert, Gerald G. "Gunfire and Brickbats: The Great Railway Strike of 1877." *American History Illustrated* 16, no. 2 (1981): 16–25.

Ellis, Richard J. "Rival Visions of Equality in American Political Culture." *Review of Politics* (2001): 253–280.

Engermann, Stanley L. "Some Considerations Relating to Property Rights in Man." *Journal of Economic History* 33, no. 1 (1973): 43–65.

Evera, Steve. "The Family Assistance Plan: 40 Acres and a Mule?" *New South* (Fall 1971): 70–74.

Fallows, James. "Washington and the Contract with America." *The Atlantic* (1994), available online at http://www.theatlantic.com/past/docs/unbound/jfnpr/jfreview.htm, accessed November 2, 2015.

Feenstra, Robert C. "Integration of Trade and Disintegration of Production in the Global Economy." *Journal of Economic Perspectives* 12, no. 4 (1988): 31–50.

Feldman, Stanley, and John Zaller. "The Political Culture of Ambivalence: Ideological Responses to the Welfare State." *American Journal of Political Science* 36, no. 1 (Feb. 1992): 268–307.

Fitzhugh, George. *Cannibals All!* Cambridge, MA: Harvard University Press, 1960.

Flanagan, Maureen A. *America Reformed: Progressives and Progressivisms, 1890s–1920s.* New York: Oxford University Press, 2007.

Frank, Mark W. "Inequality and Growth in the United States: Evidence from a New State-Level Panel of Income Inequality Measures." *Economic Inquiry* 47, no. 1 (2009): 55–68.

Frankel, Charles. "The New Egalitarianism and the Old." *Commentary* 56, no. 3 (1973): 34–61.

Franklin, John Hope. "Edward Bellamy and the Nationalist Movement." *New England Quarterly* 11, no. 4 (December 1938): 739–772.

Fraser, Steve. *The Age of Acquiescence: The Life and Death of American Resistance to Organized Wealth and Power.* New York: Little, Brown and Co., 2015.

Freeman, Richard. "Failing the Test? The Flexible US Job Market in the Great Recession." *Annals of the American Academy of Political and Social Science* 650 (2013): 78–97.

Gendzel, Glen. "What the Progressives Had in Common." *Journal of the Gilded Age and Progressive Era* 10 (2011): 331–339.

George, Henry. *Progress and Poverty.* New York: Robert Schalkenbach Foundation, 1990.

Gilje, Paul. *The Road to Mobocracy: Popular Disorder in New York City, 1763–1834.* Chapel Hill: University of North Carolina Press, 1987.

Gilman, Nicholas P. " 'Nationalism' in the United States." *Quarterly Journal of Economics* 4 (October 1889): 50–76.

Ginsburg, Helen Lachs. "Historical Amnesia: The Humphrey-Hawkins Act, Full Employment and Employment as a Right." *Review of Black Political Economy* 39 (2012): 121–136.

Gitterman, Daniel P. "Making the New Deal Stick: The Minimum Wage and American Political History." *Journal of the Historical Society* 12, no. 1 (March 2012): 47–78.

Goebel, Thomas. "The Political Economy of American Populism: From Jackson to the New Deal." *Studies in American Political Development* 11, no. 1 (1997): 109–148.

Goldin, Claudia, and Robert A. Margo. "The Great Compression: The Wage Structure in the United States at Mid-Century." *Quarterly Journal of Economics* 107, no. 1 (February 1992): 1–34.

Goodwyn, Lawrence. *The Populist Moment: A Short History of the Agrarian Revolt in America*. New York: Oxford University Press, 1978.

Gottschalk, Peter. "Inequality, Income Growth, and Mobility: The Basic Facts." *Journal of Economic Perspectives* 11, no. 2 (1997): 21–40.

Handlin, Lilian, and Oscar Handlin. "America and Its Discontents: A Great Society Legacy." *American Scholar* 64 (1995): 15–37.

Hanne, Daniel. " 'Ham and Eggs' Left and Right: The California Scrip Pension Initiatives of 1938 and 1939." *Southern California Quarterly* 80, no. 2 (1998): 183–230.

Harrington, Michael. *The Other America: Poverty in the United States*. New York: Macmillan, 1963.

Hashemzadeh, Nozar. "The Effects of Bush's Tax Cuts on Income Distribution and Economic Growth in the United States." *Perspectives and Problems in Management* 3 (2004): 111–120.

Horowitz, Irving. "From the New Deal to the New Federalism: Presidential Ideology in the U.S. from 1932 to 1987." *American Journal of Economics and Sociology* 42, no. 2 (April 1983): 129–148.

Hoschchild, Jennifer. *What's Fair? American Beliefs about Distributive Justice*. Cambridge, MA: Harvard University Press, 1981.

Houseman, Susan, Christopher Kurz, Paul Lengerman, and Benjamin Mandel, "Offshoring Bias in U.S. Manufacturing." *Journal of Economic Perspectives* 25, no. 1 (Spring 2011): 111–132.

Hurst, Allison L. "Languages of Class in US Party Platforms, 1880–1936." *Journal of Historical Sociology* 23, no. 4 (2010): 542–569.

Huston, James L. *Securing the Fruits of Labor: The American Concept of Wealth Distribution, 1765–1900*. Baton Rouge: Louisiana State University Press, 1998.

Huston, Reeve. "The Parties and 'the People': The New York Anti-Rent Wars and the Contours of Jacksonian Politics." *Journal of the Early Republic* 20, no. 2 (2000): 241–271.

Huyssen, David. *Progressive Inequality: Rich and Poor in New York, 1890–1920*. Cambridge, MA: Harvard University Press, 2014.

Jeansonne, Glen. "The Apotheosis of Huey Long." *Biography* 12, no. 4 (1989): 283–301.

Jefferson, Thomas. *Notes on the State of Virginia* (1782), available online at http://xroads.virginia.edu/~hyper/hns/yoeman/qxix.html, accessed May 24, 2016.

Jensen, Richard J. "The Causes and Cures of Unemployment in the Great Depression." *Journal of Interdisciplinary History* 19, no. 4 (1989): 553–583.

Johnson, Lyndon B. "State of the Union Address." January 8, 1964, available online at http://www.pbs.org/wgbh/americanexperience/features/primary-resources/lbj-union64/, accessed May 24, 2016.

Jones, David K., Katharine W. V. Bradley, and Jonathan Oberlander. "Pascal's Wager: Health Insurance Exchanges, Obamacare, and the Republican Dilemma." *Journal of Health Politics, Policy and Law* 39, no. 1 (2014): 97–137.

Jorgenson, Dale W. "Productivity and Postwar U.S. Economic Growth." *Journal of Economic Perspectives* 2, no. 4 (Fall 1988): 23–41.

Kantor, Harvey, and Brenda Brenzel. "Urban Education and the 'Truly Disadvantaged': The Historical Roots of the Contemporary Crisis, 1945–1980." *Teachers College Record* 94, no. 2 (1992): 278–314.

Katz, Andrew. "Congress Is Now Mostly a Millionaires Club." *Time*, January 9, 2014, available online at http://time.com/373/congress-is-now-mostly-a-millionaires-club/, accessed May 25, 2016.

Katz, Claudio J. "Syndicalist Liberalism: The Normative Economics of Herbert Croly." *History of Political Thought* 22, no. 4 (2001): 669–702.

Katz, Michael B. *The Underclass Debate.* Princeton, NJ: Princeton University Press, 1993.

Katz, Michael B., Mark J. Stern, and Jamie J. Fader. "Women and the Paradox of Economic Inequality in the Twentieth Century." *Journal of Social History* 39, no. 1 (Fall 2005): 65–88.

Katz, Stanley N. "The Strange Birth and Unlikely History of Constitutional Equality." *Journal of American History* 75, no. 3 (1988): 747–762.

Kennedy, Susan Estabrook. "Poverty, Respectability, and Ability to Work." *International Journal of Women's Studies* 2, no. 5 (1979): 401–418.

Kessler-Harris, Alice. *In Pursuit of Equity: Women, Men and the Quest for Economic Citizenship in 20th-Century America.* Oxford, UK: Oxford University Press, 2001.

Knight, Louise. *Citizen: Jane Addams and the Struggle for Democracy.* Chicago: University of Chicago Press, 2005.

Kolchin, Peter. "In Defense of Servitude: American Proslavery and Russian Pro-Serfdom Arguments, 1760–1860." *American Historical Review* 85, no. 4 (1980): 809–827.

Kolko, Gabriel. *Wealth and Power in America: An Analysis of Social Class and Income Distribution.* New York: Praeger, 1962.

Kraig, Robert Alexander. "The 1912 Election and the Rhetorical Foundations of the Liberal State." *Rhetoric and Public Affairs* 3, no. 3 (2000): 363–395.

Kulikoff, Alan. "Inequality in Boston." *William and Mary Quarterly* 28, no. 3 (July 1971): 375–412.

Kumhof, Michael, Romain Ranciere, and Pablo Winant. "Inequality, Leverage, and Crises." *American Economic Review* 105, no. 3 (2015): 1217–1245.

Kuznets, Simon. "Economic Growth and Income Inequality." *American Economic Review* 45, no. 1 (1955): 1–30.

Kwon, Ray. "Does Radical Partisan Politics Affect National Income Distributions? Congressional Polarization and Income Inequality in the United States, 1913–2008." *Social Science Quarterly* 96, no. 1 (2015): 49–64.

Levitan, Sar A. "How the Welfare System Promotes Economic Security." *Political Science Quarterly* 100, no. 3 (Autumn 1985): 447–459.

Levy, Michael. "Liberal Equality and Inherited Wealth." *Political Theory* 11, no. 4 (November 1983): 545–564.

Lloyd, Henry Demarest. *Wealth against Commonwealth*. Englewood Cliffs, NJ: Prentice-Hall, 1963.

Long, Jason, and Joseph Ferrie. "Intergenerational Occupational Mobility in Great Britain and the United States since 1850." *American Economic Review* 103, no. 4 (2013): 1109–1137.

Lovett, Frank. "Domination and Distributive Justice." *Journal of Politics* 71, no. 3 (2009): 817–830.

Magdoff, Fred, and John Bellamy Foster. "The Plight of the U.S. Working Class." *Monthly Review* 65, no. 8 (January 2014): 1–22.

Margo, Robert. "Explaining Black-White Wage Convergence, 1940–1950." *Industrial and Labor Relations Review* 48, no. 4 (1995): 470–481.

Matthewson, Donald J., and Shelly Arsenault. "Conservatives, Federalism, and the Defense of Inequality." *National Review of Political Science* 11 (2007): 335–351.

Mattson, Kevin. "Doing Democracy: An Exploration of Progressive-Era Reform and Its Legacy for American Politics." *National Civic Review* 87, no. 4 (1998): 337–346.

McCall, Leslie. *The Undeserving Rich: American Beliefs about Inequality, Opportunity and Redistribution*. Cambridge, UK: Cambridge University Press, 2013.

McCann, Charles R., Jr. "Apprehending the Social Philosophy of Henry George." *American Journal of Economics and Sociology* 67, no. 1 (January 2008): 67–88.

McClay, Wilfred M. "Croly's Progressive America." *Public Interest*, September 1, 1999, 56–72.

McGahey, Richard. "The Political Economy of Austerity in the United States." *Social Research* 80, no. 3 (Fall 2013): 717–748.

McNown, Robert F. "The Story of the Family Assistance Plan." *Current History* 65, no. 384 (1973): 57–86.

McVeigh, Rory, Kraig Beyerlein, Burrell Vann Jr., and Priyamvada Trivedi. "Educational Segregation, Tea Party Organizations, and Battles over Distributive Justice." *American Sociological Review* 79, no. 4 (2014): 630–652.

Milanovic, Branko. *The Haves and Have-Nots: A Brief and Idiosyncratic History of Global Inequality.* New York: Basic Books, 2010.

Miller, David. "Distributive Justice: What the People Think." *Ethics* 102, no. 3 (1992): 555–593.

Miller, Melinda C. "Land and Racial Wealth Inequality." *American Economic Review, Papers and Proceedings* 101, no. 3 (2011): 371–376.

Mitchell, Daniel J. B. "The Lessons of Ham and Eggs: California's 1938 and 1939 Pension Ballot Propositions." *Southern California Quarterly* 82, no. 2 (2000): 193–218.

Mitchell, Daniel J. B. "Townsend and Roosevelt: Lessons from the Struggle for Elderly Income Support." *Labor History* 42, no. 3 (2001) 255–276.

Mokyr, Joel, Chris Vickers, and Nicholas L. Ziebarth. "The History of Technological Anxiety and the Future of Economic Growth: Is This Time Different?" *Journal of Economic Perspectives* 29, no. 3 (Summer 2015): 31–50.

Morgan, Edmund. "Slavery and Freedom: The American Paradox." *Journal of American History* 59, no. 1 (1972): 5–29.

Morgan, Iwan. "Jimmy Carter, Bill Clinton, and the New Democratic Economies." *Historical Journal* 47, no. 4 (December 2004): 1015–1039.

Mouw, Ted, and Arne L. Kalleberg. "Occupations and the Structure of Wage Inequality in the United States, 1980 to 2000s." *American Sociological Review* 75, no. 3 (2010): 402–431.

Moynihan, Daniel Patrick. *The Negro Family: The Case for National Action.* U.S. Department of Labor Office of Policy Planning and Research, 1965.

Murolo, Priscilla, and A. B. Chitty. *From the Folks Who Brought You the Weekend.* New York: New Press, 2001.

Murray, Charles. A. *Losing Ground: American Social Policy, 1950–1980.* New York: Basic Books, 1981.

Murray, Charles A. "The Two Wars against Poverty: Economic Growth and the Great Society." *Public Interest* 69, no. 3 (1982): 3–16.

Murrow, Edward R. *1960: Harvest of Shame.* CBS Reports, November 1960, available online at https://www.youtube.com/watch?v=yJTVF_dya7E, accessed May 25, 2016.

Ngai, Mae. *Impossible Subjects: Illegal Aliens and the Making of Modern America.* Princeton, NJ: Princeton University Press, 2004.

Nozick, Robert. *Anarchy, State, and Utopia.* New York: Basic Books, 1974.

O'Connor, Brendan. "Policies, Principles, and Polls: Bill Clinton's Third Way Welfare Policies, 1992–1996." *Australian Journal of Politics and History* 48, no. 13 (2002): 396–411.

O'Donnell, Heather A. "The Impact of Slavery on Racial Inequality in Poverty in the Contemporary US South." *Social Forces* 90, no. 3 (2012): 713–734.

Page, Benjamin, and Larry Jacobs. *Class War? What Americans Really Think about Economic Inequality.* Chicago: University of Chicago Press, 2009.

Paine, Thomas. *Agrarian Justice* (1795), available online at http://xroads.virginia.edu/~hyper/Paine/agrarian.html, accessed May 25, 2016.

Peltzman, Sam. "Mortality Inequality." *Journal of Economic Perspectives* 23, no. 4 (Fall 2009): 175–190.

Perrin, Andrew J., Stephen Tepper, Neal Caren, and Sally Morris, "Political and Cultural Dimensions of Tea Party Support, 2009–2012," *Sociological Quarterly* 55 (2014): 625–652.

Pestana, Carla Gardina, and Sharon V. Salinger, eds. *Inequality in Early America.* Hanover, NH: University Press of New England, 1999.

Pfeffer, Fabian T., Sheldon Danziger, and Robert F. Schoeni. "Wealth Disparities Before and After the Great Recession." *Annals of the American Academy of Political and Social Science*, no. 650 (2013): 98–123.

Piketty, Thomas. *Capital in the Twenty-First Century.* Cambridge, MA: Harvard University Press, 2013.

Piketty, Thomas, and Emanuel Saez. "How Progressive Is the U.S. Federal Tax System? A Historical and International Perspective." *Journal of Economic Perspectives* 21, no. 1 (Winter 2007): 3–24.

Piper, Jessica. "The Great Railroad Strike of 1877: A Catalyst for the American Labor Movement." *The History Teacher* 47, no. 1 (2013): 93–110.

Pole, J. R. *The Pursuit of Equality in American Society.* Berkeley: University of California Press, 1978.

Prasad, Monica. "The Popular Origins of Neoliberalism in the Reagan Tax Cut of 1981," *Journal of Policy History* 14, no. 3 (2012): 351–383.

Quadagno, Jill. *The Color of Welfare.* New York: Oxford University Press, 1994.

Quadagno, Jill. "Race, Class and Gender in the U.S. Welfare State: Nixon's Family Assistance Plan." *American Sociological Review* 55, no. 1 (Feb. 1990): 11–28.

Ransom, Roger. "Reconstructing Reconstruction: Options and Limitations to Federal Policies on Land Distribution in 1866–67." *Civil War History* 51, no. 4 (2005): 364–377.

Rawls, John. *A Theory of Justice.* Cambridge, MA: Harvard University Press, 1971.

Rockman, Seth. *Scraping By: Wage Labor, Slavery, and Survival in Early Baltimore.* Baltimore, MD: Johns Hopkins University Press, 2009.

Rodgers, Daniel T. "Capitalism and Politics in the Progressive Era and in Ours." *Journal of the Gilded Age and Progressive Era* 13, no. 3 (June 2014): 379–386.

Roosevelt, Franklin Delano. "State of the Union Address, January 11, 1944," available online at http://www.fdrlibrary.marist.edu/archives/address_text.html, accessed May 25, 2016.

Roosevelt, Theodore. "The New Nationalism." *Theodore Roosevelt Association Journal* 33, nos. 1–3 (2012): 54–64.

Savage, Ritchie. "From McCarthyism to the Tea Party: Interpreting Anti-Leftist Forms of US Populism in Comparative Perspective." *New Political Science* 34, no. 4 (December 2012): 564–584.

Schiller, Bradley. "Who Are the Working Poor?" *The Public Interest* 115 (Spring 1994): 61–71.

Schmitt, Edward R. "The Appalachian Thread in the Antipoverty Politics of Robert F. Kennedy." *Register of the Kentucky Historical Society* 107, no. 3 (Summer 2009): 371–400.

Scott, Robert, and Steven Pressman. "Household Debt and Income Distribution." *Journal of Economic Issues* 47, no. 2 (June 2013): 323–331.

Sellers, Charles. *The Market Revolution: Jacksonian America, 1815–1846.* New York: Oxford University Press, 1994.

Shammas, Carole. "A New Look at Long-Term Trends in Wealth Inequality in the United States." *American Historical Review* 98, no. 2 (April 1993): 412–431.

Shankman, Andrew. *Crucible of American Democracy: The Struggle to Fuse Egalitarianism and Capitalism in Jeffersonian Pennsylvania.* Lawrence: University Press of Kansas, 2004.

Shankman, Andrew, ed. *The World of the Revolutionary American Republic: Land, Labor and the Conflict for a Continent.* New York: Routledge Press, 2014.

Sherman, Erik. "America Is the Richest, and Most Unequal, Country." *Fortune*, September 30, 2015, available online at http://fortune.com/2015/09/30/america-wealth-inequality/, accessed May 25, 2016.

Sinclair, Upton. *I, Governor of California, and How I Ended Poverty: A True Story of the Future.* Los Angeles, CA: Poverty League, 1933.

Skidmore, Thomas. *The Rights of Man to Property!* New York: Author, 1829.

Smiley, Gene. "A Note on New Estimates of the Distribution of Income in the 1920s." *Journal of Economic History* 60, no. 4 (2000): 1120–1128.

Smith, Gene. *The Shattered Dream: Herbert Hoover and the Great Depression.* New York: William and Morrow, 1970.

Soltow, Lee. "Inequality amidst Abundance: Land Ownership in Early Nineteenth-Century Ohio." *Ohio History* 88, no. 2 (1979): 133–151.

Spahr, Charles Barzillai. *America's Working People.* London: Longmans Green, 1900.

Spahr, Charles Barzillai. *An Essay on the Present Distribution of Wealth in the United States.* New York: Johnson Reprint Corporation, 1970.

Stiglitz, Joseph. "The One Percent's Problem," *Vanity Fair*, June 2, 2012.

Streitmatter, Roger. "Origins of the American Labor Press." *Journalism History* 25, no. 3 (1999): 99–106.

Suarez, Sandra L. "Symbolic Politics and the Regulation of Executive Compensation: A Comparison of the Great Depression and the Great Recession." *Politics and Society* 42, no. 1 (2014): 73–105.

Sugrue, Thomas. *The Origins of the Urban Crisis: Race and Inequality in Postwar Detroit.* Princeton, NJ: Princeton University Press, 1996.

Tabb, William K. "The Crisis: A View from Occupied America." *Monthly Review* 64, no. 4 (2012): 15–21.

Temin, Peter. "The Great Recession and the Great Depression." *Daedalus* 4, no. 9 (2010): 115–30.

Terkel, Studs. *Hard Times: An Oral History of the Great Depression.* New York: New Press, 1986.

Thompson, Michael J. *The Politics of Inequality: A Political History of the Idea of Economic Inequality in America.* New York: Columbia University Press, 2007.

Thurow, Lester C. "The Political Economy of Income Redistribution Policies," *Annals of the American Academy of Political and Social Science* 408 (1973): 146–155.

Tobin, James. "The Case for an Income Guarantee." *The Public Interest* 4 (1966): 31–41.

Valocchi, Steve. "The Racial Basis of Capitalism and the State, and the Impact of the New Deal on African Americans." *Social Problems* 41, no. 3 (1994): 347–362.

Van Gelder, Sarah. *This Changes Everything: Occupy Wall Street and the 99% Movement.* San Francisco, CA: Berrett-Koehler, 2011.

Walker, Mark. *Free Money for All.* New York: Palgrave, 2015.

Warden, G. B. "Inequality and Instability in Eighteenth-Century Boston: A Reappraisal." *Journal of Interdisciplinary History* 6, no. 4 (1976): 585–620.

Weidenbaum, Murray. "The Employment Act of 1946: A Half Century of Presidential Policymaking." *Presidential Studies Quarterly* 26, no. 3 (1996): 880–885.

Wells, Donald T. "Reaganomics: Micro-Perspectives and Macro-Effects." *Studies in the Social Sciences* 21 (1982): 53–71.

Western, Bruce, and Becky Pettit. "Black-White Wage Inequality, Employment Rates, and Incarceration." *American Journal of Sociology* 111, no. 2 (2005): 553–578.

Weyl, Walter. *The New Democracy.* New York: Harper and Row, 1964.

White, Richard. *Railroaded: The Transcontinentals and the Making of Modern America.* New York: W. W. Norton and Co., 2011.

Widerquist, Karl. *Independence, Propertylessness, and Basic Income: Freedom as the Power to Say No.* New York: Palgrave Macmillan, 2013.

Wilentz, Sean. "America's Lost Egalitarian Tradition." *Daedalus* 131, no. 1 (2002): 66–80.

Wilentz, Sean. *Chants Democratic*. New York: Oxford University Press, 1984.

Wilentz, Sean, and Michael Merrill, *The Key of Liberty: The Life and Democratic Writings of William Manning*. Cambridge, MA: Harvard University Press, 1993.

Williamson, Jeffrey, and Peter H. Lindert. *American Inequality: A Macroeconomic History*. New York: Academic Press, 1980.

Williamson, Jeffrey, and Peter H. Lindert. *Three Centuries of American Inequality*. Madison, WI: Wisconsin University Institute on Research on Poverty, 1976.

Wolfe, Margaret Ripley. "Lifting Up His Eyes unto the Hills: Harry M. Caudill and His Appalachia." *Filson History Quarterly* 76, no. 1 (2002): 1–32.

Wolff, Edward Nathan. "Recent Trends in Household Wealth, 1983–2006: The Irresistible Rise of Household Debt." *Review of Economics and Institutions* 2, no. 1 (Winter 2001): 1–31.

Yalung-Matthews, Don. "Business Perspectives on the Full Employment Bill of 1945 and Passage of the Employment Act of 1946." *Essays in Economic and Business History* 8 (1990): 331–342.

Young, Alfred F., ed. *Beyond the American Revolution*. DeKalb, IL: Northern Indiana University Press, 1993.

Zimmerman, Tom. "Ham and Eggs, Everybody!" *Southern California Quarterly* 62, no. 1 (1980): 77–96.

Index

About the Author

Jamie L. Bronstein is the author of four other books: *Land Reform in Britain and the United States, 1800–1862* (1999); *Caught in the Machinery: Workplace Accidents and Injured Workers in 19th-Century Britain* (2008); *Transatlantic Radical: John Francis Bray* (2009); and, with Andrew Harris, *Empire, State and Society: Britain since 1830* (2012). Bronstein is a professor of U.S. and British history at New Mexico State University.